# How to Forgive When You Can't

*The Breakthrough Guide to
Free Your Heart & Mind*

Healing Upsets Without Condoning
or Being Hurt Again

## Dr. Jim Dincalci
FOUNDER OF THE FORGIVENESS FOUNDATION

> **Winner - Living Now Book Award**
> in Personal Growth
> Independent Publisher Magazine

> **Finalist - Book of the Year Award**
> in Self-Help
> Foreword Review Magazine Awards.

> **Finalist - Indie Book Award**
> in Self-Help
> Independent Book Publishing Professionals Group

## Copyright ©2018, 2016, 2011, 2010 by James Dincalci.

Ruah Press Edition - All rights reserved under the International and Pan-American Copyright Convention.

The material in this book may not be copied or reproduced in any form, in whole or in part, without the express permission of the author or The Forgiveness Foundation. Send requests for permission to use the material in this book to the Permissions Department, The Forgiveness Foundation, fax to 262-244-3823 or to: RuahPress@forgivenessfoundation.org

**Profits** from this book go toward building caring families and communities worldwide by people helping each other heal blame, resentment and grudges.

Limit of Liability/Disclaimer of Warranty: While the publisher and author have used their best efforts in preparing this book, they make no warranties with respect to the completeness of **its** contents. Some of the advice and strategies contained herein may not be suitable for your situation. The information and opinions provided in this book are believed to be accurate and sound, based on the best judgment of the author, but readers who fail to consult with appropriate mental health professionals assume the risk of any problems. Neither the publisher nor author shall be liable for any loss of health or profit or any commercial damages, including but not limited to special, incidental, consequential, or other damages.

The Forgiveness Foundation books and products are available through our website. FF-INTL.com
To contact us directly call within the
USA - 919-929-0788 or fax 262-244-3823.
We also publish in a variety of electronic formats.

Library of Congress Catalogue Number

---

Publisher's Cataloging-in-Publication Data
Dincalci, Jim.
How to forgive when you can't : the breakthrough guide to free your heart and mind : healing upsets without condoning or being hurt again / Jim Dincalci.
p. cm.
Includes bibliographical references.

ISBN: 978-0-9824307-4-3

1. Forgiveness. 2. Self-acceptance. 3. Mind and body. I. Title.

# Praise for Dr. Dincalci's forgiveness book and work

This is an outstanding book. What an invaluable and needed book for our times. -Angeles Arrien, PhD, Anthropologist/Author/Teacher

I'm experiencing deep healing by forgiving others and myself. The Power Forgiveness Process in this book has been so profound.
S. Weechie Baker, MA, Counselor

This book has set me free! I was able to identify why I felt inferiority and rejection and let them go. - LeVonder Brinkley, PhD, Author/Speaker

This book helped to renew my spirit. I highly recommend this book to apply the techniques, which will last a lifetime and will be a well-spent effort on self-improvement. - G. Thomas, MD

By using methods in this book, it was easy to release upsets that I never really felt I could deal with. - Dr. Eric F. Donaldson, Researcher

Being able to work through an issue from childhood so quickly (after years of various other tools) was a thrill. - Trice Bonney

The process is much faster than I had thought possible. The surprising thing for me was that everything leads to and proceeds from self-forgiveness.
- Cate Griffiths

It gave me specific tools for guiding my own process of forgiveness—excellent content to meet any situation. - Deborah Klass, RN, PhD

I not only learned a process for forgiving, I forgave. - Evan Lloyd

This work helped me see things in other ways, and gave me tools to use in my relationships. Debbi Berto

It really put the processes of how to forgive in "layman's terms" so that I can explain and discuss forgiveness easily with others. Laura Lutz

Forgiveness is a missing link in social evolution, via the individual heart.
Kit Lofroos

This work exceeded my expectations. The personal learning was intense and profound. Harriette Linn

This work feels like the missing piece of the puzzle for deeper love, joy and peace. My overall response was excitement, empowering—New tools.
Ren Nelson

# Successes from people who work with clients

On a professional level, I am now equipped to teach my clients about forgiveness and to guide them through the process. - Sally Lobb

Dr. Dincalci's approach actually helped me deal with past emotions to find an internal peace long sought after. The book has also helped me in dealing with patients in my own practice as well as students whom I work with in clinical settings. – Paulette Mahurin, Nurse Practitioner

I now have the information to help my clients who may be struggling with forgiveness. - C. Slovonik

The Principles of Forgiveness are a blueprint for self-acceptance and compassion, and are wonderful intervention tools for clinicians.
- Suzette Dotson

It gave me the information and the process to resolve issues I was hanging onto that needed forgiveness. — It will also be useful in my work with families. - Carol Newman

I learned tools to use in my own personal life and also to share with clients. I'm excited about new possibilities in my clinical life.
- J Bennett Jordan

I gained insights and competency for working with clients.
- Jacqueline Doyle

Extremely helpful information framed in a useful way. Every process gave me insight. - Tawny Martin, MFT

The reading is infused with evocative and inspiring quotations which enrich and sustain the reader's focus throughout. This book is best viewed as a reference to return to again and again as one attempts to pursue the forgiveness process thoroughly. - Nicholas Morano, Ph.D., ABBP
Diplomate in Clinical Psychology

# DEDICATION

To my daughter, Erica,
and the young people of the world.
May this book bring you the means to a better future.

To my parents, Grace and Tony,
I guess I will always miss you.

To Rita who enriched my mother's life,
And to all those who take care of people.
May this book lighten your heart.

To those who have been to hell from terrible trauma.
May this book help bring you peace.

# Contents

**Foreword** .................................................................. 11
**The Opening** ............................................................. 15
   Stages and Phases of Forgiveness ................................. 16
   The Very First Step Is ................................................. 16
   Search for What Works ............................................... 19
**How It Works** ............................................................ 21
   The Best-kept Secret .................................................. 21
   The Myths of Forgiveness ............................................ 23
   The Forgiveness Battle ............................................... 23
   The Effects of Trauma and High Stress ......................... 24
   Understanding our Reactions ....................................... 24
   The War of the Brains ................................................ 26
   Quieting the Stressed System ...................................... 27
   Success in Forgiving .................................................. 30
**What Forgiving Really Is** ........................................... 21
   How Do You Know You Have Really Forgiven? .......... 35
   Effects of Hostility ..................................................... 38
   The First Essential Aspect .......................................... 40
   The Major Barrier to Forgiving: ................................. 42
   Forgiving Big Issues .................................................. 44
**The Proven Benefits of Forgiving** ............................... 35
   Research Results ....................................................... 35
   Changes in Others ..................................................... 38
   Happier Relationships ................................................ 39
   Positive Results with Children .................................... 40
   Dealing with Marriage and New Relationships ............ 40
   Physical Healing ....................................................... 41
   The Real Consequence of Holding on to Upsets .......... 44
   The Seldom Used Act That Brings Big Results ........... 45
   The Simplest Forgiveness Practice .............................. 46
   Hope for Humankind ................................................. 47
**The Blocks to Forgiving** ............................................ 48
   The Myths of Forgiveness .......................................... 48
**Making Sense of Our Thinking** .................................. 64
   How the Brain Works Best ........................................ 76
**Breaking Out of Prison** ............................................. 78

    Dealing with Emotional Pain ................................................ 78
    The Deadly Rules, Judgments and Expectations .......... 85
**Making Forgiving Easier**.................................................... **103**
    The Best Strategy for Dealing with Difficult Situations 105
    A Technique to Make Forgiveness Go Faster .............. 105
    Getting Needs and Wants Met ...................................... 106
    The Secret Attitude That Aids Forgiving ...................... 107
    The Overlooked Brain Function .................................... 110
    Do Positive Affirmations Work? .................................... 114
    The Secrets of Forgiveness Work .................................. 115
**The Power behind Forgiving** .............................................. **117**
    Love and Forgiveness ..................................................... 119
    Our Healthiest State of Mind ......................................... 119
    Real Healing .................................................................... 122
    Gratitude .......................................................................... 125
**Working on Upsets** ............................................................. **129**
    Vital Steps and Actions to Remember ........................... 129
**Forgiving Permanently** ...................................................... **134**
    The Defenses that Prevent Forgiving ............................ 137
    Stressed Thinking That Sabotages Forgiving ............. 1443
**Self-Forgiveness and Empowerment** .............................. **137**
    The Keys to Self-Forgiveness .......................................... 137
    Guilt, Pain and Punishment .......................................... 137
    Help in Gaining Self-forgiveness .................................. 157
**Dealing with Stress and Trauma** ..................................... **158**
    The Signs of Stress Overload and Exhaustion .............. 160
    What You Can Do ............................................................ 163
    What Do Trauma Survivors Need to Know? .................. 164
    Trauma's Long-Term Consequences – PTSD ............... 165
    Compassion Fatigue ........................................................ 168
    How and Why Self-Forgiveness Helps ......................... 169
**The Power Forgiveness Process** ..................................... **179**
    Part 1 – Facing the Unforgiven In Your Life ................ 169
    Part 2 – Working on an Incident .................................. 181
    Part 3 – Transformation ................................................ 192
**Continued Healing** ............................................................ **195**
**The Ultimate Result** ........................................................... **191**
**The Appendix, Notes, bibliography and Index**…… **193-207**

# About the Author

For the past twenty-five years, Dr. Jim Dincalci has worked on methods to help people forgive. His sources can be found in modern psychology as well as centuries of spiritual methods and cross-cultural healing practices. He has spent over forty years using emotional, spiritual, mental, and physical techniques to help people feel better and heal their lives.

Dr. Dincalci began his psychology training in graduate school at New York Medical College in 1968. He received a Master's Degree in Transpersonal Counseling Psychology and doctorates in Religious Studies and Divinity.

His 35 years of counseling experience includes three years of facilitating domestic violence groups and working for the Hawaii Departments of Health and Education as a clinical therapist in the state's school system. And Drug rehab work.

His book, *How to Forgive When You Can't*, integrates fifty years of studying world religions and their practices, including cross-cultural indigenous healing ways, effective thought and emotional processes of psychology, time-proven spiritual methods, perspectives such as prayers and meditations, and inspirational viewpoints that all aid in forgiving.

In 1974, Dr. Dincalci started presenting public seminars. Since then he has presented at The 2017 World Peace Conference and at professional conferences including: the Association of Transpersonal Psychology, the Campaign for Forgiveness Research, Keynote speaker- Wholistic Women's Empowerment Experience - Durham, NC, Florida Hospice & Palliative Care Association-2017, Florida Council on Crime & Delinquency-Criminal Justice Training 2016

He has taught his forgiveness work in many venues including colleges, hospitals, schools, and churches, Duke University in North Carolina, Florida State University, plus Sonoma State University, John F Kennedy University and California Institute of Integral Studies plus several other colleges and universities, all in California.

He has presented internationally at Cayetano Herrera University Medical School in Lima, Peru, The Stress and Anxiety Research Society 37th Annual Conference 2016 in Zagreb, Croatia. The 31st International Congress of Psychology 2016 in Yokohama, Japan.

# Acknowledgments

No one writes a book alone. Everyone who helped me on this book is dear to me. The trite term "I couldn't have done it without you." is true. The changes I went through while writing this book were due to their support. I am blessed to have such first-rate friends, who have all been enthusiastic and encouraging about the book.

Thank you to Angeles Arrien, Ph.D., whose support through my psychotherapy training and far beyond has been invaluable. The influence of her trainings in cross-cultural healing carried me through my own forgiveness transformation in 1993.

Thank you to Dr. Fred Luskin, a forgiveness pioneer, who acknowledged the validity of my original premises of the *Power Forgiveness Process* and for his encouragement through the years.

Thank you to Loralee Denny, Robert Williamson, Dr. Ken Lebensold, and Dee Cseh for their work on formatting and the final edit of the book; to Ginnie Ward, Cate Griffiths and Gayle Shirley for editing earlier version of the book; to Ken Urquhart for his work on permissions for the book; and to Chris Many for is help in naming the book.

Thank you very much to Tami Dever at TLC Graphics for her wisdom, blessings, coordination, and skill to produce a lovely book inside and out. Praise for her staff – Marisa Jackson for her stellar work on the cover and Erin Stark for the aesthetic eye to make the inside appealing.

Thank you to Terri Gamboa, Jocelyn Callard, Nancy Many, and Laurel Davar for their ideas, work, and support in the early phases; to Susan Johnson for giving substance to the initial writing by transcribing one of my university classes. Thank you to the late Michael Berkes, Ph.D. for helping laying out the plan for the book.

I am grateful to Abagayle, Rosie, Chris Loukas, Kokoman and Aesha Clottey, and Kima Douglas for their personal stories.

Thank you to the SW Florida Writer group whose support was priceless through difficult times while writing the book, with particular thanks to Hana Whitfield, my old friend. Special thanks to our teacher, Ginnie Ward, who was so enthusiastic about my initial work that she renewed my own enthusiasm. You all helped me become not only a better writer but also a happy writer.

Thank you to my students and clients through the years. Your willingness and success to move beyond your upsets and find peace and freedom kept me persisting in writing this book. Your stories make it rich.

A special thank you to the forgiveness researchers around the world who are making forgiveness more accepted in psychology and the scientific community; to the legal professionals who are calling for its use to resolve hurtful situations and to the therapists, spiritual advisors and church leaders all over the world who encourage its use every day.

# PERMISSIONS

I GRATEFULLY ACKNOWLEDGE permission to quote from the following copyrighted works:

- To Dr. Fredric Luskin for permission to quote from *Forgive For Good: A Proven Prescription for Health and Happiness*
- To Dr. Jerry Jampolsky for permission to quote from *Out of the Darkness into the Light: A Journey of Inner Healing*, and from *Teach Only Love: The Twelve Principles of Attitudinal Healing*,
- To Paulo Coelho for permission to quote from *By The River Piedra, I Sat Down and Wept: A Novel Of Forgiveness*
- To PuddleDancer Press for permission to quote from *Nonviolent Communication- A Language of Compassion* by Dr. Marshall Rosenberg.
- To Cindy Funfsinn and David Smith for permission to quote from *Anatomy of the Spirit* by Caroline Myss – www.myss.com
- To Luzie Mason for permission to quote from *Fire in the Soul: A New Psychology of Spiritual Optimism,* by Dr. Joan Borysenko
- To Julie Noordhoek of Baker Publishing Group for permissions to quote from *Return From Tomorrow* by George Ritchie.

All scripture quotations, unless otherwise indicated, are taken from the Holy Bible, New International Version®, NIV® ©1973, 1978, 1984 by Biblica, Inc.™ Used by permission of Zondervan. All rights reserved worldwide

# Foreword

I am the Director of the Stanford Forgiveness Projects and have written two bestselling books on forgiveness, Forgive for Good and Forgive for Love. My work is used all over the world to help people to forgive. I consider Jim Dincalci to be my peer in this work. He is one of those teachers the New York Times has not yet featured. My work has been featured in the New York Times and all other major media. That is in part because I developed my forgiveness work while working at Stanford University. Jim developed his forgiveness program through his life experience, desire to be of help and his multidimensional education. The bottom line is we are both saying the same thing. We are preaching from the same pulpit.

This is a really good forgiveness book. It is clear, helpful and wise and anyone who brings a hurt or grievance to this work will be helped. I recommend *How to Forgive When You Can't* both because of the book and because of Jim. I have known Jim for seven years. Since our first meeting, I have known him to be sincere and determined to help people forgive. The first time we met was before I was to give a book talk at a bookstore near Jim's home. Before the book talk, he contacted me to meet, and we talked forgiveness for a long dinner and walk.

When Jim and I first met in Sonoma, California, we talked about the projective defense mechanism where we picture our wounds. He said to me that we make forgiveness permanent by this simple process, which I found creative and strong:

A. To pull back the projection (forgiving the other because we have done the same thing in similar manner). Then
B. To do self-forgiveness so that there is no need to project the personal guilt onto anyone else through blame.

Jim is the only person that I know of who worked full time on forgiveness work outside of those employed in a University setting. The last time I saw Jim was on the other coast and again we talked of forgiveness and of life over a long dinner. Again, I found that mostly we were on the same page and that Jim was sincerely committed to helping people through forgiveness.

Not only does this book have a strong psychological basis but Jim has added a spiritual but non-religious dimension. Thus, his book can be used by pastors, ministers and chaplains to help their parishioners forgive, in addition to therapists, lawyers and counselors in general. As Jim says in the first chapter, he set about to create a manual to help people learn how to help others forgive and of course to do their own forgiving. It took him 9 years and he has used all of what he found in his classes to create this book. Jim is clear that his vision of forgiveness has been a driving force in his life, and this book attests that it has been fruitful.

This is not a Moron's Guide to Forgiveness or a Forgive for Dummies book. It is thoughtful and complete and is the product of a lot of hard work and effort. It is for the person who wants to truly leave their wounds behind and who is willing to work at it. And, as importantly it is for the professional who wants to help his/her clients forgive and live more peaceful and fulfilling lives.

Frederic Luskin, Ph.D.

---

**Please Note:**
There are raised letters and numbers at the end of some sentences. These are either references to publications on where I found the information or notes giving more data on what was said. See the "Notes" section at the end of the book for the references in each chapter.

Readers should be aware that Internet Web sites offered as citations and/or sources for further information may have changed or disappeared between the time this was written *and* when it is read.

# Introduction to the 4th Edition

I've been teaching and counseling forgiveness, stress management, conflict resolution, and reconciliation for over 25 years. Not only has it helped me and others, sometimes immeasurably, but also from this experience, I give you throughout this book real-life successes and examples of 40 different ways to help you forgive.

I am grateful to all of my students and clients. You will learn from their stories and find out what worked for them. To preserve anonymity, I have changed names and circumstances, but the situations are all real.

The 2nd edition (available on Amazon) is published in seven counties. The 3rd edition was not available on Amazon as it was a private printing and reformatting of the book that publishers used in two other countries. This 4th edition is re-organized, completely reformatted and re-edited:

1. The brain science data has been updated and added to.
2. Even more importantly, I have included what I consider the most effective affirmation/prayer/meditation people have used in this work. It came about through an exceptionally difficult forgiveness situation that I had. It helped greatly. Every person I've given it to has remarked at how powerful it was for them. I use it every day to quickly clean up upset. It is also a very effective and researched meditation.
3. Valuable data is expanded on Trauma, PTSD, Moral Injury and Complex PTSD giving more ways to help with these.
4. A clarification on acceptance and forgiveness because of the confusion between them.
5. Plus, I've added important actions from conflict management for you to use with people you want to keep a relationship with.

Over 120 references to research and data are cited in the Bibliography at the end of the book.

I wish you all the best on your forgiveness journey.

Jim Dincalci
Tallahassee, Florida
May 2018

# THERE ARE FIVE PARTS TO THIS BOOK:

*Part I – Opening to a Different Way,* helps develop knowledge and skill in forgiving.

*Part II – Taking It Deeper,* deals with more difficult situations.

*Part III–The Truth Behind the Resistance to Forgive,* goes into aspects that prevent forgiveness, so that understanding and compassion increase.

*Part IV – Doing the Work,* presents a working model to apply what has been learned.

*Part V – After the Process,* looks at how to maintain and strengthen the positive effects of doing this forgiveness work.

# The Opening

*"To forgive is to set a prisoner free
and discover that the prisoner was you."*

DR. LEWIS SMEDES

Being happy, having more love in your life, satisfaction in your relationships, contentment in your work, and peace in your heart – we all want to achieve these goals, but even when we do, they are often short-lived. This book shows you why.

Forgiveness is not only the key to achieving these aims but also, the way to make them permanent. It provides you with proven methods to help you forgive even the seemingly unforgivable.

Forgiveness is letting go of resentment, grudges, negative attitudes, and upsets that occupy your mind, sap your ability to love and destroy your peace of mind. It is not about turning the other cheek to be hurt again, reconciling with your victimizer, or condoning what they did. These regrettable interpretations have given forgiving a terrible name.

Forgiveness is universal, common to all religions, and integral to the human experience. It is the most significant tool we have in this time of war, terrorism, and crisis around the world.

Most people I have met admit they know forgiving is the right thing to do, but they don't know *how* to do it. Now, for the first time in history, we have made immense progress through university research in learning how to apply this timeless lesson.

Neither psychology nor religion adequately addresses this subject. It is only when you begin to understand your mind, emotions, and spirituality that you discover vital aspects about yourself that are essential to the process of forgiving. Forgiving is so difficult because there are essentials and even secrets that are not being used sufficiently even today.

**Please note:** It is important to first get the knowledge about the mind and the facts around forgiveness that are in the early chapters so that you can apply the forgiveness process to get the best result. **Please don't skip over the early chapters.**

With the understanding you get from these early chapters, you will have tools to control your stress reactions and difficult emotions so that once again love, compassion, joy, and vitality for living will be a normal part of your life. And your spirituality can bring forth wisdom and inner resources in challenging times.

In the past thirty years, I have collected over forty different methods on how to forgive others and oneself. I have taught them in universities, colleges, hospitals, churches, public workshops, schools, and individual counseling, and have watched joyously as people transformed their lives for the better.

The question of forgiving, though, is not only "What methods can help me to forgive?" It goes deeper for it seeks to find "What keeps me from forgiving?" A book of methods provides little value if you do not address the blocks in your mind and the attitudes that prevent you from forgiving yourself and others, and then identify the specific resources available to get you past your barriers. The methods in this book take you all the way.

## *The Issue of Evil*

There are people who seem to be quite evil. People who show no emotion or regret for the violence they have caused, and who will probably commit the crime again while blaming their victims. This cannot be denied. Prisons are full of them. You may even have been the victim of one.

This book is for you and your healing, not theirs.

## *Stages and Phases of Forgiveness*

Forgiveness is a complex subject in our world and for us as individuals. Each person is different, and each will forgive uniquely according to his or her own timing. What works for you may not work for another.

## *The Very First Step Is Willingness*

Without being willing to do this work, nothing will happen. You, of course, are willing in some way or you wouldn't be looking at these pages. If you are thinking of others who need to have this information and these techniques, keep reading. You will come to understand why people do not or cannot forgive. Some people will find they do this work more easily in a group, some with another person, and some together with the presence of a Higher Power.

In studying and teaching this subject, I have noticed that forgiving is a skill developed through resulting in increasing levels of awareness and success. Mindfulness is being aware of what's going on in your mind. It's a popular tool right now. There's a lot of research on it. Each chapter has exercises to help with this.

> "We may not know how to forgive, and we may not want to forgive, but the very fact we say we are willing to forgive begins the healing practice." LOUISE HAY from *YOU CAN HEAL YOUR LIFE*

The questions, information, and insights given in the first chapters of this book will increase your understanding of the essential aspects of letting go of resentment and hate. The practical exercises offered will help you apply what you have learned.

By doing the suggestions, questions, and exercises, forgiving another person and yourself can bring astounding results. I call this work "Power Forgiveness" because it is intended to heal a lifetime of guilt or resentment, as well as for an isolated situation.

After attending my first forgiveness class, a dear friend asked me for a summary of steps on how to forgive. Through the years, no summary has been adequate. Instead, I found that a series of questions that cover all the bases in a logical sequence—proven by trial and research—worked beautifully. This series became *The Power Forgiveness Process*.

The heart of Power Forgiveness is letting go all of your regrets, guilt, and self-blame. Self-forgiveness and self-compassion hold the key to releasing upsets permanently. Self-forgiveness is necessary because your own guilt and shame will keep you trapped in your negative thoughts and feelings, and they, in turn, keep you convinced that you do not deserve better. YOU DO!

## *My Story and Transformation*

In July 1993, while driving through the redwood trees on my way home, I realized that my life was no longer worth living. It looked okay on the surface; I had a pleasant home, a lovely daughter, a master's degree in counseling and a supportive community of friends. Yet I felt that I had utterly failed to become the person I dreamed of being when I was young. And, my spirituality—so essential to me for years, and a source of security and peace—was gone.

Even though I had studied different psychologies and healing methods since 1960s and eventually taught them in graduate schools, I could not help myself. I didn't know how to start. I'd lived with anger, hate, and resentment for years and thought them normal. Even when I hit rock bottom, I didn't think them were a problem. I accepted the same old justifications not to let go of the trauma and abuse I had experienced earlier in my life while a vicious militaristic organization.

Finally, at a point of utter despair, I saw that my anger was destroying me rather than being a source of effective energy. In my search for help in those dreadful hours, I scanned books on psychology and spirituality and realized clearly that to have the experience of Divine Love that I yearned for, I had to forgive.

In fact, forgiving *every* upset seemed my only way out. The skills I had developed from doing inner work for so many years came forward and helped me understand how to forgive others as well as myself.

I wrote my upsets for hours – no sentences or paragraphs, only people, situations or organizations with each thing they had done to me, over 30 pages of single line items. After many hours in seclusion, I was able let go of every upset and trauma that I could remember. With them went all the resentment, anger, and hate I had accumulated in my life. The change was miraculous. My happiness and appreciation for life returned. My soul felt free. Love radiated to and from me, and was with me constantly for the following eight years.

In discussing his book, *By The River Piedra I Sat Down and Wept: A Novel Of Forgiveness*, Paulo Coelho related a similar experience: "One morning, going from Death Valley in California to Tucson in Arizona, I made a mental list of everyone I thought I hated because they had hurt me. I went along pardoning them one by one; six hours later in Tucson, my soul felt so light, and my life had changed much for the better." [1]

## Search for What Works

Thus began my journey of helping others let go of their anger, bitterness, and hate. When I first started teaching these principles in 1996, I believed I could change the world through the same process I had experienced. Most people, though, didn't understand what I was talking about. From this disappointment, I began my quest to find out what would truly help others forgive.

I kept giving classes in forgiveness at universities and in public seminars as well as in my private counseling practice. I continued learning what worked and what did not. I read all the research, books, and articles I could on the subject of forgiveness.

The result of my extensive search is *The Power Forgiveness Process*, the most complete system available at this time to help people let go of residual anger, upset, resentment and fear from past hurtful experiences. This book, with its viewpoints, case studies, and exercises, will carry you through to forgiving even the most awful things. *The Power Forgiveness Process* may be used for a single difficult situation. It can also address a lifetime of negative emotions down to their source.

In forgiveness work, do not try to let it all go at once. If it does not seem right, do not force the procedure. Take an emotional break before moving to the next stage or incident. Accepting where you are is central to the healing process. Resting, remembering, and releasing are all cycles in healing. Be patient with yourself. You will learn methods in this book to move you through the detours, such as denial, depression, blaming, and alcohol or drugs, until you feel you can face the situation and forgive.[3]

"If you're going through hell, keep going." WINSTON CHURCHILL

## In Summary

This book makes forgiveness possible because it uses proven methods from psychology, and time-honored spiritual practices, resources and perspectives to allow a person to move past the emotional obstacles that prevent forgiving. It also addresses brain patterns and emotional defenses to enable you to gain a deeper understanding of why forgiving is difficult and how to simplify it.

Reading this book <u>in sequence</u> enables you to learn how and why the mind holds onto harmful ideas. Your responsibility is to answer the questions and do the exercises provided. In doing so, the pain of a lifetime will disappear, and you will enjoy freedom you have not experienced for years.

Forgiveness is necessary not only spiritually and emotionally, but also socially. It is the ultimate choice that brings us closest to the human and divine ideal of love and peace. It could even be the magic pill for many social ills like violence and addiction, and situations involving anger or guilt.

By using the perspectives and methods in this book:
- You will be able to let go of anger, resentments, negative feelings, and attitudes of ill will.
- You will have more peace of mind and joy in your life.
- Your life will get better because you will understand how, when, and where to forgive.

"True forgiveness deals with the past—all of the past, to make the future possible. We cannot go on nursing grudges even vicariously for those who cannot speak for themselves any longer. We have to accept that we do what we do for generations past, present and yet to come."

DESMOND TUTU From: *NO FUTURE WITHOUT FORGIVENESS*

May all your deepest dreams come true. I wish you an enlightening and rewarding journey as you read these pages.

# CHAPTER ONE

# How It Works

Forgiveness is the most powerful action you have to change relationships and heal your own life. The forgiving mindset is able to engage tragedies and trauma at a higher level and bring about true healing.

I've read that hunters catch small monkeys by putting peanuts into a gourd with a hole just small enough for the monkey to reach its hand inside. The gourd is then tied to a tree. When the hunters return, they find monkeys trapped by their unwillingness to let go of the peanuts to free their hands. This is what holding onto our resentments and unforgiven hurts do to us. We clutch onto the little peanuts that imprison our mind and heart, preventing love, peace, and joy from filling our lives.

Why do we hold onto the peanuts? What are these negative thought patterns and emotions that keep us from forgiving? Why do we listen to them? If we can answer these questions, we will have the tools to forgive.

## *The Best Kept Secret*

Luckily, recent years have seen a blossoming of research on forgiveness. It has also demonstrated the considerable emotional and even physical benefits that forgiveness[1] brings. Brain studies have pointed to systems and patterns that can slow or prevent forgiving. Psychology has revealed the mechanisms in the mind that keep in place old, inhibiting patterns and emotions, such as hate and anger. We have gained good knowledge of how the mind works and how it sabotages us. And now we have the perspectives and tools to help us forgive more easily.

With all of the new understanding about forgiving and its notable results, psychology in general still ignores the power that forgiveness generates. Dr. Carl Thoresen, a retired professor of psychology and psychiatry at Stanford University and researcher for the Stanford Forgiveness Project, has called forgiveness "one of the best-kept secrets" and notes that he and his colleagues "have come across few people who understand what forgiveness is and how it works."[2]   Why is this? There is speculation that in the mid- to late 1800s, most psychologists, Freud in particular, rejected church control and interpretation in matters of mental health. I believe with other researchers[2a] that psychology rejected forgiveness because it was associated with "The Church" and its doctrine. As a result, forgiveness was lost to the professional therapy community and remains so today.

Finding a therapist or doctor who understands forgiveness is not easy. One of the reasons I've written this book is to assist professionals and lay people to do a better job of helping others learn how to forgive.

Because religion has not done much better in helping people to forgive, I also hope this book helps clergy and pastoral counselors. For centuries, clergy have prescribed forgiveness without offering clear ways how to achieve it. Therefore, it has not worked well. What does work is using the many forgiveness methods that are available today and which are brought together in this book.

## *The Types of Forgiveness*

For some, it is easier **not** to look at all of the negative influences in a situation and just decide to forgive. This is difficult. I call it, *direct forgiveness*. It is often influenced by the belief in Divine Forgiveness and Love. Most of us are not able to make direct decisions to forgive. In fact, they often do not even seem possible.

If a person experiences great emotion around an upset, direct forgiving is often too difficult. Merely deciding to forgive can open you up to *false forgiveness*, a situation where you have the intention to do so yet still hold resentment and may even seek retribution. If you decide to forgive without going through some sort of inner work, the decision usually must frequently be repeated due to the emotional turmoil that has not yet been released.

Today, the majority of forgiveness research, therapy, and spiritual counseling tries to get a person to the point of deciding to forgive.[3] This book and its exercises are for those who are not able to make that decision easily. It addresses how to deal permanently with resentment and guilt. You will find as you continue reading that your upset will change and letting go of the upset will take place.

## *The Myths of Forgiveness*

Several significant university studies on forgiveness deal with the false ideas that prevent us from forgiving. In Chapter 3, I've gathered many of these wrong and harmful beliefs that give forgiveness a bad reputation and discourage its use.

Here are five of the most detrimental myths that most people believe about forgiving that are not true. They think that it:

1. Needs an apology
2. Condones harmful acts
3. Comes from weakness
4. Requires you to reconcile with the person
5. Causes you to be hurt again as you must "turn the other cheek."

Our culture tends to agree with these myths. Yet forgiveness does not condone evil or wrongdoing, nor does it insist on reconciliation. It is not an act of weakness, and it does not need an apology. All it does is encourage you to let go of the upsets that are harming you, and to set limits on yourself and others to keep you safe.

True forgiveness frees your heart, soul, and mind. Should an abused woman forgive her husband and let him go on hitting her? Of course not! In the rest of the book, we will go over what works and what does not. In this way, you will learn *how* to forgive difficult situations.

To overcome these myths, it is useful to recognize that there are two opposing aspects of human survival, attacking those who threaten us, i.e., the enemy, and caring for those close to us—family, friends, and lovers.

These drives, however, are not as stable as we might wish. Sometimes a friend or spouse is seen as the enemy. Without forgiveness, the "enemy" label keeps getting bigger. Popular sentiment is to withhold forgiveness when a friend becomes an enemy, as in a legal problem or divorce.

## *The Forgiveness Battle*

There has always been a debate as to whether to forgive or not. Revenge, not forgiveness, fills our media. This is mostly due to the two parts of the survival drive discussed above, the split between our highest and true self vs. our basic survival self. Both are part of us. The former gives us our highest vision and goals of community, peace, and kindness. The latter protects us by setting limits. But, when it is in control, it keeps us separate, depressed, and vengeful.

To get past the basic, survival-self you need to understand its mechanisms so that your highest or authentic self—that part of you that enjoys life, thinks clearly, loves others, and generates peace—can be the dominant self in your life.

My strong background in medicine and science drew me to study recent research on the brain. This research provides ground-breaking insight and understanding into why we do what we do and say what we say, particularly in high-stress situations.

Many of my students were able to achieve full forgiveness only after gaining a basic understanding of the brain's stress responses. I provide this information because it is crucial in forgiving as well as in understanding what might be occurring in your life. And it is vital for anyone dealing with people who are upset.

If you sail down the river not knowing where the snags, sandbars and old shipwrecks are, those hazards will inevitably hurt you. This book is a chart you can use to navigate the rough waters of life and arrive at a destination filled with safety and satisfaction.

## *The Effects of Trauma and High Stress*

I have found when someone cannot forgive, often he or she is still suffering from the effects of trauma and/or intense stress. This pain needs to be dealt with for your forgiveness work to be entirely successful. Forgiving the trauma done by or to another is fundamental. In later chapters, I address how to get past these types of experiences. Terrible incidents that happened years ago can still have deep effects on an individual in the present. The suicide rate for Iraq war veterans is twice that of other Americans. "They are the casualties of wars you don't often hear about."[4] It is also higher for veterans than non-veterans. The suicide rate for Vietnam veterans is higher than the combat fatalities in that war.[4a]

## *Understanding our Reactions*

Important contributors to veterans' suicides is believing the myths of forgiveness, the controversy around forgiving, and the difficulty in forgiving under extremely stressful conditions. To understand this, we need to look at how our brain functions under stress.

Brain research has uncovered significant insight into:
- Why we act as we do
- Why stress makes us react in unusual ways
- How to cope with stress reactions so that our responses become more appropriate.

Most people know the brain as a processor of information—the computer inside our head that deals with thoughts and body functions. You need a broader understanding than this when you try to forgive terrible behavior. Actually, most people's present understanding of the brain hinders forgiveness.

The impact of the brain's stress responses has not yet been sufficiently or appropriately acknowledged. Better familiarity with how stress negatively impacts our brain functions will greatly improve our responses to others and life in general. Your new understanding and compassion do not justify what was done to you, but they will help you to let go of the upset and restore your peace of mind and heart.

We forgive all the time to offset the errors that we know occur from being human. We have relatively smooth functioning on our roads, in our cities, and at our workplaces, because people are inherently forgiving. If they were not, we would have full-blown chaos and violence. Forgiveness is a normal action of the human mind when it is not trapped by the reactive systems of our brain. The more strain we have, the less we are likely to forgive.

More stress equals less forgiveness. Yet forgiving is essential for success in any endeavor that involves others. And self-forgiveness is essential to succeed in any personal undertaking. Learning how your survival mechanisms affect you enables you to look at negative situations in your life in a different way.

During an offense, forgiving is more difficult if the stressed-brain reactions are going on such as the loss of job, property or a loved one because all future memories of the incident become trapped in the stress response. Thus, each time that memory recurs even years later, a flood of deep reactions surface into awareness as well. Naturally, people prefer to avoid such painful recollections.

However, avoiding your memories is not really in your best interest because this upset remains just under the surface of your awareness negatively coloring your life. Many unforgiven, unresolved events can, unknowingly and much of the time, keep your mind in a damaging state. If you include the ongoing stress of the threat of loss of job, home, or loved one, your situation could look quite hopeless. But it isn't. Forgiving is a powerful way out. You will find your answers as you progress through this book.

## *The War in our Brains*

Brain research in the 1960s and 1970s revealed that we seemed to have three brain systems operating within us. Though modern research has shown that this isn't exactly true, that early research pointed out the opposing reactions in the structures we do have within us. In general, our various brain structures function in concert with each other resulting in our best thinking, happiness, and goal achievement.[5] They function together best in a safe environment. Safety enables our mind to work as a symphony instead of a war zone. The war begins when we become overwhelmed by stress and/or fear.

Through the eons, our brain structures have adapted, expanded, and built onto themselves.[6] Thus in the present, we still carry the reactions of our ancient ancestors as well as those of mammals and reptiles. These adapted early brain structures help us not only to survive, but also to have important social qualities, and even to feel love. However, in threatening or hopeless situations, the "primitive" or reactive brain structures can override our newest thinking part of the brain, the neocortex.

The neocortex is our largest brain. It provides us with language, logic, ability to analyze, and importantly for us, forgiveness.[6a] When the brain's reactive systems shut down, the neocortex in a survival emergency, we respond immediately by fighting, fleeing, or freezing. We lose our ability to think clearly, speak intelligently, and solve problems.

In stressful times, the survival reactive brain structures over-influences our thinking resulting in regretted decisions and inappropriate actions.[7] In prehistoric times, to survive we simply reacted without thought, action or speech. In our modern culture, our survival responses are often inappropriate to achieve a positive outcome.

Isaac is an easy-going guy and always ready to give a fellow employee an acknowledging smile and help if needed. However, when his daughter was diagnosed with cancer, not only did his work suffer, but he became a terror, yelling at people for even small mistakes. The office went into chaos until they learned about Isaac's tragic situation. His coworkers rallied around him, helping him through the difficult weeks of the initial shock.

Each time we are thrown into an emergency our earlier brain structures activate our sympathetic nervous system resulting in the specific body responses that manifest as stress. Besides the typical immediate reaction of heart pounding, tense muscles, and tunnel vision, we also identify stress by our emotional reactions, such as fear with the urge to run, anger with its urge to attack, numbness, and confusion resulting in an inability to do anything.

Each person has a different threshold of stress. When we reach that over-stressed point, our sympathetic nervous system has become fully engaged. The earlier brain parts keep us stressed until we feel safe again.

To regain your true self you must find safety. Your system will then calm down. However, if you cannot experience "safety" or find a safe space in your workplace or home, turning off the sympathetic nervous system may be difficult, and may result in some of the abuse and violence so prevalent in our society today. We will go over many methods to help you calm down, start thinking and acting effectively again, and begin forgiving.

## *Quieting the Stressed System*

"The reptilian brain" is one of the names given to our earliest brain structures by the US National Institutes of Health[8] researcher, Dr. Paul MacLean, who brought these brains to light. Though this is not now accurate it does point to how our stressed reactions can become chronic as opposed to being an isolated reaction. The result is to poison us with fear and/or anger, or any of many other negative emotions. Forgiveness is *the* key choice for helping us out of the continual reactivity.

**NOTE:** Feelings might resurface as you start looking at your upsets and you might not want to continue. This is just a smoke screen put up by fear. In nature, the <u>hunted</u> will often turn to fight. When monstrous situations from the past haunt you mercilessly, attack is sometimes the best defense. If you are committed to slaying your demons and facing them head on, they will lose their power to frighten or harm you.

The thought of facing our most painful situations often feels as though it will kill us. But running from our demons gives them power. The defense mechanisms that have protected us now hobble our efforts to change this chronic pattern of response to enable us to become fully alive.

Fear keeps our stress system going, not only preventing forgiveness but also stopping the joy of life. We see it all around us today—fear of loss of work, fear of spending, fear of loss of home, fear of a terrible future, and more. These are all real. A better life, though, demands that we step out of fear. Whether or not we forgive, **fear must be quieted**.

We know that people do not compete well when afraid, and as you have probably seen, showing fear will not get a person the job they want. Exhibiting fear does not evoke confidence from others or attract them. Some people use food, drugs and alcohol to quiet fear. These are poor and temporary fixes. There are plenty of ways to quiet fear without resorting to overusing substances that will cause more harm.

To have any kind of decent, fruitful life, your continuing stressed-brain responses **need to be resolved.** Of course, you will say "How, when there are bills to pay, children to feed, and a family to support?" I understand the challenges. I am only reminding you that your stress response, though seemingly normal, is not in your best interest and certainly not to anyone around you, especially children. This book will guide you through the changes you need. There is hope.

For now, remember that there is far more complexity going on inside your brains than you realize. Under stress, rationality may be too easily overcome by strong emotions and impulses, giving way to "inhuman" behavior. This is because logic, problem-solving and analysis are relatively new functions of the brain. When the earlier organs of the brain are running the show, there will be difficulties and even chaos. We see this in violence, mass shootings, and terrorism, as well as the trauma of war; and more subtly in depression, hopelessness, and in the escalating numbers of suicides.

Forgiveness helps quiet the fearful mind. It's not easy when the fight and flight brain is actively in control. You can regain control over this by finding a safe place in your thoughts or your environment.

Several ways to achieve the state of quietness are through meditation, prayer, visiting a place of worship, talking with a close friend, listening to calming music, finding someone to take care of the kids for a while, doing something enjoyable, reading something inspirational, exercising, or even taking a shower.

**Note:** It only takes about 20 minutes of quieting activity to notice a dramatic shift away from the stressed brain's reactivity.

Remember that you are not those reactive responses. Your responsibility is to become aware of them, resolve them, and take back the reigns of your life. When you identify with the more primitive brain responses, you give up who you really are as well as your abilities to control them. It's just a case of mistaken identity.

When the stressed brain reactions take over, people will not feel like themselves and can even feel like they are obsessed or possessed. In a way, they are. If this happens, it is urgent to quiet the system, become calm, and try not to react. I know, easier said than done!

### *Write It Down*

A helpful way to claim yourself, your true self, from the more primitive reactions, is to write down your upsets as they occur or as you remember those in the past. This simple action is your commitment to deal with them.

As you read this book and look at your life, upsets with others and with yourself will inevitably come up. Write them down so that you can come back to them later.

There are two reasons for keeping a record.
1) To ensure you will address them later.
2) To use those memories during the practical exercises and questions throughout this book.

Situations will come up that you have not thought about for many years. The incidents were hidden as part of your mind's defenses to prevent mental anguish. If an event still upsets you in the present, it has not healed. It will continue to affect you beneath the surface of your awareness until you take care of it.

In her book, *Molecules of Emotion: The Science Behind Mind-Body Medicine*, Dr. Candace Pert, noted researcher, says that studies have shown that when trauma victims write about their experience, physiological changes actually occur.[9]

A companion workbook now exists to use as you read this book. Keep a journal as well to record upsetting incidents that come to mind. Include what you worked on, how you did, and what you realized. This is important work so buy a nice journal, something you will enjoy using. Writing will help this process.

## *Success in Forgiving*

Letting go of upsets does not come easily to most people, but we all have the ability to develop the skill. As with any activity, success takes work and practice. So please do the exercises.

To find happiness you must face the demons that keep you trapped in resistance, hate, or the desire for revenge. Forgiveness releases these negative thoughts and emotions. Once free of them, you have greater control over your energy, thinking, and ability to make decisions that benefit yourself and others —decisions that arise out of positive emotions.

**Please note:** Forgiveness is sometimes not an easy path because it can open up painful memories. For this reason, and because of the confusion of emotions connected to the subject, we recommend that you keep this work private, at least until you feel secure about it. At such a vulnerable time, you do not want to open yourself to others' criticism, ridicule, or unforgiven stories. You don't need those sentiments right now.

I've known clergy who preached about forgiveness but couldn't do it themselves, and certainly never gave it the respect or emphasis it deserved. I've been told that only saints can forgive, and perhaps that was true at one time, but things have changed. Anyone can forgive. Do your own work, and perhaps others will notice and ask you about it.

**It is imperative** NOT to tell someone you have forgiven her or him, unless they specifically asked for forgiveness in the past that you did not give. Telling a person, you have forgiven him/her may seem arrogant. You may create more turmoil because they might not have seen the situation as you did. You don't have to say how wonderful you are for forgiving them. Words are not needed. Your changed attitude will suffice.

People who oppose forgiveness see it as weakness. Actually, it requires extraordinary courage. "The weak can never forgive. Forgiveness is the attribute of the strong," said Gandhi. Nevertheless, vengeance is popular in our culture, not forgiveness.

An acquaintance, whose son was killed by a drunk driver, got the man prosecuted for murder, not manslaughter. Later, she realized that the young man did not deserve to spend the rest of his life in jail, and that he had a mother who was grieving for him. Her choice to forgive and help him get out of prison caused trouble for her family.[12] After Sue Norton forgave her grandparents' killer, friends would move to the other side of the street to avoid her. Even so, neither of these women regretted their forgiving.[13] Promote forgiveness by all means, but only when you are totally secure in your perspective and gains.

Forgiveness wipes away the damage of the past whether the hurt occurred thirty years or thirty minutes ago and allows us to experience the present moment fully. It produces clarity of thought because it removes the negative emotions that cloud the mind and heart. With that clarity, you start making beneficial decisions in all areas of life.

What Picasso said about art, I will say about forgiving:

*Forgiveness washes away from the soul the dust of everyday life.*

I heard a story from a woman who was driving on the freeway when a driver intentionally swerved in front of her and cut her off. Though frightened, shaken and upset, she quickly regained control of her car without a mishap. Being practiced in forgiving, and because the upset was impairing her driving, she released the anger and even said a prayer. A few minutes later, the man cut another driver off causing it to careen into a second car and then a third. Suddenly, cars were crashing into one another all around her. In her composure, she avoided them and pulled off the road undamaged. She credited her safety to having let go of the upset and clear her thoughts. She knew for sure that if she had not done so, she would have also been involved in the multiple collisions.

> "It should be clear that continuing to haul around a heart full of bitterness will not get you what you want. Therein lies the power of forgiveness. Something did, in fact, happen to you, but you still, in the interest of yourself must lay it down and move on."
>
> DR. PHIL MCGRAW, TV PSYCHOLOGIST,
> FROM HIS BOOK, *SELF MATTERS*

The following is a conversation with Paolo Coelho and a friend of his about his novel on forgiveness, *By The River Piedra I Sat Down and Wept*.

"Those are fine words, but I don't know if I am capable of pardoning ingratitude so easily."..."It's very difficult. But there is no choice: if you don't pardon, then you'll think about the pain they caused you, and that pain will never go away. I'm not saying that you have to like those who do you wrong. I'm not telling you to go back to that person's company. I'm not suggesting that you start seeing that person as an angel or as someone who acted without any hurtful intentions. All I am saying is that the energy of hate will take you nowhere, but the energy of pardon which manifests itself through love will manage to change your life in a positive sense."

CHAPTER TWO

# What Forgiving Really Is

Forgiveness means "to stop blaming or being angry with [someone] for something they have done, or to ask someone not to be angry with you."
THE CAMBRIDGE INTERNATIONAL DICTIONARY OF ENGLISH

This definition makes forgiving seem like a one-time act when it is really a way of approaching life. "Forgiveness is not an occasional act; it is a permanent attitude." - Dr. Martin Luther King, Jr.

Making it a constant presence in your life takes more than simply understanding the nature and practice of forgiveness; we must also overcome misconceptions or myths about it (Chapter 3) and recognize benefits that inspire us to forgive (Chapter 4).

## *Release of a Debt*

The most effective way that I have found to explain and define forgiveness in my classes and counseling is to use the example of forgiving a financial debt—letting go of money owed.

Simply said, **the act of forgiving is letting go of what you feel another owes you.**

In a painful situation, forgiving is letting go of the physical or emotional debt that you expect to see paid. When you forgive, the person or group no longer owes you what you expected them to give, understand, or experience. In your mind, they no longer need to feel the physical or emotional pain that you suffered, nor the desire to have them apologize to you. In truth, they might have seen the situation in quite a different way. This also means letting go of the spiritual debt of God punishing them, or their going to hell.

*The Lord's Prayer* in Christianity says it quite clearly: "Forgive us our debts, as we forgive our debtors." Just as forgiving a debt means letting go of what is owed to us, forgiving an injustice means letting go of the punishment or the payment we believe our wrongdoer owes us.

It means no longer seeking an "eye for an eye." But it does not mean turning the other cheek or inviting further injury. As Mahatma Gandhi said, "If we practice an eye for an eye and a tooth for a tooth, soon the whole world will be blind and toothless."

Often people change their ideas of what they need from the offender when they think about it more deeply. You have an idea of what it would take to let go of a particular upset. The problem is that you have not received it and probably never will. There could be many reasons for this, but the bottom line is that you might have to reevaluate the reality of your expectation and the possibility of getting what you want.

An example of forgiving a debt came from Luke, a minister, who attended one of my first forgiveness therapy classes, *Teaching How to Forgive*. Though he knew the value and necessity of forgiving, his emotions prevented him from going further because someone had lied about him to his congregation. The lie caused a huge rift in his church. Luke needed the man to tell parishioners that he had lied. He laughed as he told us, because he knew the parishioner, believing the lie, would never apologize. He saw that it is silly to expect an apology that would never come. Luke added that the rift, a matter of allegiance, probably would have occurred anyway because his style was different from that of the previous pastor.

By merely making a statement of a debt owed, I have seen insights arise. Some people have the experience and ability to look more deeply within themselves. This is not, however, a place most people to get to right away. Luke had done a considerable amount of inner work and he understood the repercussions of his unrealistic expectations and the misery they caused him.

The second part of this exercise asks the question, can you let go to gain peace of mind? This is a basic in forgiving. You need to be *willing* to consider the possibility of not getting what you feel is owed to you. Being willing to reflect on letting your expectation go, will help greatly.

This is not the end of the road, though. It means that the next step in your forgiving is to find another way to forgive, a way that does not involve the other person because he or she might never change, may never have the realization or punishment that you desire for him or her.

By forgiving, you release anger, hate, grudges, and resentments held in your mind and heart, and set limits on your negative and self-destructive attitudes. It is a gift to yourself. In situations that involve values of community well-being, family harmony, or couple's reconciliation, it is also a gift from one heart to another.[1]

Forgiveness is an act of love. It is a personal choice that relieves the forgiver of the effects of pain, hurt, resentment and anger around a hurtful and injurious situation. It takes letting go of animosity and ill will. It requires that you step out of a fixed and limited emotional stance into a grander, deeper part of yourself. It is an act of courage for it requires letting go of a justified upset.

> "Forgiveness is me giving up my right to hurt you for hurting me." ANONYMOUS

## How Do You Know You Have Really Forgiven?

The following quote tells you what to look for and how to know you have forgiven. I have used it for years with clients and students because it is especially clear.

> "You know you have forgiven someone when he or she has harmless passage through your mind." [2] REV. KARYL HUNTLEY PASTOR, GOLDEN GATE CENTER FOR SPIRITUAL LIVING

When you think of the offender, does he or she move cleanly through your mind? Or does the person crash and burn?

Renowned author and theologian, Dr. Lewis Smedes, says in his book, *Forgive and Forget: Healing the Hurts We Don't Deserve:* "You will know that forgiveness has begun when you recall those who hurt you and feel the power to wish them well."

Noted forgiveness researcher Dr. Robert Enright and The Human Development Study Group (1996) define forgiveness as the "absence of negative affect, judgment, and behavior toward an offender and the presence of positive affect, judgment, and behavior toward this same offender."[3] This is a clear result—positive feelings, opinions and actions toward the offender *and* yourself—**with no negativity.**

**Note**: I have seen forgiveness occur with only the release of the negative attitude toward the offender, and without positive thoughts entering, especially with victims of abuse and torture.

This same forgiveness research group emphasizes that self-forgiveness entails not only facing one's wrongs but also letting go of the negative thoughts, feelings and actions against the self and "replacing them with compassion, generosity and love."[3a] Forgiveness toward yourself must result in positive feelings, actions and thoughts for you, or it is incomplete.

## *Lovingkindness*

In recent years, people in my counseling, classes, and groups have had significant success in forgiving using Lovingkindness meditation, also called a compassion affirmation or prayer, as it directly addresses the well-being for another – the end-result of forgiving. For those who practiced it daily, there were significant positive changes in the brain and body, including lowered stress response and even reduced inflammation. Participants reported being more satisfied with their lives, an overall sense of well-being and experiencing fewer symptoms of depression.[4]

I've found that it has helped people mend when they hit tough times, even in drug and alcohol recovery and loss of a loved one. I put all the different Lovingkindness variations I found on the web into one meditation/affirmation/prayer. Say it sincerely for others, and you will get the same blessing as someone saying it for you. It is best to do it with 100% intention and meaning along with visualizing the result for the person.

> May you be safe.
> May you be well.
> May you be happy.
> May you be free from suffering.
> May you be filled with love and kindness.
> May you be at peace and at ease.
> May you be filled with joy.

With the most difficult forgiveness I did in my life, I was able to clean it up by using this affirmation for the person, saying it over and over for days. It worked. At first, I had to fake it, but I finally made it to where I wanted those intentions for the person. I realized that if s/he really had the above, the situation would not have happened.

## *Justice, Revenge and Punishment*

The question of justice usually comes up when considering forgiveness. People will say that it's not right to forgive a person because then there will be no consequence for what the person did. The unforgiven person broke your personal, familial, or cultural rules of behavior yet you have to forgive him? Where is the justice when you have been wronged?

It seems unjust to let a person get away with having done something awful to you, particularly when it is wrong. You may even want to teach the offender a lesson. That kind of thinking, though, perpetuates the emotional pain you feel. I have yet to find someone happy in his or her life who is also punishing another.

Researchers are showing that punishment, often through revenge and justice, were built into our brain reactions in early times when there were fewer people and smaller groups. In those times, revenge/justice would have been effective at changing people's minds.[4a 4b 4c]

Thinking about revenge activates the brain's reward pathways, much like drugs do for a drug addict.[4d] But, contrary to popular belief, research shows that punishing others causes the punisher to think about the transgressor more, not less, and can even increase the desire for more revenge—revenge does not bring closure.[4e] This is because the drive for revenge comes from the more primitive emotional centers of the brain.[4f] Also, revenge can create a cycle of retaliation causing even more trouble.

Dr Michael McCullough in his book, *Beyond Revenge: The evolution of the forgiveness instinct*, says that forgiveness has evolved to restrain our reaction to be vengeful as we not only have less possibility of ever seeing the person again as societies grew, but also it alleviated the stress that revenge puts on us. Forgiveness comes from our highest functions, the prefrontal lobes of the neocortex.[4g 4h] The only time that revenge seems to be fruitful at all is when the punished offender understands why the punishment occurred.[4i] However, often the offender who is punished feel that the punishment was too much and then retaliation can occur making the situation even worse.[4j]

You would not need to forgive if you did not have an expectation of punishment for the offender or repentance for his behavior. The emotional effect of that desire is the problem.

S/he may claim to be happy to get back at the offender, but look carefully and you will find no joy in life, as the researchers have found. When a person wants to punish and attack another, he or she is being controlled by the reactionary brain of where joy and love are not components.

The intent to punish may continue even when the offender is no longer in someone's life. Many people hold onto upsets with parents who have been dead for years. They still attack the parent *in their minds* even when the attack is painful only to themselves.

> "Before you embark on a journey of revenge,
> dig two graves." — CONFUCIUS

The question of right and wrong seems vital. When you feel right and justified in your anger, you will have difficulty in your personal, family, and work life.

We expect to receive justice when values, rules for behavior, or ethical principles of a person, group, or country are broken. Ideals, laws, and rules maintain a culture and hold a society together. They are also the glue of family bonds and relationships.

When a person or group goes against our values or breaks our rules, whether, in a one-to-one relationship or a societal setting, the person or group is usually cast out. It is only after the individual or group makes sufficient reparation for their offense, are they permitted back.

In the legal system, this may occur after fulfilling a prison sentence or public service. A personal situation might require an apology or payment for the damage. It is easier to forgive someone who has tried to repair the result of his or her act.

When the person or group disagrees with your values or rules of how you expect them to behave, forgiving becomes difficult. How do you forgive then? How does justice occur? How do you release the pain, anger and hurt when there is no apology or repair when the offender sees the situation differently and feels justified in what he or she did? This book contains many methods to attain relief.

## *Effects of Hostility*

Women who score high on anger and hostility have a higher risk of a cardiovascular event.[5] Earlier research showed that it is not Type-A people who necessarily have heart attacks, but those who score high on the hostility portion of the questionnaire.[6] (See note A ) Dean Ornish, MD, and author of *Love and Survival,* cites forty-five studies connecting hostility and coronary heart disease.[7]

A Duke University study shows that students who score high on a hostility test are in greater danger of dying younger than their peers, concluding that students who are prone to anger are at more risk than those who smoke, have high blood pressure or cholesterol.[8]

If you often find yourself angry and hostile, consider this: Somewhere along the way, for your health and happiness, you might think about resigning from the job of judge and punisher.

## *Important Points for Effective Forgiving*

**Always Be Aware Of The Small Shifts of Heart and Attitude.**
The most significant discovery I've found in forgiveness work is how quickly it can occur. As you do the exercises, you will experience small shifts of heart and thought. Positive energy accumulates from these shifts and enables a transformation. If you feel relief while working on a question, that might be enough for the moment. Take a break or go to the next action.

I call these changes of feeling and attitude the "felt shift." It's a sensation of warmth in the chest area, an opening of your heart, with a relaxation of the muscles around the ribs and throat, often accompanied by a realization. It is like the "felt sense" that Dr. Eugene Gendlin describes in his book, *Focusing.* It's a little movement of the heart coming back in tune.[10]

The whole secret is a sense of "aha," often a smile, and a feeling of relief. It might be because of a compassionate thought or a new understanding of the person. If you look at the shift more closely, you will see it involves a change in attitude toward the person. Often that little movement is sufficient to change your whole day, and sometimes even your whole life.

> "Forgiveness does not change the past, but it does enlarge the future." - PAUL BOESE 1668 – 1738 DUTCH PHYSICIAN

With each felt shift, you regain some of the energy you tied up in the emotional upset. As you continue to look at different areas of your life, gain understanding of them and forgive, you recover more and more life energy. This process becomes increasingly easier and quicker because the released energy and power boost your life and increase your ability to forgive, live, love, and heal.

## A Clarification on Acceptance and Forgiveness

I had this discussion on these two subjects on a Los Angeles NPR radio interview I had several years ago.

Acceptance is a natural step in forgiving because you must look realistically at the situation and the feelings that are going on around the upset, but it does not necessarily result in forgiveness.

The best definitions for *accept* that I've found were at learnersdictionary.com:
- to stop denying or resisting (something true or necessary), i.e. "The truth is sometimes hard to *accept*."
- to admit you have or deserve (something, such as blame or responsibility), i.e. to *accept* blame or "I *accept* responsibility for the accident."

You can accept what happened, and even accept blame and responsibility and not feel forgiven for or forgiving toward another. True forgiveness results in letting go of the upset. Acceptance brings about forgiveness when understanding and compassion happen. Effective forgiving dissolves the upset so that it no longer has any negative emotional effect.

The problem with acceptance is that you can acknowledge the presence of the upset and then avoid it. I've seen people intentionally avoid and deny the impact of the upsetting situation. For some, this might work. I've seen people completely accept the state of their mind and their depression and wallow it "acceptingly." It's my experience that depression dissolves when real and complete forgiveness is done. We will get into this later in the book.

This quote in the A.A. Big Book brings us the closest to the ideal of acceptance: "Acceptance is the answer to ALL of my problems today. When I am disturbed, it is because I find some person, place, thing or situation- some fact of my life- unacceptable to me, and I can find no serenity until I accept that person, place, thing, or situation as being exactly the way it is supposed to be at this moment…; unless I accept my life completely on life's terms, I cannot be happy. I need to concentrate not so much on what needs to be changed in the world as on what needs to be changed in me and in my attitudes."

This type of acceptance brings us to the point of being willing to forgive. But forgiveness – letting the upset go – is the change that is needed. Forgiveness relieves the body and mind of the upset and returning them to a natural connection to Life. Even my meditations went much deeper after my forgiveness transformation.

## *The First Essential Aspect*

Throughout the book, I reveal essential actions for doing this work. The primary one is: **Hold the highest possible vision or goal for yourself that you believe forgiving can bring.**

Without this incentive, it may be too difficult to look at upsets, and you will probably give up. You will do well, though, if you have a high ideal for yourself.

In my own experience with forgiveness, I have often needed to choose my highest vision. Because my highest goal was to experience the unconditional love of God, I would ask myself, "Am I willing to let this upset go to experience unconditional love?" It worked every time. Each time, I would have relief in my heart and joy flow through me.

Set your vision and goal, by asking:
A. What do I want in my life from this forgiveness work? Is it to experience Healing? More Love? Calmness and peace? Divine Love? A deeper connection to God?
B. What would inspire me to let this upset go?
C. Other than myself, who benefits from my forgiving?

**Journal Questions:** To help you, I have included an exercise used successfully for centuries by Christians:

"Forgive us our debts, as we forgive our debtors."

You don't need to go any further with this book if you can apply that prayer right now. Few, however, have been able to, so let's look at this idea further.
1. What does that person owe you? An apology? Groveling on their stomach in grief? Hanging by their toes in pain for three days? You beating them to death with your fists? Electrocution?

2. What punishment do you need to see? Just what is it that you expected, didn't get, or don't expect to receive? That is their debt to you. {If you are working on forgiving yourself for something, you are looking for what you owe the other or yourself.}
3. At this point, write down what the person or group owes you (or you owe another). No one is going to read this but you, so let it all out. You can be as vile and vicious as you'd like.
4. After you have written all you want, look and see if this is the justice you want. How do you feel? Then ask:
    a. How likely is it that I will get the punishment or behavior change I would like?
    b. How long am I going to wait to get it?
    c. Am I willing to let this upset go?

## *The Major Barrier to Forgiving:*

*Feeling overwhelmed*

This often comes from trying to forgive too much at once. The objective of *The Power Forgiveness Process* is to forgive everything in your life that you have not yet let go of, not just one act. But to do it successfully, you need to b*reak it down to smaller parts.*

The first thing to do with a consuming situation is to break it down into workable parts. It's too much to try to jam a whole plate of food into your mouth at one time and try to swallow. You take bite-size pieces. It is the same with forgiving. See how you can break a difficult situation down into smaller, more manageable parts.

Tom's upset with a building contractor entailed writing down all the contractor's upsetting actions He found that it calmed him. Tom was then able to sit down with the man and come to an understanding.

Sometimes writing all your negative experiences down at one time is too much. Marjory was upset with several doctors for mishandling her illness. She became too angry writing all her upsets down, so she took one doctor at a time, wrote her upsets with him, then forgave each perceived wrong. After that, she took the next doctor following the same method. In the end, her anger and underlying fear of doctors had vanished, and she was able to undergo a procedure that helped her healing.

You need to take care of yourself first. The most important thing I have learned from counseling, couple's therapy, conflict resolution and reconciliation work is that each person must **always** feel safe. This includes yourself when working alone. If you feel to upset,stop. Relax, work on something smaller less reactive. Any forgiveness work you do helps.

## *Dealing with Large Organizations*

If you have difficulty forgiving large institutions or organizations, it's because you be overwhelmed by the magnitude of your upset. Again, breaking it down into bite-size pieces makes a difference.

Similarly, when you try to deal with offenses committed by governments, organizations, corporations, or churches, you accomplish nothing by addressing the whole group, or seeing it as "them." Break it down into specific situations and specific people and then work on each one. When you get to the specifics of a situation, you get closer to the truth.

When you work on offenses, address all the smaller parts of the upset to achieve full forgiveness.

People form and run organizations, movements, churches, societies, political groups, and governments. *People need forgiving.* Break down the upsets by thinking of who represents that organization. As you think of one, others will come to mind.

I worked with a woman who had been in a cult for many years. She thought that writing all the upsets she experienced in the cult would be too overwhelming. Instead, she found it was more overpowering to let them boil in the dark subconscious emotional sea and the horrific storms they created in her everyday life. She started writing them down and, to her surprise, she started feeling increasingly better.

The feeling of betterment, though, is a good start. You have to continue and forgive the upsets.

## *The Key Question*

Breaking down the situation often brings up a key question about what happened or the people involved. The answer is found by looking at all the pieces of the situation and forgiving each person involved to bring full resolution.

It took Gilbert and Kaitlin a year after their divorce to sit down and talk about what had happened. Both shared their experience. Gilbert found that he had only one question. "Why did you stay with me when I was so terrible to be around and our life was so bad?" Kaitlin's answer stunned him. "I didn't mind it. The kids were doing okay. The place was nice. And you weren't as bad as you think." Note that a completely different answer may have satisfied another person with different values.

Gilbert was lucky. People do not often get the chance to have the key question answered directly. It helps to talk with someone about your upset, especially if the person is objective, does not take sides, and who can provide insights.

## *Truth and Reconciliation Commission*

In 1995 when South Africa was trying to forge peace after many years of a racially oppressive government, it set up a *Truth and Reconciliation Commission* to consider amnesty for perpetrators of crimes committed under apartheid's reign. The democratic government did not give a blanket forgiveness amnesty because it knew it would not work. The commissioners gave amnesties, person by person, to those who came before them. There was confrontation by victims, and confessions of guilt.

The movie, *Long Night's Journey into Day: South Africa's Search for Truth & Reconciliation*, skillfully depicts part of the Commission's work. In 2000, it was awarded the Sundance Film Festival -Best Documentary.[11] This amnesty model, under various names, has been used in eleven other countries emerging from periods of internal unrest, civil war, or dictatorship.[12]

## *Forgiving Big Issues*

Behind broad issues in history or the world that you do not like—racism for instance—there is a person or group who represent that injustice in your thoughts. You might have to explore your past to find them.

Marion was trying to forgive the Catholic Church for the atrocities against women during the Inquisition in the Middle Ages. She remained upset until noticed pictures in her mind of the inquisitors as dark, sinister men in black robes. She knew she had to forgive those priests. This awareness put her on a journey to understand the mindset of priests of that time. Equipped with that recognition, she could let her upset go.

To forgive the German Nazis, Jacob thought of each Nazi soldier and supporter he had come across in his life. He gave a prayer of forgiveness to each individually until he felt complete with that person. Because certain guards were difficult, he kept on praying until he felt relief. He could see how others were caught up in the lies about Jews. Only then was he able to let go of his upset. It was a long process for Jacob, and it became easier with each step he took.

Margaret was in a particularly difficult court suit. After years, several lawyers, and no resolution, she was even more upset and almost penniless. While she needed to get on with her life, she could not forgive the legal system, much less the person against whom she had filed the suit. She went through the *Power Forgiveness Process* in several counseling sessions. She forgave each legal representative she could remember on both sides of the suit. The result was a new perspective that enabled her to forgive the person and quickly resolve the suit to her satisfaction.

## *Forgiving God*

"How do you forgive God for allowing the terrible atrocities that people do to each other every day?" Harvey thundered at me one day. "I cannot and will not forgive a God that allows brutality and the decimation of peoples and cultures in his name!" To resolve his conflict with God, he had to look at how he perceived God, God's role, and where and when he learned about them.

He also had to look at the atrocities he attributed to God. In the middle of this searching of mind and hear, Harvey looked around the room, shook his head, and said, "This is not about God! It's about men acting out of fear and hate. And, many times, even believing they were doing right! God does not do these things, we do. There is nothing to forgive God for."

Forgiving God seems self-centered. It is. That is exactly why we need to forgive. Our perspective is always self-centered when we see only from our own eyes.

Forgiveness requires that we walk in the other person's shoes as much as we can. That includes God's shoes if we are to forgive God. It often requires us to reevaluate the God of our childhood. This exercise of reviewing our earliest concepts of The Almighty can bring us understanding, a deepening of our faith, and new humility.

When Adam, a young police officer, was in a personal crisis, he went down his list of gripes with God. He felt better, but it brought him to a basic question of theology. He told his pastor: "God should change the minds trapped in evil ways." Many have this deep question of the natures of God and man. He told me later, "I was stymied when my pastor asked me about the importance of free will. In our discussion, I finally understood that without free will we are just trapped robots. Our free will gives us our life." That insight gave him understanding and forgiveness.

**Journal exercise:** To forgive God, as with any other big upset, you must:
1. Break down the upset,
2. List all the upsetting things you feel God has done, then
3. Answer the key questions that come up.

Spend time now looking at your upset or upsets and see if you can break them down as far as possible.

## *The First Hurdle*

By understanding: •what forgiveness is • what you need to let go of to forgive • getting past the biggest barrier • understanding and noticing the small shifts • and focusing on your highest vision for yourself, you have passed the first hurdle to forgiving.

However, you are not expected to forgive everything this soon. But if you already have good results, go on to the next person you need to forgive.

Initial research on forgiving occurred in forgiveness training classes at universities. There, students were taught what forgiveness was and was not. Often significant forgiveness results were obtained just through this step. You are doing much more than that here.

CHAPTER THREE

# The Proven Benefits of Forgiving

## *The Mind Transforms through Forgiving*

When you let go of the bitterness of the past, mental, spiritual, and physical energy becomes more available. How much life energy returns depends on how much energy you expended holding onto resentments from the past, and how much letting go is completed.

## *Research Results*

Research conducted at prestigious universities shows that forgiveness results in an increase in cardiovascular functioning, lowering both blood pressure and heart rate. Findings also include an increase in psychological and emotional well-being, less anxiety and stress, reduction in depression and hopelessness[2], less anger, more confidence, and higher self-esteem.

When held too long, grudges and resentments damage the heart and blood vessels. All age groups noted these effects. The gains remained long after the forgiveness training ended. In both short-term and long-term well-being, people who were more forgiving had fewer chronic conditions and physical symptoms of illness, and more vitality and emotional resiliency. It seems there is no negative outcome from learning to forgive.[3]

In his bestselling book, *Forgive for Good, A Proven Prescription for Health and Happiness,* Dr. Fred Luskin, of the Stanford Forgiveness Project, tells us that researchers have found that just the idea of forgiving someone allowed some people to feel better psychologically and emotionally. Conversely, if the participants in the study imagined themselves as unforgiving, they had negative reactions, such as high blood pressure.

He cites forgiveness research has revealed these general results:[3a]

- People who are more forgiving report fewer symptoms of stress and health problems.
- Failure to forgive may be more significant than hostility as a risk factor for heart disease.
- Even people with devastating losses can learn to forgive and feel better psychologically and emotionally.
- On the other hand, people who blame others for their troubles have a higher incidence of illnesses such as cardiovascular disease and cancer.

Forgiveness training in scientific studies has been shown to:[3b]
1. Heal relationships
2. Increase hopefulness, personal growth, and self-confidence
3. Decrease depression, anger, and anxiety
4. Improve compassion, spiritual well-being, and quality of life.

## More Research Results on Forgiving

*In addition to the above section, here more forgiveness research results, compiled and written by Michelle Pender, MPH for the Forgiveness Foundation.*

When people fail to forgive a past upset, they prolong the pain and anger caused by these upsets. Unforgiveness keeps us reliving past events over and over again, and places our bodies through the same strains as the actual event itself, causing numerous negative health outcomes.[I] In contrast, the act of forgiving has been associated with fewer reported physical symptoms of illness, fewer medications taken, a stronger immune system, improved cardiovascular activity, and decreased blood pressure.

Failing to forgive and hanging on to hostility has been proven to be hostile to our health. Numerous research studies have demonstrated a strong connection between hostility, anger, and poor cardiovascular health.[II] Feelings such as anger and other feelings associated with unforgiveness are strongly associated with chronically elevated blood pressure and platelet aggregation, which, can lead to blood clots and increase a person's risk for heart disease.[III]

Another study found that participants who relived stressful moments experienced increased heart rate, blood pressure, and facial muscle tension.[IV] On the other hand, experiments suggest that forgiveness is associated with lower levels of blood pressure and our body's ability to recovery from a stressful event, lowering blood pressure levels more quickly.[V] In fact, research has shown very positive results with forgiving on cardiovascular health that scientists have suggested incorporating forgiveness therapies into existing cardiac rehabilitation programs.[VI]

An essential factor in forgiveness having such a strong impact on our health is the prolonged nature of forgiveness.[VII] It provides our bodies with a long protective factor against reliving past upsets and stressful events or allows us to remember these events without the feeling the same stress and anger so detrimental to our health.[VIIb]

The stress and negative emotions caused by an upset and then prolonged by unforgiveness can wreak havoc on our immune systems. This, in turn, has very real negative consequences on our health including susceptibility to infectious disease and the inability to heal from wounds.[IX] A search of the web will show numerous the link between forgiveness and the health of people living with HIV/AIDS. One such study found that depression, a symptom strongly associated with unforgiveness[VIII], decreases CD4T-Cells that alert the immune system of viruses and bacteria, which are an essential part of slowing the progression of HIV.[X]

Unforgiveness affects our immune system in less direct ways as well. The feelings of anger, resentment, animosity and other negative emotions associated with unforgiveness can often lead to social isolation, as friends and family are driven away. There is strong evidence to support the connection between strong, healthy personal relationships and strong, healthy immune function.[XI] Lack of social support among HIV-positive men was associated with a more rapid decline in CD4 T-Cells than among men who had social support from friends and family.[XII]

While social isolation has negative consequences on our immune systems, disruptive social relationships can also have a similar impact. A study revealed that couples who exhibit more hostile and negative behavior during conflict showed a decrease in their immune systems and an increase in stress hormones.[XIII] Altering immune function in this manner inhibits the body's ability to heal wounds, fight infections, and increases the risk for contracting diseases, prolonging illness[XIV] and tumor growth.[XV]

Since our minds have such a powerful impact on our bodies and consequently our health, addressing the mind through forgiveness therapies and/or meditation are a way to combat health problems. Studies have found that meditation can increase levels of melatonin in our bodies, which enhances our immune systems and slow the growth of malignant prostate cancer tumors.[XVI]

Holding on to negative emotions can be harmful to our health. One experiment found a direct link between emotions and the physical makeup of our bodies. This experiment placed human DNA strands in containers. These containers were then exposed to feelings and strong emotions of researchers. Findings revealed that the DNA changed shape depending on the type of emotion they were exposed to. When exposed to emotions of gratitude, love and appreciation the DNA strands relaxed and unwound. However, when they were exposed to emotions of anger, fear, and frustration and stressed the DNA strands tightened up and became shorter in length.[XVIII]

## *Forgiveness Therapy Results*

Drs. Robert Enright and Richard Fitzgibbons have a textbook on the benefits of Forgiveness Therapy called *Helping Clients Forgive: An Empirical Guide for Resolving Anger and Restoring Hope*. Their studies show that Forgiveness Therapy can be beneficial for treating:[4]

- Anxiety disorders, including generalized anxiety disorder, separation anxiety disorder, panic disorder, social phobia, obsessive-compulsive disorder
- Post-Traumatic Stress Disorder (PTSD)
- Depression, including Bipolar Disorder
- Children with conduct disorders, such as Oppositional Defiance Disorder, Attention Deficit Hyperactive Disorder (ADHD), and impulsivity
- Substance abuse and eating disorders; Impulse control disorders, such as gambling, pyromania, and kleptomania
- Personality disorders, such as paranoia, borderline, histrionic, narcissistic, and any condition where strong anger is involved

## *Increased Energy and Uplifted Spirits*

Unforgiven situations can cause depression by keeping your life energy low. Upsets and resentments do not remain in your mind without effort. You are investing your life energy on upsetting thoughts. When you let them go, you regain zest and life.

Salespeople who had a one-day workshop on forgiveness and emotional competence with regular forgiveness coaching over a six month period sold two and a half times more than their coworkers who had none of this training.[5]

## Changes in Others

Years ago, a friend's daughter and the daughter's fiancé were brutally murdered. The murderer was found, convicted and sent to prison. My friend, Aba Gayle, who was miserable for years, finally said, "I just can't hate like this!" She needed to find out why he did it. She went to the prison to meet the murderer. In hearing his story, she realized she had to forgive. Over time, she made friends with him; his humanity moved her.[6a]

## Happier Relationships

Forgiving improves relationships because you can be emotionally present and communicate a deeper level of love. In intimate relationships, you and your partner are more in tune with each other. Loving thoughts can come forward releasing upsets more easily. When there is an upset, there is more compassion, rather than a determined defense of your position.

My dear friend, Kima, sent me this note after I asked her how she and her husband, Michael, had managed to remain so happy in their marriage for 35 years. Whenever I'd talk with them, they'd say, "Our relationship hasn't been better!" Here's what she wrote:[6b]

> "After several years together and things not going well, we spent many days going over situations where our feelings were hurt. We looked at our relationship from every angle, talked about every one of our upsets, and let them go. These were not big things, but when they accumulated, they caused big hurts. From that forgiveness work, we have managed to build a rock-solid platform for our marriage.
>
> So, I want to say that when you are dealing with couples, what is left unsaid can be a vicious sting later down the line, especially if it seems silly or embarrassing to one person. Those things come up later to harm the relationship."

This was intense work, difficult for couples to do without help. Michael was a psychotherapist. They both knew the value of doing this "cleanup work." I would recommend getting a counselor initially to help you to get to that level of communication.

## *Positive Results with Children*

Paul was quite angry after his divorce. He was unloving toward his three children because they reminded him of the painful divorce and his financial troubles. He did not behave rationally or tenderly toward them. Of course, they did not want to be around him, but Paul did not see how he was creating the estrangement.

Luckily, his girlfriend dragged him to a forgiveness class. In it, he finally could see his responsibility in the estrangement from his children. A month later in his summary paper for the class, he said that he was able to recreate a loving bond with them instead of blaming them and his ex-wife.

## *Dealing with Marriage and New Relationships*

Statistics show that second and third marriages are NOT likely to be more successful than first marriages. As with computers, old programs from parents and failed relationships are still in our conscious *operating system*, disrupting the new relationship until it is *corrupted*. The problems will increase until the system *crashes* in another ruptured relationship, or a health problem.

You owe it to each new relationship or life endeavor to look for and clean up anything that might contaminate it. Forgiveness presents an opportunity to change destructive family patterns.

To install a new operating system, you must uninstall the old one. You are doing that with Power Forgiveness. To *install* a better inner system for higher possibility and happiness, remove as many old resentments and grievances as you can. Look at the *Power Forgiveness Process* as an antivirus program, removing vicious incidents that are ruining your life.

## *Physical Healing*

Research published in the *Journal of General Psychiatry* showed that hostile marital interactions slowed physical wound healing and caused an increase in an inflammatory protein in the blood. This data also shows "hostile or abrasive relationships affect physiological functioning and health."[7a] Chronically elevated levels of this "hostile" protein can contribute to cardiovascular disease, arthritis, certain kinds of cancers, and other conditions.[7b]

> "There's something called the 'physiology of forgiveness.' Being unable to forgive other people's faults is harmful to one's health."
> HERBERT BENSON, MD, NOTED AUTHOR, RESEARCHER

Julia came to a weekly forgiveness group for two months. Life was getting better for her, but she still had trouble forgiving her abuse as a child. On the fourth week, the group gave Julia the whole evening to work on the issues she still had with her parents, who had been dead ten years. She felt good after the session. Two or three weeks later she revealed that the pain in her knees that she had suffered for years, was gone. She said it all went away that night when she finally forgave her father.

When Hank felt miserable and hopeless from a fever and sore throat, he decided to look for an unresolved upset that could have caused the illness. After looking for only a few minutes, he said, "I remembered an assistant at work had demanded a salary equal to my own even though he didn't have the years of experience or skill. I was quite upset with him." Hank used the forgiveness process outlined in the workshop.

Later he said, "When I realized that the guy was just being himself and did need a raise, I felt fine about him. You know, all of a sudden, the sore throat started clearing up, and the fever started coming down. I was well in less than three hours. Wow, Amazing." Although this result is unusual, mastering forgiveness can help maintain better health.

## *Chris Loukas*

Even the devastating effects of trauma heal faster with forgiveness, often miraculously. Chris Loukas, a deeply spiritual man, and old friend, lives forgiveness. One night, years ago, a drunk driver collided with Chris' van. For six weeks, he lay in a coma suffering from multiple fractures. When he regained consciousness, the doctors told him he would never walk again.

With the prayers of many and forgiveness for the fellow who hit him, he did walk again. When he recovered, Chris not only befriended the young man who caused the accident but treated him as a son, helping him to get off alcohol and find work. Chris held no resentment. His forgiving attitude not only facilitated his physical recovery but also left him with peace of mind.[8a]

After my workshops, some people are so convinced of the benefits of forgiveness; they check to see whom they haven't forgiven when the first symptoms of illness appear. Often, the symptoms will clear up quickly and sometimes go away within a few hours of performing this action.

When you find yourself sick, ask,:[9]
1. When did it start?
2. What was going on in my life at that time?
3. Who do I need to forgive?

## *Experiencing Deeper Spirituality*

All of the above research and examples show the mental, emotional, and physical benefits of forgiving. Even more significant are the spiritual benefits.

Spiritually, the clear and forgiving mind can sense The Divine and Sacred in life. In letting go of upsets, life becomes full, the heart becomes peaceful, and the mind, calm. Joy is then a natural consequence, love is renewed, and true self-esteem is reestablished. Then we experience the truth of who we are through the connection to the Essence of Life.

Those people who live the forgiving way of life, the way of letting go of upsets, tell us and show us that Love is an essential part of our natural state of being.

Some people have deeply religious experiences after forgiving. They say that they have a deeper understanding of life, love, and God. Lewis Smedes, in his book, *Forgive and Forget* suggests:

> "When you forgive the person who hurt you deeply and unfairly, you perform a miracle that has no equal. Nothing else is the same. Forgiving has its own feel, color and climax, different from any other creative act in the repertoire of human relationships."[10]

Forgiveness work is effective in changing our lives because we are realigning our mind with the Primary Principle of Existence—God, Higher Power, Allah, The Great Spirit, etc. This empowers us to go beyond thinking about the way things should be. This act of quieting our self-centeredness and realigning with a Highest Power calls forth a higher magnitude of healing power.

Because something was terribly negative or continued for a long time does not mean its release must be comparably difficult or drawn out. Psychotherapy is often caught in this false thinking. In Power Forgiveness, we are talking about a different approach. Standard psychotherapy often addresses the issue from the level and mindset of victimhood. In forgiveness counseling, the practitioner and the person working on his or her upsets are attempting to hold the mindset of the Highest Potential available.

> "No problem can be solved from the same level of consciousness that created it." ALBERT EINSTEIN

The highest potential perspective will bring our thoughts back to our highest capacity. Holding grudges, resentments, anger, revenge thoughts, obsessing about a hurt, or avoiding something are all manifestations of lack of love and lack of connection to the highest within us. By the willingness to realign to our highest potential or power, we call forth resources both personal and universal to assist us.

## *The Real Consequence of Holding on to Upsets*

Sometimes people believe there is a benefit to not forgiving. So, let's look at this. The first look at **the payoff** for not letting go of the upset. Generally, people have a good reason for doing or not doing something. Even though a decision we've made might not seem to be in our best interest, if we look deeply, we'll find a belief that the choice made was the best one possible at the time. Often however, we are influenced by lower brain activities and stress.

**Ask yourself:**
- What do I get by keeping the upset going? Write down any benefits. Who benefits and how?
- Is being right more important than being happy?

Sometimes you don't notice how much the upset affects you. Here are questions to ask:

1. What am I really getting out of this upset? List the negatives and the positives.
2. What is happening to the people closest to me by my holding onto the upset?
3. In my life, how strong are love, peace, and joy?
4. Could forgiving this situation increase my happiness and those around me?

The following are questions about being a victim:
   a. Have I seen myself as a victim of others?
   b. How long have I felt victimized?
   c. How long is it okay to let others be in control of my happiness?
   d. Am I a contributor to the problem, not just the victim?

## *The Seldom Used Act That Brings Big Results*

*Prayer for Inner Help* – Even though many people have a religious or spiritual perspective in their life, they seldom pray for help in forgiving. We do have deep inner help available. It can show us a different way of viewing any negative situation and can unburden us if we are willing to accept it. I call it Divine Help because it seems to have much greater wisdom and honesty than I have. Accessing this Power beyond our small unforgiving-self is effective. You are empowered by realigning with the Creation Principle of the universe—opening your mind to possibilities and perspectives other than your own.

To connect with this Divine Help: Take time to relax and contemplate the highest in yourself as you do this forgiveness work.

♦ Take a moment now to ask for inner Divine support through a prayer to assist you in forgiving.

**Note**: An extremely useful prayer, is, **"Please help me to see this in a different way."**

If you bog down at any time during this work, be silent, and make a sincere request for Help. *Have faith in Divine Love.* When you have done all you can do, let the struggle go and listen. I cannot tell you how this help will manifest or how it will occur, but I know that it is there to assist you.

**Writing Dialogue:** Writing about what is going on with you now concerning a specific incident or person is an effective tool in forgiving. I use what I call the *Dialogue Process*. It is a writing technique that helps you get underneath the upset and gain a different view. This shift in viewpoint is critical in the entire process of letting go.

To do it talk with yourself in writing about your upset until you come up with the next logical question. For example, if you are upset with your husband, you write about how upset you are until a question comes up. Perhaps, "How could he do that?" You then write, answering that question until the next question comes up, as "Was his mother like that to him?" This goes on until understanding, or compassion arises.

This is a valuable method. The questions and answers never fail to surprise. If I start out with a prayer for guidance and help, I find the help always comes. When emotions come up, accept them and keep writing, or ask another question, like "what's behind this emotion."

## *The Simplest Forgiveness Practice*

At first, I was skeptical of Rosie's forgiveness beads and prayer. When I met Rosie Rodriguez, a sweet and spiritual woman in Santa Rosa, California, she had been teaching her work and having people make "pay-it-forward beads" for over a year with terrific results. There are 490 beads in all, resembling Catholic rosary beads, which some people use for this. This number comes from the Bible (KJV)– Matthew 18:21-22:

> "Then came Peter to him, and said, Lord, how oft shall my brother sin against me, and I forgive him? Till seven times? saith unto him, I say not unto thee, until seven times: but, until seventy times seven."

None of the forgiveness methods I had used for ten years were as simple as this one. The first time I used the beads I tackled a big forgiveness issue that was bothering me. I simply prayed "I forgive," with strong prayerful intention on each of the prayer beads. After ten beads there is a gratitude bead where I said something I was grateful for from that situation. At the end of that session, the upset was gone and never came back.

Self-forgiveness is difficult inner work. So, a few months later, I decided to tackle an area of my life where I felt guilt. Again, I used Rosie's method. Again, I broke down the big upset into bite-size pieces. On each of the smaller upsets with myself, with strong intention, I just prayed, "I forgive" repeatedly with a grateful thought after ten to twenty repetitions. I was pleased with the changes from pain to relief that I had within five to seven minutes on each small issue. I continued for 45 minutes until there were no small upsets. I felt great—the big upset was no longer there.

It is effective for people with both large and small upsets.

## *Hope for Humankind*

Our highest self comes forward in a calm, unthreatened state of mind. Then, our brain begin to synchronize, making sense of our lives and giving meaning to our actions. Forgiveness makes that state of mind stable so that we can function at our highest level and fulfill our deepest dreams.

Forgiveness, then, is the hope for humankind, because forgiving readily brings the highest function of the mind and heart to the forefront, assisting us to let go of unreasonable expectations, fears, and attack. It enables us to undo the chronic primitive brain reactions, fear and fight, allowing the highest functioning of the brain to occur. Also, we have the connection to the Divine, enabling us to reach our highest capacity.

Forgiveness is not the highest function of the human mind. It is, however, the most powerful way you have to quell the storm of emotions and primitive stimulus-response mechanisms that you experience. Through a forgiving mind, you can function at a higher level of kindness, peace, problem-solving, and openness to the highest creative power available to you—a state to which humanity aspires.

## *The Second Hurdle*

By being convinced of the power of forgiveness, you have passed the third hurdle in forgiving. You know what it can do in your life, and what not forgiving has done to you. This might not have brought you to forgiving your main upset, but for many, this information helps sway the thoughts of forgiving toward the positive. By this time, you should have found an excellent reason to forgive, and, are working on forgiving some people in your life.

"To carry a grudge is like being stung to death by one bee."
WILLIAM H. WALTON

# CHAPTER FOUR

# The Blocks to Forgiving

## *The Myths of Forgiveness*

In addition to their stressed-brain reactions, people resist giving up their upsets because of misconceptions about forgiving. I call these *The Myths of Forgiveness*. Sadly, these myths prevent us from letting go of resentments even when we know they are not true. Here are some of the most common ones.

*Myth 1 – The person is deceased or no longer around, so forgiveness is not needed!*

You might think, "out of sight, out of mind." But, if you still carry upsetting emotions and thoughts about the person, the injury remains alive inside you, in your mind. At some level, harboring any resentment, large or small, affects your life and relationships. Though forgiveness may be an act of compassion toward someone who is gone, it is intended, mainly to relieve *you* of your self-inflicted torture of hate and anger. I've frequently had students and clients forgive their long-gone parents and then experience major changes in their lives. In one of my forgiveness groups, after a woman in her forties forgave her father for abuses in childhood, the pain she had in her legs for years went away.

*Myth 2 – I don't have to forgive because I never want to see them again!*

Forgiveness is not reconciliation. Reconciliation, the reunion of two upset parties, is not necessarily the outcome of forgiving. A person may forgive an abuser and still choose to protect herself from further abuses by never seeing that person again.

For effective reconciliation, forgiveness of the offense must happen. Extensive research with couples who have experienced infidelity attests to the positive healing power of forgiving each other.[1a]

Rick Warren, the noted pastor and writer who gave the invocation at Barack Obama's inauguration in 2009, tells us that the Bible teaches three things that are essential to resuming a broken relationship: repentance, restitution and rebuilding trust. "In fact," he stresses, "trust is something that's rebuilt over a period of time. It must be re-earned." [1b]

## *Myth 3 – If I forgive, I will be condoning or justifying their offense.*

Forgiveness is not condoning bad behavior or justifying an offense. As Dr. Fred Luskin points out in his excellent book, *Forgive for Love: The Missing Ingredient for a Healthy and Lasting Relationship*, if we condone, we believe the offense was okay, and thus forgiving is not necessary. Forgiveness is always needed when we are hurt and grieving.[2] The family of a drug abuser may forgive him for his behavior but does not condone his misuse of drugs. They will probably do everything in their power to have him stop.

That a child may break something and be forgiven does not mean the parents condone the act. In fact, the child might receive a consequence appropriate for his or her age. The consequence, however, is given with love and understanding, so that the child learns. Applying it with anger instills fear and fosters resentment. Studies show that consequences are more effective when given without anger.

When I worked as a school psychotherapist, I often saw that parents felt guilty at the prospect of hurting their child's feelings and possibly losing their love and approval, so they wouldn't enforcement the consequences they originally set. Thus, the child didn't learn the lesson. Ideally, there are understood and pre-established consequences when rules are broken.

Another aspect of this myth that men often get into is - *People will think I am weak to let the other person win.*

If this is present in your thinking, consider this: Are you winning by carrying hate, anger and the physiological problems that those cause? Remember, forgiveness is for you, not them. It might help them; it might not. We only know for sure that it helps us.

## *Myth 4 – I've tried, but I can't.*

You may have many reasons why you can't forgive, but that doesn't mean you can't let go of the upset. You are gaining the tools now so that you can succeed. Sometimes a person will forgive and then regret it. This is not unusual. Often there are deeper aspects that need to be looked at, not only concerning the other but yourself too.

## *Myth 5 – I'm just too angry! (or too hurt!)*

It's essential in forgiving to be aware of your feelings. You can see the effects of too much emotion in the violence caused by anger. Each time anger and hostility arise, your whole physiology automatically gets stressed. The stress then continues to activate the reactive brain.

Allowing anger and resentment to remain in your heart and mind is harmful. It is a temporary fix that does not work. Being assertive and angry are not the same; you can learn to set limits without the negative emotion of anger.

The ability to set limits without anger comes from a perspective of strength and peace as opposed to anger and resentment. Forgiveness has its timing. You need to calm down to do effective work. Meditation, Tai Chi, prayer, contemplation, being in nature, massage, yoga, exercise, and talking with friends are all useful methods to regain your calm. Often even, praying for the person helps.

## *Feelings under the Surface*

Becoming aware of emotions other than your dominant one will help deal with every upset. Most often, a person is angry at what happened. When I facilitated groups of men who were abusers, their predominant emotion was anger. We always noted, though, that for these men, anger was the easy surface emotion.

Mike saw this when we worked on an upset about his girlfriend, Susan. He knew that he controlled her with anger. The show of anger is central in most mammalian behavior; it establishes dominance. So, it is with us.

One day, Mike became extremely angry with Susan over something small she had done. Later, he admitted that "it was really nothing." Nevertheless, at the time he blew up and broke something. In his mind, it was her fault. And in our anger control group, he went on and on about her.

Another man in the same group, Nick, remembered that two weeks before, Mike's buddy had died. Nick knew quite well that the first response of many men to an emotional situation is anger. He also knew there were deeper emotions under the anger. He asked Mike if his anger was really about his friend's death and not his girlfriend's mistake. Mike's eyes teared as he saw the truth. And his upset with Susan disappeared. He even said later that it was easier to cope with the anger about Susan than to feel the deep loss and sadness of his buddy's death.

We often saw this in anger control groups. As a result, I tended to call anger a false emotion for these men. Anger was too easy for them. It covered deeper and much more uncomfortable emotions.

In forgiveness work, you will often find other emotions below anger. Changes occur by contacting those emotions, perhaps fear or grief. Likewise, where anger is not an acceptable emotion, which is more often the case for women, being aware of anger beneath the surface might be what creates movement toward resolution of the upset.

Use the feelings list in the Appendix to help you find other emotions that you might not be aware of in an upset.

## *Myth 6 – They do not deserve it!*

You may believe that certain people don't deserve forgiveness. You might be right; they might not. However, you are practicing forgiveness for yourself, for your benefit, as well as your relationships. I've seen compassionate people forgive a person who doesn't deserve it because they felt the person needed love somewhere in their life. Dr. Everett Worthington, noted forgiveness researcher and author, includes giving "the gift of forgiveness" as one of his forgiveness steps.[2a]

We see the effect of this gift in a true story told to me by Aeeshah Ababio-Clottey, one of the authors of *Beyond Fear – Twelve Spiritual Keys to*

*Racial Healing*. The story occurred in Ghana in the hometown of Aeeshah's husband and coauthor, Kokoman.

A troubled boy was bullying other children in school. Everyone disliked him. The principal decided to punish him on stage in front of the whole school assembly, so that other children would feel justice was done. Kokoman's sister was a teacher at the school and had taught all of her students about forgiveness. When the troublesome boy and principal were on stage, the students in her class started chanting, "Forgive him!" Soon the whole school was chanting, "Forgive him!" The principal stopped and let the boy off stage.[2b]

The story does not end there. The children's loving act toward the bully transformed him. He became a kinder person and good student. That act of compassion changed the whole situation at the school. In later years, the Clotteys heard this story first hand from the man who was that boy. He was working for the Attitudinal Healing Center in Ghana.

> "Your attitude is everything and determines how you experience every aspect of your life. You cannot always control what happens to you in the world, but you do determine how you react to it many times a day by your attitude."
> JERRY JAMPOLSKY, MD AND DIANE CIRINCIONE, PHD

## Myth 7 – *I just want to forget about it.*

"In forgiving, people are not being asked to forget. On the contrary, it is important to remember, so that such atrocities do not happen again. Forgiveness does not mean condoning what has been done. It means taking what happened seriously not minimizing it; drawing out the sting in the memory that threatens our entire existence." BISHOP DESMOND TUTU[3] - *NO FUTURE WITHOUT FORGIVENESS*

Forgetting about an injury might not be forgiveness but denial. The negative results of denial impinge insidiously under the surface of your mind. Remember, you know you have forgiven someone when he or she has harmless passage through your mind. [4]

Forgive and forget is a myth. The brain is no set up to forget. However, forgiveness allows the upset to fade in the mind because it is no longer being activated. This allows you to refocus on the positives in your life.

## Myth 8 – Before I forgive, I need an apology!

You may wait forever and never get the admission of guilt you yearn for. The person who caused the upset may have a different perspective of what happened and feel that an apology is unnecessary. In fact, he or she might expect an apology from you. If you can let the upset go by forgiving it, you will regain your happiness and peace of mind, and not be dependent on the whims of another person. And, you will stop being their victim. Even if they do apologize, it might not be heartfelt if it comes at your insistence. Forgive without the apology and save yourself time, energy, and heartache.

## Myth 9 – There is too much to forgive!

Sometimes, it may be too difficult to forgive someone because he or she did so much wrong. The principle mentioned in chapter two applies. <u>Break it down</u>. List all the offenses you can see the person committed, and forgive each one at a time.

Anna Marie said she came out of her marriage "abused and broken." "It is impossible for me to forgive the years of abuse I suffered from my husband." Her rage toward him continued for six long years. One wrong glance or comment by any man demanded that she attack him verbally for his disrespect. Of course, people avoided her.

The few friends she had left told her she had to forgive and get on with her life, which is why she came to my class. "How do you forgive that many years of hurt?" she asked. Her task was first to write down each hurt from her husband that she could remember, then start forgiving the small ones. Because she did not like the person she had become, she determined to do this. In far less time than she thought, she reached a place of peace.

**Questions:** If you are having difficulty forgiving, see if your situation is too big. Spend time breaking the situation down to its smallest level, and then forgive each person involved.

Is there someone or a set of people who represents the organization to you? I call this "Finding the who."

Here are further questions to help find out more about the general situation.

1. Who are the people you think of when you see this upsetting situation?
2. What is it about what they did that upsets you?
3. What does their face look like, what did they specifically do?
4. Was every person similar to "them" doing the same thing?
5. In your experience, have all of "them" been the same way?

## *Myth 10 – I cannot forgive because they keep doing it!*

If a person continues to hurt your feelings intentionally or not, out of habit, or because they do not know any better, forgiving is beneficial, although, admittedly, quite difficult. Forgiveness wipes away the effect of the hurt even if it occurred fifteen minutes ago or repeats fifteen minutes from now.

Physical and emotional abuse is a very different situation. In the presence of physical abuse, you must protect yourself. But if there is no option, and sometimes there doesn't seem to be (which we see far too commonly), forgiveness can help.

Inspirational author, Dr. Bernie Siegel, tells us in his book *Prescription for Living*, "Forgiveness is at the heart of a healthy and happy life. Forgiveness protects relationships. It also protects the person who does the forgiving."

He relates the story that psychiatrist and author, Dr. Robert Coles, told in his book, *Children of Crisis: A Study of Courage*, about Ruby Bridges, the first African-American child to integrate a Southern elementary school.

In 1960, federal marshals had to escort Ruby every day through a crowd of adults who spat at her and called her terrible names. Dr. Coles was puzzled by the amazing fact that this five-year-old did not seem to be emotionally damaged by the ordeal. He discovered that Ruby prayed every day asking God to forgive her persecutors.[5]

Letting go of an upset, even if it is still occurring, also involves self-forgiveness. By refusing to be respectful to yourself, you stay in the loop of "what goes around comes around." And you will continue to get what you've been getting. To change the situation, you have to stop the destructive cycle by first removing yourself from the abuser and the abuse. This might require professional help.

At a teen forgiveness group, I talked with Cristy, whose previous good friend was spreading vicious rumors about her. Depressed by the unfairness of the situation, her life was deteriorating. She could not let her hurt go. When we went through the forgiveness process, her attitude changed toward her abuser. Even her body language changed. This resulted in her sending a different non-verbal message in school. She began to feel less like a victim. Not only did she feel better, but the ex-friend perceived a softening in her attitude and backed off her attacks. Ultimately, Cristy forgave her former friend. As an added result, her relationship with her boyfriend improved.

## *Myth 11 – They will just hurt me again if I forgive!*

Fear keeps the reactionary stress system going. It is true that "love is letting go of fear"[6] because both cannot occur at the same time. When our basic survival system becomes activated by fear, what we consider "higher" functioning drops away and we are only concerned with saving our life. This self-protection is important, but it can be a strong obstacle to forgiving, especially if we fear being hurt again.

Forgiving does not mean turning the other cheek to allow the offense to occur again. Jesus' original meaning of "turn the other cheek" was to show your strength in your faith. Its broader meaning includes, but is not limited to, forgiveness. You can forgive someone completely and still hold him or her to a standard. Similarly, you can forgive a business associate for doing something damaging and warn him/her that if it happens again, it will end the business relationship.

The fear of being hurt again if you forgive is real. But if fear drives your life, you exist only at basic survival. Your fear needs to be resolved. It may require assistance from professionals. Meditation, prayer and faith help. So does a walk in nature or listening to your favorite music. There are many methods in this book that can help. Do what you can to release the reactionary fearful mind.

When you have quieted your fear, even for the moment, do forgiveness. Remember, you can forgive *and* set limits so that you will not be hurt.

When forgiveness work occurs within an abusive relationship, feelings of love for the abuser can return. And the person may go back to the abuser feeling healed. Fear about forgiving an abuser comes from a very real concern that the abused person will bring the abuser back into her life and the violence will continue.

**WARNING:** Abuse continues only because the abuser has not done inner work on his anger. Therefore, the abuse will probably occur again.

Abusers, men or women, do not recognize that their victims are not the cause of their anger and thus do not deserve to be hurt.

Because abusers have a short fuse and explode quickly, they need to learn how to remain calm in stressful situations. Until an abusive person acquires these skills, he or she is not safe to be around in stressful situations. If you want to be with an abuser, make sure they do an extensive anger control program, not just a short ten-week course for one night a week.

In general, I have found that one of the most efficient tools for lowering the threshold of anger is forgiveness. A perceived hurt often drives anger. For an abusive person, that hurt is far deeper than the present upset. Dealing with the pain of the past is necessary to lower the intensity of anger in a current situation. Healing the wounds takes in-depth work. If an abusive person is not willing to work on his or her anger, he or she will probably abuse again.

Forgiveness does *not* mean letting the person back into your life to abuse another time. A woman might forgive her abuser and still have the police issue a restraining order to protect her and her children. An abuser **must** learn self-restraint no matter how emotionally upset he or she is. Limiting harmful behavior helps the abuser get out of the stressed-brain reactions. The chronic abuser needs to learn continual inner discipline and practice to stay above the stressed brain.

**When a relationship has reached the point of physical or emotional abuse, it is in deep trouble. Outside help is needed.** Limit-setting on the abuse is urgent. Working on a domestically violent relationship requires at least a psychotherapist trained specifically in this area. **It is not work that you do alone.** Groups on abuse, domestic violence, and anger control are effective, not only because they teach good methods, but also because in a group the abuser learns to find healthier ways to have connections with people other than a spouse or partner.

## *Myth 12 – God will deal with them; I don't have to*

This myth is untrue. You will continue to carry the upsets as you wait for the person's divine punishment. Waiting does not bring relief from the upset.

Though we may speculate on how God might judge someone, we cannot possibly know God's perspective on a situation because we are unable to take the 360-degree God's-eye-view of that person or circumstance. We cannot see the past, and often even the present situation that made the person do what he or she did. We cannot know all the dynamics involved in their life. We often do not see the forces involved in our own lives that cause us to make a particular decision. Thus, all we can do is our work, and let God do His. In our own life, forgiveness *is* up to us.

You can, of course, ask for Divine Help. You can say prayers for the person or meditate on the situation asking for insight. You can do much with the Inner Help that is always available to you. Throughout the book, many ways are presented to get the help you need and to use it.

- **Look at** your present concept of God to see if your perspective is influenced by views from childhood that are no longer accurate.

## *The Myths of Forgiveness Summary*

In summary, there are concepts about forgiveness that are *not* correct and that cause problems when people attempt to forgive others. When we look at what forgiveness is and is not, we reveal these myths.

Forgiveness **is**:
- **not** condoning bad behavior, justifying an offense, or turning the other cheek
- **not** reconciling with the offending party
- **not** the same as, out of sight, out of mind
- **not** dependent upon an apology
- **not** dependent on the other being alive or in touch with you
- **not** dependent on whether the offender deserves it
- **not** taking the easy way out of a situation
- **not** forgetting or taking no responsibility
- **not** dependent on a belief in God

**Myths of Forgiveness Detection:** To assist your forgiving complete this exercise.
- Recall a situation in your life where you have been unsuccessful in forgiving another person.
- Look and see if one of the Myths of Forgiveness stands in the way of your being able to forgive. Write down the myth.
  1. Would dispelling that myth allow you to see the situation from a different perspective?
  2. Could you forgive the other person now?

## *God as a Block to Forgiving?*

A strong influence on whether people forgive or not is their concept of a Higher Power. Some people are trained to see God primarily as a judge and condemner. With this perspective, they probably justify condemning and harming others. They will also judge themselves, which then justifies their suffering, depression, and lack of peace, love, and forgiveness.

I mention this because people raised with these concepts may have difficulty forgiving until they change their idea of God to loving and forgiving Being. If you have feelings of unworthiness, then self-forgiveness is a vital area for you to work on. Gaining compassion and understanding for yourself is crucial.

## *Self-Forgiveness*

There is a problem with *love your neighbor as yourself*. If you have no love for yourself, then there is often no love to give to your neighbor. To follow the truth of this principle in its full meaning would be first to regain self-esteem, love, and worthiness. You do this by gaining self-forgiveness. As author Paulo Coelho says:

> "Pay attention to every moment because the opportunity — the 'magic moment'—is within our reach, although we let it pass by because we feel guilty." [9]

I use the term, "gain self-forgiveness" because you cannot always do your own forgiving. You must see how you feel. Sometimes you need to make amends for what you did, as in the 12-step programs. Or, you might need to turn to a Higher Power for help in releasing your heart from self-torment.

This self-torment is often misplaced because it was, perhaps, the result of a lower brain reaction/take-over. In that case, an act to help gain self-forgiveness would be effective to learn how to control those reactions.

To gain forgiveness from his dead father for the way Simon, his son, treated his dad through the years, Simon did a daily ritual from Judaism for his father. At the end of two months, he felt significant changes. He carried on doing this ritual, not only because it continued to help him deepen his connection with life, love, and God, but also because it helped him feel calmer inside and less reactive to situations on the outside.

Ruth felt that her anger at her mother in her mother's last months was unforgivable. Even though she knew the forgiveness process, she couldn't find relief. My suggestions were of no help. Her choice was to pray regularly at a beautiful cathedral. Ruth wasn't Catholic, but her mother was. At one service, she said, "I felt a change inside and felt my mother's love and forgiveness."

Sometimes we need to **get** forgiveness from those we have hurt to feel right about ourselves. This often takes at least an apology. In her book, *The Power of Apology,* Beverly Engel gives us a fine three-step method for giving a meaningful apology:[9a]

1. State your regret for causing the situation.
2. Accept responsibility for what you did.
3. Give a way to repair the harm done, perhaps a pledge or act.

Her book gives plenty of helpful ideas on doing these steps.

For some, gaining self-forgiveness might mean looking deeply at their family of origin to gain some objectivity. For others to regain their self-esteem, it might be a donation to or working for a cause they feel is important. You won't know what will work until you are in the process. Sometimes the most powerful action you can do to gain self-forgiveness is to ask for inner spiritual help with deep sincerity.

## *Is It True That Only God Forgives?*

Some religious factions teach that people are incapable of forgiveness because humans are inherently evil and thus only God forgives. Thirty years of research shows, however, that people of all lifestyles, religious or not, forgive regularly, much to their benefit and the benefit of others. Those without any religious orientation can enjoy the same positive benefits from letting go of old hates and resentments as a religious person.

I've worked with atheists and people from many different religions, all of whom have experienced radical changes in their lives through forgiving. Forgiveness is a movement of the mind and heart toward compassion, kindness, and love. It is an act of peace, which results in joy for the forgiver, regardless of religious belief.

<u>Forgiveness is given by anyone to anyone</u>—anyone can help another to forgive. We have the methods and outline of how to use them. We have only to do it.

## *Awareness of Feelings*

In Myth 5, we talked of feelings under the surface, and that lack of awareness of other emotions concerning a situation can keep us from forgiving. When we carry old hurts and trauma, they affect us in our subconscious mind. Have you ever been driving and noticed suddenly that your neck hurt and felt tense? It did not seem to hurt a minute before. Nevertheless, when you thought back, it had been hurting for a while, but not in your conscious awareness. Once you become aware the tension, you feel the pain. Then you can act to alleviate the pain.

Our subconscious protects us from the emotional pain of old injuries by putting them out of our consciousness. Although the old events may be out of our awareness, they can still harm us. They may appear as physical symptoms, irritability, or general anger, which can explode and cause serious damage in our life. These old injuries and the negative attitudes from them continue to affect us destructively in the ways we interact in the world.

When you bury past hurts, they can control you and, even seemingly, to possess you. In those situations, where you don't feel like yourself, you will probably do things you regret.

Awareness of our emotions is a key to letting go of an upset. Remember, if you are not aware of it, you cannot deal with it. Just finding the emotion below the surface of an unforgiven situation, such as sadness, grief or hurt, can change the reaction drastically.

## *Valuable Points to Remember Concerning Feelings*

- Forgiveness is not just an intellectual course of action. Strong feelings will surface.
- Feelings are the entry point for forgiving.
- Feelings are often multilayered, particularly anger which may be driven by fear and grief.
- Avoiding difficult feelings is normal but not helpful in this work. You can't let go of something that is hidden.
- Being willing to feel what might be underneath the surface and not resist it, takes honesty and courage.

Help for awareness of your emotions is in the Appendix; you will find the page: *How We Are Likely to Feel When Our Needs Are Not Being Met.* AND *Feelings Likely To Be Present When Your Needs Are Being Satisfied.* These are from the outstanding work of Dr. Marshall Rosenberg, the author of *Nonviolent Communication – A Language of Compassion.* He found that people are heard better by others when they say the emotions that are affecting them at the moment.[10]

Here are some things to do to help you understand what you might be feeling other than the typical anger, hurt or resentment. Often by knowing the deeper or more accurate emotion, people can understand the whole situation better.

1. Think of an upset you are working on.
2. Go down the list in the Appendix: *How We Are Likely to Feel When Our Needs Are Not Being Me*, and notice how your experience changes when you come upon feelings involved in this situation.
3. Go through the list *Feelings Likely To Be Present When Your Needs Are Being Satisfied.* Notice how you feel better just thinking of these emotions. Do this anytime to feel better.

## *The Third Hurdle*

By identifying the major barriers to forgiving, and by being aware of emotions under the surface, you have passed the third hurdle to forgiving. You know the best way to handle a difficult situation and you have cleared up the misunderstandings about it. I hope that you have achieved some relief through understanding and awareness. The core of our work so far is 1. increased awareness of what is going on inside you concerning the upset, and 2. the **willingness** to let it go.

All of the results from forgiving can easily be attributed to your mind and heart finally returning to their natural state. This "natural state" is more than a release of control by the lower brains; it is also spiritual. That spiritual connection is influenced by the functioning of your brain systems working in concert. We will look further at the implication and potential of your brain in the next chapter.

From a Buddhist story:[10]

"A man is struck by an arrow from an unknown assailant. Rather than tending to the wound, he refuses to remove the arrow until the archer is found and punished. In the meantime, the wound festers until finally, the poison kills him. Which is the more responsible for this death: the archer's letting go or the victim's foolish holding on?"
COLIN BERG AMERICAN AUTHOR/TEACHER

# PART II

# GOING DEEPER

- Making Sense of Our Thinking
- Breaking Out of Prison
- Making Forgiving Easier
- The Power behind Forgiving
- Working on Upsets

CHAPTER FIVE

# Making Sense of Our Thinking

## *Our Complex and Fascinating Brain*

The greatest accumulation of nerve cells in our body is in our brain. Surrounding the outer edge of the brain, closest to the skull bone, is the gray matter. It is only a quarter of an inch thick (6 – 7 mm), yet in it, there are 100 billion nerve cell bodies. The nerve cell, or neuron, is made of the cell body and its arms, which send and receive messages to and from other nerve cells, muscles, and organs. Each neuron body can have up to 10,000 connections to other cells. The white matter of the brain, which takes up the most volume in our skull, is where the arms from the cell bodies connect.

The number of these interconnections is astronomical (100 billion times 10,000). If you spent fifteen hours a day tapping your finger on the table every second, without any days off (not even to go to the doctor for your finger), it would take you 50 years to do just one billion taps.

All that you learn and do creates new neural connections in the brain every second until you die. The hundreds of trillions of nerve pathways enable you to access all of your memories, skills, and life activities from the womb to death.

Look at these connections as your brain's highway system for your thoughts, emotions, and actions. The impulses around the brain go at 200 miles per hour (320 kph). There, you have everything from ten lane highways to walking trails to map your experiences.

## *Why Habits Are Hard to Break*

Frequent repetition generates the highest number of nerve connections. These would be akin to a freeway or major city highway artery. Lesser-used responses have fewer neurons involved.

Anything new that you try will take effort to become a habit. It's like following a well-worn path through the woods. When you try to create a new trail, it is initially difficult but becomes easier each time you take it. At first, you will need to remove branches and rocks that are in the way. As you remove the obstacles in the path and continue to use it, your way becomes easier. Likewise, what you are trying to learn needs to develop a large enough nerve pathway to become easy.

When you do something repeatedly, you create a neuron *superhighway*. This is a habit. Habits can help you function better and do your work more efficiently. For example, you drive your vehicle out of habit, barely aware of what you are doing. This is helpful for many activities, but not when you want to change.

If you spend forty years rehearsing resentment about someone, you develop a nerve *freeway* to that resentment. If you are speaking or thinking of a negative situation, you are reinforcing and adding to that negative pathway in your brain, which will not only consume your thoughts but can also cause physical problems and lack of happiness.

Though habits keep you in ruts you do not like, changing them can be frustrating. Repeated attempts to change will normally bring success unless the stressed brain reactions are active, which they often are.

## *What's behind Your Thoughts*

To deal with and make sense of all the information we receive, we sort and catalog incoming data according to our past associations and experiences. In addition, the mind stores and retrieves data through a personal symbolic shorthand—a code—known only to us and based on our own experiences. You can't really know what another person is thinking because you don't know their code, and they usually don't either because this all takes place below conscious awareness.

Since we associate our experiences in unique ways, problems may occur because every new experience we have, integrates with an *already formed* group of experiences. The most probable nerve pathway that already exists incorporates the new experience. This merging is also dependent on the most activated pathway at the time.

*The new piggybacks onto the old.* Thus, each person takes in his or her new experience differently.

A girl raised in a loving family might connect her new boyfriend with loving family experiences and feel secure about their relationship. The woman with a terrible family relationship might also connect her boyfriend with her *family neural pathway*. If her family security was nonexistent, she will probably expect abuse like that given by her father or ex-husband and thus, not trust the boyfriend. This is a formula for failure even though the boyfriend might be a fine guy.

## *The Brain*

There is incredible inter-connection between all parts of the brain. However, back in 1960, Neurophysiology researcher, Paul Maclean, MD, proposed that we had three separate brains that had evolutionarily developed, which he called the Triune Brain.[A] In reality, modern researchers have shown that those brains share functions, and cannot be split into three. However, for 50 years these three brains, the Neocortex, the Limbic and the Reptilian brains, have been discussed, many books have been written on them, and the terms are still being used.[1]

I've found through the years in my many courses and workshops that breaking down the brain functions to the three areas of focus, as the early research talked of, has helped people understand the complex influences of the brain on our life. Though our discussion in this chapter of these three functional areas is an oversimplification of what is going on, they do give us a basis for understanding on how they affect forgiving.

### *The Neocortex*

The brain most people are familiar with is the neocortex, which is the main storehouse of our information and memories. Within the neocortex in the front part of our skull, there is the Pre-Frontal Cortex, which mainly differentiates us as humans. Some say that this is even the fourth brain. Brain studies have shown that this area seems to be where forgiveness occurs.[2] Each side of the prefrontal cortex is responsible for controlling the responses of earlier brain functions. Magnetic resonance shows that when a person is depressed, the limbic system is overactive and the left prefrontal cortex is much less active.[3]

The neocortex/prefrontal lobes:
- Generates our ideas, gives us our capacity for concentration and uses symbols to produce our ability to read, write, talk and do math.[4]
- Helps us to be not only logical and systematic but also intuitive and imaginative. [5]

- Overrides and suppresses unacceptable social responses of the earlier brains. [6]

In its highest functioning, it is not only the agent of invention and creativity but also governs prayer and the spiritual experience.[7]

Even if we didn't have all the forgiveness research results, you can see that just functioning in the neocortex more of the time would be a positive result.

This newest brain enables us to:
1. Give meaning to our life and world.
2. Analyze different perspectives and alternative possibilities to make choices among them.
3. Coordinate with the lower brains – enabling us to have empathy and better judgment.[8]

## *Our Emotional Brain*

In the center of the brain is our emotional center—the limbic system, which is a series of interconnected structures. With the development of the limbic system in birds, mammals and some reptiles, our nurturing and loving connections became more established, thus enabling:[9]

- nursing and protection of offspring and family
- activities like friendship, love and affection, laughter and playfulness and control of aggressive behaviors

It gives our life and language interest, and even passion.

"Emotion is the messenger of love," Drs Lewis, Amini, and Landon tell us in *A General Theory of Love*. They add that emotions carry the signals of our heart to one another and that, for many of us, feeling deeply is one and the same with being alive.[11]

This sounds good, doesn't it? The problem occurs when this love is inhibited for whatever reason. Then other strong emotions like misery or rage, to name a couple, can take hold and cause terrible reactions and consequences.

(There is controversy among neuroscientists as to which structures compose the limbic system. Our focus regarding forgiveness is the fear mechanism and the amygdala, the structure that activates fear reactions.[10])

The limbic system gives feelings to our life events, feelings through an entire range of emotions, from terror and grief to excitement, joy, and passion. These feelings help us remember both positive and negative events because our memories always have emotional content.[12] In fact, greater emotional stimulation around a learning event increases a person's retention of that event.[13]

In stress and emotional turmoil, our control of aggressive behavior decreases. In those times, anger, revenge, and jealousy can increase, causing even more difficulty. This turmoil can shut down "rational behavior." In the legal system, this is *temporary insanity* and in society *crimes of passion*.

Ralph was disappointed in himself for not being able to forgive his sister for a hurtful comment she made at a family gathering. When we discussed how he felt, he said, "Feelings have nothing to do with this; I should still be able to forgive her." Difficult unforgiven situations always have strong emotions tied to them. Avoiding how he felt prevented real forgiving. I'm not saying wallowing in feelings is good, but acknowledging how you feel does help you let go of an upset.

Ongoing trauma or tension enlarges the amygdala, the instigator of the fear response, which then predisposes it to create more fear. When this response goes on too long, the person is said to have Post Traumatic Stress Disorder (PTSD). We will go into this in Chapter 12.

**Remember:** Forgiving can take time because of intense feelings that may be present.

The limbic system sets the tone for our response to events and our enjoyment of life. It is the switchboard that coordinates all the information between the external and internal world. Either it feeds incoming data to the neocortex for conscious thought, planning, or problem-solving, or it feeds the data to the stressed/ fight or flight brain for a survival reaction. It decides which way to send the messages by immediately comparing the present conditions with similar past experiences.[14]

This information switchboard creates problems, however, when a person is emotionally upset. At those times, all data coming in is classified as unpleasant even when, normally, it might not be. Then, when the limbic system compares new information coming in with the distorted information already gathered, there is inaccuracy, and the new data is reacted to or classified as dangerous. A person in chronic pain or an ongoing threatening situation will have an enormous store of negative memories and probably be in constant reaction mode, feeling quite upset, and being unpleasant to be around.

Alex, a therapist, was not able to forgive his father for his childhood abuse and harshness towards him even into adulthood. Their relationship had always been strained. When Alex started having work and physical problems, he came to forgiveness work out of necessity. Though he could forgive everyone else in his life, he couldn't forgive his father, thus his work and physical condition were getting worse. Initially, I was unable to give him perspectives or processes to help him to forgive his father. Finally, after two months of decline and struggle, he remembered that his father had been in continual pain all his life. With that insight, he understood why his father had been so angry and mean all those years. Alex's forgiveness was automatic, and his work and physical condition started turning around within a week.

We learn two key lessons from Alex's forgiveness work. The first is—**just one unforgiven person is enough to prevent healing.** The second came from Alex several months after forgiving his father. He visited his dad and told me that they had a better time together than they had ever had. In addition, they had no arguing or disagreeing. His father was even friendly. As a result, Alex saw that *his own negative mind-set had affected their relationship*.

With that attitude gone, replaced with compassion and understanding, his father acted differently. "We even had a peak experience one night just chatting and listening to music. Dad even said at the time, 'It doesn't get any better than this!'" The second lesson is—**we affect our relationships by our subtle attitudes toward one another.**

> "Who you are speaks so loudly, I can't hear what you are saying." – RALPH WALDO EMERSON

When the negative memories become stronger than the positive, the limbic system can cause: [15]

- moodiness, irritability, clinical depression
- increased negative thinking and perceiving
- decreased motivation and drive
- appetite and sleep problems
- decreased sexual responsiveness

- social isolation.

Sadness, hopelessness, and an overabundance of automatic negative thoughts also occur.[16]

Psychiatrists Lewis, Amini, and Landon in their book, *A General Theory of Love* points out that we cannot direct our emotional life as we can our muscles. We cannot force ourselves "to want the right thing or to love the right person or even to be happy after a disappointment or even to be happy in happy times." This is not because we have a shortage of discipline, but because *will* is limited only to the newest brain. "The emotional life can be influenced but not commanded," the doctors say.[17]

There are spiritual teachers as well as brain scientists who maintain that people can learn to direct their emotions, but this requires sustained practice. Thus, if the person you are trying to forgive has reacted emotionally and you are condemning them for not changing, you must understand that they might not be able to change in the time and in the way you would like.

Martin was a responsible man; he took care of his family quite well. He was devoted and worked hard for them, even doing work he didn't like. He did it because he wanted to provide a decent home for his family. Because he did not like his work, he was often grumpy and tired. After a few years of this, his wife became fed up and asked for a divorce. He went crazy and almost killed her. (Here we see how emotions can drive us in positive and negative directions.)

In a similar example, Rick not only disliked his work but also hated the city where he and his family lived. He stayed there because his wife, Natalie, liked it. When she tired of his lack of enthusiasm for her and his life, she decided the marriage was over. When she took the kids and filed for divorce, Rick was lost in his emotional upset and tried to kill himself. Natalie could not understand his grief and upset at all. She said, "He never showed much interest in me or the kids when he came home."

In the first case, Martin could not forgive his wife for years because he could not understand how she did not see that he was sacrificing for the family doing work he didn't enjoy. Also, he felt she had no regard for what he went through every day at work. In the second case, Natalie could not understand how Rick could get so upset when their marriage seemed to be nothing. When she examined the relationship from his point of view, she understood.

Our emotional circuits can drive us to behave in bizarre and irrational ways in the name of love (and hate). This is because the emotional system develops before, our ability to analyze, which is the last to be developed. In teenagers, the neocortex is not yet fully developed until well into adulthood. Teens can be difficult to deal with because the amygdala, which develops early, is responsible for immediate reactions including fear and aggressive behavior. But the area of the brain that controls reasoning and helps us think before we act, the frontal cortex, develops later.[18]

The limbic system is also involved in alcoholism, drug addiction, impulsive gambling, and compulsion for sweet foods.[19] This is why a person cannot just decide to quit addictions but must make a strong, ongoing, and concerted effort to do it. Because we are social beings, working with addictions in a group can have great results, a fact the Twelve-Step movement found long ago.

In summary, the limbic system gives passion and interest to our lives. It decides how we will react to events, and even colors those events with emotions. In coordination with the neocortex, it adds a richness to our lives and memories. On the other hand, when it activates our stressed reactions brain, we may go for a very rough ride.

## *"The Early Vertebrate Complex/Reptilian Brain"*

In earlier editions of this book, I used the term "reptilian brain," "R-complex," and "snake brain." Since these terms not accurate per the latest neuroscience research, I have removed these terms, to keep it simpler. Some researchers have proposed this area be called the early vertebrate complex.[20]

The following basic brain activities around territory and sex are still accurate and important to be understood for forgiving. In addition to its physiological actions, here are the basic life activities that these base brain areas can affect.[21] They are:

- **Domination and control of territory** – Our space is our empire, our territory. Here is the source of reaction to strangers or people who are *different*. This starting place of prejudice comes out of our basic need to protect what is ours. Under stress, it becomes "I will attack any stranger who enters my space." In driving, we see this in road rage, which often results from a violation of one's space or "territory."

- **Courting and mating behavior and displays** – These actions guarantee the survival of the species. This includes sexual aggression and submission. The answer to why a woman sometimes submits against her better judgment to sexual aggression, and why men and women may become overwhelmed with sexual desires, is here deep in the brain.

- **Control of interaction with others** – This is the drive for social maintenance and dominance through establishing a *pecking order*, a chain of command. At the deepest level, we are social beings. This is why we have a tendency to follow the crowd and its standards, and have awe for authority.[22]

- **Ritual behavior** – Following regular rituals and having ceremonies is valuable in keeping people part of the social matrix and having them feel included as part of the group.[23] Thus, routines and patterns give us a basic sense of security. This is why we organize. Here is the force behind religions, governments, and institutions.[24] Under stress, these rituals and activities may become compulsions where the person becomes obsessed with doing them and even becomes fierce about forcing these routines on others.

This level of the brain usually keeps our social and group interactions at a priority. At its highest influence, it is the impetus for forgiveness; at its lowest, it breeds violence and fascism.

Out of this desire for social interaction and control comes imitating, copying, and deception—all to be part of the group. Fads, pop culture and the fashion industry are built on this drive.

Change in any of the above areas can bring about strong reactions. Fear drives the reactive responses. It produces our basic fear reflex which is displayed as aggression or submission.[25]

When this brain influence takes over, you might feel obsessed or even possessed in some way. These are ancient responses. Any of these areas of response are alien to the highest sense of the person you identify yourself to be. So, of course, you will feel strange. These reactions can be very strong.

It doesn't incapacitate us on purpose; it's just doing its survival job. It's what causes a person to attack, be violent, run away, or withdraw. It can make a human a victim. The program it follows is survival, and all it knows is its reactions when it perceives threats.

**Make no mistake about it—this is not you!** It's normal for a person to misidentify these stressed-brain reactions as one's own. They're not. It's like calling a computer program the computer. The program might be faulty, and cause trouble with the computer's functioning, but the program is not the computer. They are both quite different.

Realize also that the program can be repaired to function properly. We are a complex mixture of mind, body, and spirit, not an ancient programmed reaction. When we misperceive our self or others as this program, we set ourselves up for unhappiness.

Some people find forgiveness by seeing that this reactivity is a misperception to be corrected rather than a sin to be perpetually condemned. Of course, you can't say, "The devil made me do it!" for we still have responsibility for dealing with that devil. Noted analyst Dr. Michael Conforti, emphasizes that we can feel possessed by patterns of life, innate qualities, which appear to be bigger than us, and seem to take us under their spell. I associate many of these patterns in this book with these survival brain activities.[26b]

Additional responses when it is in reactive control include:[27]
- nervousness and panic attacks
- ongoing prediction of the worst that can happen
- conflict avoidance or aggression
- low or too much motivation

Discomfort with change and maintaining the status quo are the hallmarks of this stressed brain's control. It repeatedly repeats the same behaviors, never learning from past mistakes.[28] Action without rational thinking is its drive under stress. Its key motto then may become, "Might makes right!" For another, the motto could be, "Hide!", or for another, "Run!"

Rod seemed to be stuck at this level of stressed brain control. He could not understand situations he found himself in very well or solve problems. He was in fights regularly and had been in and out of jail since he was an early teen. He abused his wife sexually and physically. He controlled her money, where she went, and the people she met. He wanted immediate compliance with his orders. She submitted to all of his demands for the safety of her young child. But when he started becoming controlling and violent to the child, she realized the terrible danger they were in. She sought help through a women's counseling center and left him to hide at a "safe house." He did all he could to find her. Luckily, he was unable to locate that shelter for women and children.

When he talked about his early life, I could understand how he ended up as he did. His father was an alcoholic who beat him with a belt or his fists as early as age two. He never knew when his father would go into a rage and beat him. By hearing this, I realized why he lived his life as he did. He had known no other way to react.

If I had worked with his wife, I would never have recommended she go back with him, but I would have counseled her to try to understand why he was the way he was so that she would not hate him, or herself for having been with him. What he did I don't justify or condone, nor would I ask her to. I would encourage her, through forgiveness work, to release her rage so that she could heal and move on with a positive outlook on life. Thus, she could avoid traumatizing her child and others with her negative attitudes and actions.

**Note**: People who have not dealt with their deep trauma are more likely to react to the stressed brain response because it has had control for so long. They often have not learned any other way to respond when they are under pressure. Even respectable people, when placed under constant stress, such as a war zone or a cult, may start reacting from this stressed brain more and more, and act in ways they would not have normally done. This is crucial to know if you are trying to forgive yourself for terrible ways your stressed brain's reactions and the limbic responses overwhelmed a person. The survival functions of these earlier deeper systems are powerful. Given enough ongoing stress/fear, I believe anyone may start manifesting ongoing stressed brain behaviors. That said, don't use it as a justification for continued reactive behavior. Luckily, there are many tools to assist you to come back to your true self. Forgiving is an indispensable tool that can move you out of being trapped in basic survival and into full joy of life and human functioning.

On-going stress needs to be lowered in your life. Also, most importantly, you need to see and understand you are being controlled/possessed, and **do** everything in your power to get out from under the power of these primitive reactions. It takes strong determination and resolve. No one else can do it for you. This is where professional or perhaps pastoral counseling can be of assistance. The 12-step programs can also be helpful.

Reggie was a good guy. He was friendly and helpful. He went to church regularly. But, sometimes he would go crazy with rage. Forgiveness helped him, but it wasn't enough sometimes. His PTSD from the Vietnam War still could occasionally overwhelm him when he was threatened or became fearful. As he said, "Sometimes I would know that I was out of control. Now I know that in those times I cannot afford to feed that possessing energy anything at all—not even a little taste—because it will eat me up in a moment."

## *Management by Fear*

By understanding the stress responses of this brain level, we see why *management by fear* is the least effective of all management styles. It may create results, but in the end, it not only sabotages the employees but also the company itself.

If you were part of an organization that used fear or had a manager like that, it is vital to realize that the people you are trying to forgive were likely functioning at their most stressed level. It's possible you were too. Cults and some religious sects function at this level. They might even profess, "God is love" but they certainly don't live it; they live and promote fear. Keeping people in fear and under constant pressure is part of brainwashing and may cause the victims to do things they wouldn't normally do.

To avoid being controlled by these base brain area, you must be willing to look at your behavior as an observer—as if it were not your own.[29] In truth, it is not you. From that detached perspective where you are not reactive, you can ask questions of yourself and understand what might be creating the reaction. I recommend doing this with another or others who can hold an objective viewpoint with you. If you get reactivated, they can help you out.

Distinguished educator, Dr. Elaine De Beauport says that this basic brain resists against any new desire from your limbic brain or any new decision by your neocortex. She feels that this resistance is why willpower alone, "however strong or well-intentioned" is not enough to significantly change behavior.[29b]

Dr. Conforti, who I mentioned works with life patterns, says that first, it takes realizing you are, in fact, possessed by one of these patterns, and then going deeper with it, actively reflecting on and engaging with the patterns and seeing how they repeat in your life. This is most effectively done with a therapist.[30]

In summary, this brain affects our behavior concerning:
- Our immediate physical domain,
- Mating
- Social contact.

Change in any of these areas can bring about strong reactions. Fear drives the reactive responses; it produces our basic fear reflex, which is displayed as aggression or submission.[31]

♦ Now, look at your unforgiven situation more carefully and see how this information helps you to understand the person in a different way.

## *How the Brain Works Best*

Given the number of stimuli and reactions that occur each moment, the brain's ability to orchestrate our life into a symphony of action and decisions is incredible. Our brain structures intermingle and communicate, yet they differ in structure, properties, and chemistry. Even though they have separate structures, research has shown quite clearly that they do not work independently.[32] Our exceedingly complex brain has many levels of interaction all occurring at the same time. They function best together in a safe environment which enables our mind to be a symphony instead of a war zone.

Built into our nervous system are survival functions that do not always allow us to be the perfect functioning individuals we wish to be. Survival in dangerous situations depends on the quick action of these mechanisms, which developed over hundreds of thousands of years. In the high stress of threat (fear) and hopelessness, the earlier brain systems can more easily take over control, and we lose our compassion and our ability to think through our difficulties clearly. Fight, flight or freeze are only a few of these survival responses. When they occur at the wrong time in our modern and highly complex society they can cause embarrassment and social disapproval and can even have legal consequences.

**Note**: Since the brain does its magic best when it is not threatened, make sure you put yourself in a comfortable environment when you do this work or any time you have an upset. Then your emotions can calm down, and your higher thinking abilities can work in harmony to deal with your unforgiven stressful situation.

We often seem to be imprisoned by our stress reactions. And yet, it is this same brain that can bring us our best times. In the next chapter, we will examine better ways to manage frustrations, anxieties, and unforgiven areas in your life.

> "When we harbor negative emotions toward others or toward ourselves, or when we intentionally create pain for others, we poison our own physical and spiritual systems. By far the strongest poison to the human spirit is the inability to forgive oneself or another person. It disables a person's emotional resources. The challenge .. is to refine our capacity to love others as well as ourselves and to develop the power of forgiveness."
>
> CAROLINE MYSS, www.myss.com
> from ANATOMY OF THE SPIRIT

# CHAPTER SIX

# Breaking Out of Prison

"Hold no one prisoner. Release instead of bind, for thus are you made free. The way is simple. Every time you feel a stab of anger, realize you hold a sword above your head. And it will fall or be averted as you choose to be condemned or free."

*A COURSE IN MIRACLES*- LESSON 192

## *Dealing with Emotional Pain*

The stressed mind can often seem like our jailer, punishing us and others. In this chapter, we will look at ways to put the stressed brain to rest.

### *The Overlooked Aid for Empowering Yourself*

*Finding Outer Support* – The value of external support in helping to forgive is often overlooked. Surrounding yourself with those who practice forgiveness assists you to forgive. Seeing others who are skilled in forgiveness helps you learn how to do it.

Group or individual help can be surprisingly useful when you are stuck and cannot seem to progress. Often you are not able to see the patterns in your life, particularly if these patterns go back to your earliest years.

Is there a support group, counselor, minister or 12-step program that could help you cope with a negative life situation so that you can be more positive about your life? Find one appropriate for you. If you belong to a church or meditation group, take advantage of the support to continue your work in forgiveness.

Dr. Donald Hall's research at Vanderbilt University showed that social support and contact affect: [1]

- How well people cope with stress in life, and how happy and content they are.

- How effectively the body's immune system functions and survival when a person faces crises or serious illness.

Social contact is even a predictor of how long a person lives.

> "Love and intimacy have a powerful effect on our health. Social support and interaction are as powerful in improving health and longevity as are not smoking, exercising, and eating healthfully."
> Dean Ornish, MD [2]

- Is there someone you can talk with to help in your forgiving?

## *Our Comfort Zone*

When we are forced to move away from what is familiar, our brains give us uncomfortable signals we call stress. We all have different thresholds of stress. Some people can comfortably handle running a company of hundreds of employees. That same executive might be extremely anxious in intimate settings. Another might not stand being the responsible one, but is comfortable in intimate settings.

Being in our comfort zone allows us to feel safe. Threatening environments cause discomfort, fear and even panic, removing our ability to think clearly. Thus, the best learning environment is a non-threatening one.[3]

Our comfort zone is not always the healthiest place for us, but it is the most familiar. For example, because of familiarity, people who live in war zones sometimes go back to their home even though the situation is dangerous and they are more likely to be harmed there. Often, we think we are doing the best thing when in reality, we are putting ourselves in danger by going back to familiar family patterns and old ways of acting even though they do not work.

A friend gave me a personal example of this. "Walking across a bridge with a railing I noticed that my fear of heights made my list toward the traffic side of the walkway instead of the railing. If my foot slipped for some reason, I would fall into traffic rather than the railing. Even though I felt certain the traffic was a greater risk, it still took strong effort to keep myself in the safer place."

As a child, Mario hated being hit by his father for not obeying. He hated his father and left home at a young age. He became upset when anyone yelled. Yet when his son disobeyed, Mario would hit him and shout at him just like his father had. His outbursts made him not only feel guilty but also depressed because he had no idea why he did this or how to change it.

In stressful situations, strong emotions, earlier events and defenses attack us below the surface of our awareness—subconsciously. Thus, we *must* consider the role of stress in situations that require forgiveness of others or our self.

We have a high level of complexity in our society because forgiving is built into our highest functioning as human beings. However, when we are emotionally upset, depressed, overwhelmed, angry or resentful, for example, we are not able to function at our highest level. At these times, forgiveness is essential though more difficult.

## *Making Sense*

An interesting activity of the neocortex is to even out our visual impressions. Our eyes make tiny jumps as they sweep across a field of view. But, the points <u>between</u> where the eyes land are blurry. Nevertheless, the neocortex creates a coherent perception out of them, filling in the gaps of the jerky feed, so that what you see is continuous and smooth. But in truth, it is not.[4]

Though it works well for jumpy eye movements, there is a problem with this fill-in-the-gaps work of the neocortex. In his book, *The Accidental Mind*, Dr. David Linden, a professor of neuroscience at Johns Hopkins University, tells us that this creative brain can also take the raw material of memory, and in the same way, weave it into a consistent, yet a bizarre story.[5] Thus, each person at a crime scene or accident can have a different story as to what happened.

We see this in stage hypnosis where the person is given a post-hypnotic suggestion to do a certain behavior. When he is brought out of hypnosis and then acts on the suggestion, he will make up all sorts of excuses why he is acting as he is. The excuses are the neocortex trying to make sense out of what is happening.

Depending on how your stress system is activated, the neocortex will use what you see and the "facts" to create a story incorporating all the factors to have a smooth flow. The neocortex uses the data available at the time but often through the lens of emotion. A person caught in a fear response will see fearful circumstances and justify their response even when the response is bizarre.

The implications of this in forgiving are critical. The story you tell yourself, from what you saw and the "facts" you have, might not be accurate. It may easily be a story created by the neocortex to smooth out the event. We like to think we see and think clearly, but in truth, we don't. There are gaps. We have a brain not built on reasoning but reaction. This must be taken into account when forgiving yourself and others. !

## *How Our Outer World Reflects Our Inner One*

The world we see is often upsetting. But what we are seeing is just particles or waves of light in patterns. Physiologically, this light comes through the eye and registers on the retina which sends these light patterns through the optical nerve to the brain. The brain interprets those patterns before we even know what we are seeing. To do this, the brain accesses its "experience and information data stockpile," which provides an interpretation of what it sees, and the emotions attached to it.

In our first years we rapidly fill our information stockpile. We learn to identify our surroundings from the first people in our lives. They teach us what things are and what they do. Also, they convey their emotional bias about those items. We interpret all our other experiences through our first teachers—Mom, Dad, siblings, and others close to us, and our experiences with them. Our mother is our primary emotional and information source; this information is even transmitted through the womb.[6] Your initial teachers have a tremendous influence, not only upon **how** you see and experience the world, but also on **what** you view and sense.

Even something as simple as color may create a strong emotional reaction. For example, if a mother hates red because of a trauma she experienced, she will pass that bias along to her child. The child does not have to be told red is bad. He or she will pick it up in voice inflection and facial expression.[7]

A child raised in an abusive household will often see the world as unsafe, to be feared. Similarly, a child raised by a paranoid parent often will be fearful of people and surroundings. When the parent and child have fear, their lower brains are more active, and there is less opportunity for rational thinking and positive emotions like joy to be present.

Conversely, a child raised with love feels safer and sees the world as a safer place than one who is beaten or abused in some way. The child who feels safe will think more rationally and be happier. Studies have shown that children raised in their first year of life with no touch tend to die, and if they do survive, they have poor emotional responses to people and life.[8]

What is going on inside of us determines how we see the world, because *how* we react to what we see comes from our parents, our family members, our original religion, and native country. People from diverse cultures and families often respond differently to the same event. The stressed-brain reactions are influenced especially by our familial, cultural and religious teachings and bias.

Oddly, we still accept and use our early programming from persons we do not respect or agree with. Therefore, to change an habitual reaction, you have to look at your original indoctrination and make a strong effort to transform it. This is not easy because your early training and emotional responses have been a part of you for many years and often come from the earlier brains. The freedom gained by examining your behavioral rules and expectations is invaluable. Psychotherapy can certainly help in this examination.

At age 55, Allen was discouraged about ever finding a partner to care about and grow old with. He was a professional, good looking and smart, yet had never been in a long-term relationship. In class, he had a tough time forgiving his mother. Because of his difficulty, he decided to look deeply at all his original training from his mother—he called it "brainwashing." He especially searched for her subtle messages and rules.

"This was the toughest thing I've done in my life," Allen admitted. "I hated the way my mother treated me as a kid. She was too protective and too concerned about everything I did. She was hurt when I didn't give her enough attention. What surprised me when I looked at our relationship is that I expected other women to give me extraordinary attention.

When they didn't it was obvious they didn't like me." He added, "No wonder I have never been in a long-term relationship. I never gave anyone a chance. The truth is, I didn't want ever to be smothered again, and even worse, I felt I could never do enough for any partner. I saw women as a bottomless pit. That was unfair to every woman I went out with." He understood why his mother was that way, and forgave her, but as he said, "It looks like I will probably never have a decent relationship. That's what's sad."

This shows us how Allen's outer world reflected his inner world. Women were not interested in him because he judged them. Allen's ability to see how his early programming ran his life was profound, as were his insights. It had taken him many years of inner work to be able to look inside himself with skill. Because our paths crossed socially, I was aware that within a year, he developed a loving relationship that seemed to be leading toward marriage.

> "We don't live outside ourselves; life goes on within us, and our thinking determines the experience."
> 
> JIM ROSEMERGY, AUTHOR & UNITY MINISTER

In children, we often see this example of negative programming. Again, the outer world reflects inner beliefs. A person who is taught early on that another race is inferior will always see people of that race in a certain way until there is a different set of messages put into the brain. We are given many prejudices and negative responses in our early life. These continue to run us even as adults unless we consciously choose to look at these early patterns. The forgiveness process enables us to change our habitual response so that we can pursue truth more effectively.

Perhaps you have had the experience of driving through a town when you were hungry. Because you were hungry, maybe the lack of restaurants influences what you thought of the town. If you are angry, you might only see the unfriendly people and problems. Another person in the car might be affected by something else and have a different reaction to the town. When asked about the town, each person in the car will have a different response, some, even strongly emotional.

## *Changing our Responses*

Because our survival responses are habitual, changing them takes real examination and reevaluation. What you are feeling and seeing is only your reaction and may not be reality. During an upset, if you can remember this, you might try to relax, breathe deeply, perhaps say a prayer to help change your experience. Remember, if you don't like what is going on in your life, you have the capacity to re-look and shift your reaction.

The best understanding can do is bring humility. It carries with it the humble insight that there is another way to view what you see. Yours is not the only way. This opens the door to peace and to forgiveness, which will bring the emotional shift you seek.

## *Our Standards*

We can hold others and ourselves to unrealistic standards due to our expectations of perfection. Identifying our standards and re-evaluating them is central in forgiving and to being content.

The noted Stanford Forgiveness Project researcher, Dr. Fred Luskin, calls these our rules. Effective Communication expert, Dr. Marshall Rosenberg, calls them our values. Both are useful words to enable us to go deeper in looking at how we judge people. These judgments are what keep us from forgiving.

Though we like to think that critical analysis helps us to function better, we often misuse this analyzing to judge and condemn. Thus, we keep others and ourselves in the debris of failure instead of enabling us to get up, brush off, and move on.

We need standards, values, and rules for living as these are necessary to the fabric of our social, religious, and personal development, expression, and expansion. The problem comes when our judgments lead to condemnation and attack of others or ourselves.

When we attack others, in our mind or the world, it brings unhappiness at the least and tragedy at the extreme. Just look at the decimation of peoples and cultures in Rwanda and Bosnia in recent times, and the ongoing threats of jihad and terrorism.

I am not advocating lowering standards, but looking at where your standards come from and if they are truly appropriate. I am promoting being less judgmental toward yourself and others when those standards are not met. If the standards are valuable, keep using them.

The original meaning of "sin" is from Greek. It really means—**to miss the mark**. When you miss the mark, you keep trying to do well and keep practicing until you hit where you are aiming. Forgiveness through reevaluations of your unrealistic expectations and focusing on your valuable targets is the key to attaining what you want.

Unrealistic expectations come most often from the opinions of other people. Members of Murder Victims Against Capital Punishment are sometimes harassed and even receive death threats because they have forgiven the offender and chosen not to be a victim of hatred.

**Try this:** To find out how others influence your decision to forgive, look at family and friends' opinions about any situation you are finding difficult.
1. What are they saying that prevents you from forgiving?
2. What will people think of you if you forgive?

Addressing these questions will allow you to go deeper into the social and cultural assumptions that keep you from forgiving.

## *The Deadly Rules, Judgments, and Expectations*

If you do not like the world you see, this section is indispensable. One of the ways to have the subconscious affect us less is to be aware of the attitudes that run us. As we mentioned in the previous section, under the surface of our action and thinking are rules, judgments, and expectations that are often driven by the survival mechanisms of the lower brains.

As I mentioned, much of the difficulty we have in forgiving comes from the emotional and survival rules taught to us as children by our family, religion, and society in general. From these, we make our judgments. These judgments and the rules behind them determine our standards and whether or not to forgive. Under intense stress, our perception and understanding of these rules become more distorted, even when the rules are valid.

Our family, peers, teachers, society, religion, and country all have emotionally influenced:

A. What we value,
B. How we should act, and
C. What we expect of others.

**Important Note**: Not all of what we are taught is necessarily the truth or of value. Religious and social values may be extremely different from family to family—even in the same country. These differences are even wider between countries or cultures. It is up to us as responsible adults and citizens to reevaluate what we were taught as children, especially when we have expectations that are not being met.

When people break your rules and you get very upset, you can be pretty sure that the emotion behind that reaction has not come from the highest place within you but the lowest. I'm talking here about strong reaction, probably anger and the desire to attack and harm others when a person perhaps only voiced an opinion or did something that was socially okay with others. I'm not talking about the abuse or violation of person or property, but even then, the level of our reaction can get too extreme.

Emotions give you zest for life. But, when they are running your life and making it unhappy, then it is essential to reevaluate your rules, expectations, and judgments with an eye toward forgiveness. The function of the neocortex is to control these earlier brain attitudes and acts. You must set limits on the emotions that are ruining your life.

Ned's mother had always told him, "You are just like your father." This was a negative image for him to carry because Ned was not like his father. For many years, Ned could not see his father's goodness. Then, in a guided forgiveness meditation, he remembered that his mother's opinion of her father was terrible because of abuse in her childhood. Ned realized that this experience had polluted her opinion of *all* fathers, and all men in general. This understanding of her perspective enabled him to forgive her for her constant criticism.

Forgiveness entails taking a different perspective than your habitual one so that past associations can change. Rules for behavior may come from negative sources. Reevaluating these rules lets you see whether they are useful to you now.

Mary was an only child raised in the country and had spent most of her time alone. Pete, from a large Italian family, was raised in the city. At first, these differences were exciting to them. Mary loved being with his large family. Pete saw that she brought peacefulness into his life by creating personal time for them alone. He was also comfortable having his family around. After a while, she resented not having her own personal and private time so started criticizing Pete whenever the family was around. Pete attacked back. Soon they felt their differences were irreconcilable.

Then Pete discovered forgiveness training. When Mary was upset with him, he just tried to let go of the upset and find calmness within himself to save the marriage. Instead of reacting, he found that by remaining calm, he began to understand Mary. "Finally," he said, "when I started listening through the 'ears of forgiveness,' we were able to come up with helpful solutions to our differences and save our marriage."

Pete had the good sense not to stick to his way as the only way. He stopped going to all the family gatherings, though he wanted to. Mary appreciated that he did this for her, and became more willing to go to the gatherings. During this work of reconciling their differences, they agreed to leave the family functions much earlier than they had in the past. Mary noticed that in leaving early, she did not mind being there. By going through this process, they gained understanding.

## A journal process for you:
To deal with the validity and reality of rules:
1. List the values, laws, rules, or moral codes that you feel your offender has broken.
2. Looking at each, ask:
   a) Where did this rule come from?
   b) Is it a valid rule or code? Or one that needs revision?
3. Then ask:
   **a)** Do I have an unrealistic expectation of another to follow that law, value, or rule, especially if I have done the same thing in some way to others or myself?
   **b)** Do I have an unrealistic expectation for myself to obey that law, value, or rule?

## *The Letters Practice*

This practice of writing three letters is one of the best tasks I've found to help in forgiving. (You will learn the third letter later in the book.)

Communication is fundamental to our existence. Babies in orphanages in Communist Romania who had little human contact either died or became overly withdrawn and even antisocial. When we look at unforgiven situations, often a communication problem was hurtful, rejecting or absent. Even if you don't want the contact reestablished, you must look at what happened, because the way we manifest our upset is often through communication or the lack of it.

I first came across a similar letter sequence by Dr. John Gray from Robert Plath, past founder and director of The Worldwide Forgiveness Alliance. Bob was a caring lawyer who has dedicated his life to having forgiveness used more in the world. One of his primary goals is to establish International Forgiveness Day as a globally celebrated holiday.[10]

The sequence of these letters is from our own human experience. It is how we often interact when we're upset. First, we confront the offender. We might get angry and tell the person why. Then they respond. Ideally, the upset is cleared up, and the connection reestablished.

## *The Hurt Letter*

Because forgiveness is an emotional action, we first need to be aware of the feelings involved, and to release them.

Write a letter to the person you wish to forgive. In the letter, spell out **exactly** how this situation hurt you and how you feel about the person now. Use the letter to vent all your feelings and thoughts about the person and the situation. Do not give him or her the benefit of the doubt in this letter. Just write down how upset you are.

This is where you voice all of your distress and disappointment with the person. You say just how displeased you are. It is crucial to write all of this down so that you don't fall into emotional attack or overwhelm that may occur if you happen to see the offender face to face, or even think of them.

Make sure that you look at these questions:
1. How did they hurt you?

2. What are the things in this situation that are unforgivable?
3. What in my past reminds me of this?
4. Is there something about this that robs me of the strength or willingness to consider forgiveness?

Write down the feelings that come to mind. You may find these questions helpful:
1. What do I feel when I picture the person involved in the situation—sad, depressed, angry, guilty, hurt, anxious?
2. Apart from the main emotion, are there others, such as embarrassment, humiliation, or shame, beneath or mixed up with the main one?
3. Am I willing to engage these feelings and not avoid them?

In the middle of this letter, if you remember a similar but earlier situation you had with that person or someone else, it's valuable to immediately write about what happened at that earlier time. Remember, the earlier distress may often hold the later one in place because the later event is most likely neurally connected in the brain to the earlier one.

In this *emotional* letter, you keep writing until there is nothing left to say. Reread it to see if there is anything to add. Then, put it to the side. Some people have made a ritual of burning the letter. Though you might want to send it, hold off. It is not from the first letter but the second that understanding arises.

Now we move onto the next letter.

## *The Response Letter*

I learned the effectiveness of hearing the other person's viewpoint not only from my training in marriage and family counseling but also in my work in Hawaii in a family healing process and ritual called *Ho'o Pono Pono*. This is an ancient traditional Hawaiian practice where family members come together when there are relationship problems and disharmony in their immediate family. This may be a large family gathering of up to 20 people or more.

In traditional *Ho'o Pono Pono*, each family member, from child to elder, says how he or she is affected by the disharmony and by any offense that took place. Forgiveness is expected all around and harmony is reestablished. The sharing can become involved and may take a long time, even days, so that everyone has their time to say how they feel, and sort out what happened. The willingness to forgive all parties involved is integral to the reestablishment of harmony and goodwill.[11]

Write the second letter from the offender's point of view. Use it to answer each of your upsets, but with his or her experience as the primary one. Write the letter to yourself as if it came from the offender. You are being their voice, saying exactly what happened and why solely from their perspective.

Somewhere in the letter, after they explain and justify their past, write what you would like to hear from them. Have him, or her explain how they were affected by your grief or upset. It is important to get what you want. If you want an apology, write it. If you need the offender to have an insight, hear it from that person in the letter. Though this is a wishful letter, you might be surprised how insightful and useful it can be.

Even though you know it is from you, something often happens in writing from another's perspective. I have had several students say that the person would never say that. In realizing this, they recognized the futility of wanting what they would never get, and let the upset go.

To assist at this level, I have done hypnotherapy with clients having them picture themselves getting what they want. You can do this yourself: relax and picture receiving an apology or whatever you would like. Research has shown that the mind does not often know the difference between what happens in the hypnotic state and in real life. Thus, giving yourself what you desire in a deeply relaxed state of mind enables you to feel better about the situation.

To truly understand a person's worldview, **walk in their shoes.** Here are guidelines that might help:
1. Write down what you believe to be the governing moral code that this person lives by, and that should have influenced their behavior in this situation.
2. How do they see the world? What do they fear and love, like and dislike?
3. What was it like growing up in their family?
4. What was it like to come from their culture or time?

5. What were their issues?
6. What is their emotional intelligence?
7. What was their expectation of you, of others?

If you cannot answer these questions, then you do not know enough to condemn this person.

Relief will often come as you write. Understanding always brings a decrease in emotional turmoil. Compassion brings forgiveness.

If you don't seem to be able to let go, that is all right, just go to the next chapter. Forgiveness work has snowballing results. If you do your best at each stage, you will move through the process. At some point, there will be a shift and you will let go of the upset.

There is a third letter, the Gratitude Letter that I recommend also doing. It is in Chapter 8- The Power behind Forgiving. (at p. 126)

## *The Fourth Hurdle*

Your reaction to the world and people in it comes from the programming in your own mind. When you look for the truth, you can take control of your life. You now have some tools to do just that.

This is a major hurdle because you can stop blaming others for your condition and you can take control of your reactions. This is not easy but is more rewarding than anger and resentment. When bad things happen, you do not have to look outside of yourself for ways to deal with them. Rather, the problem becomes a challenge and an opportunity to get past your early training, see the situation in a different way and forgive.

> "Be not angry that you cannot make others as you wish them to be, since you cannot make yourself as you wish to be. If you cannot mold yourself entirely as you would wish, how can you expect other people to be entirely to your liking?"
>
> THOMAS A KEMPIS, *THE IMITATION OF CHRIST*
> FROM THE 15TH CENTURY

# CHAPTER SEVEN

# Making Forgiving Easier

"He that cannot forgive others breaks the bridge over which he must pass himself; for every man has a need to be forgiven."
GEORGE HERBERT (1593 – 1633)

## Find Meaning in Forgiving

It's essential to find meaning in your forgiving. Here are two stories that show its power.

### Amy Biehl

During the apartheid violence in South Africa in 1993, a young black man killed Amy Biehl, an American Rhodes Scholar and exchange student. Her parents, who had supported her apartheid protests, came from the U.S. to visit the family of the young man who killed their daughter as a way of paying tribute to her and her ideals. They forgave him and then testified in court on the young man's behalf so that he would receive a pardon. They said they were only able to do this because they knew it would be their daughter's wish. [1]

Her parents were able, out of love for their daughter and her highest vision, to shift their perspective and embrace her point of view. This meaning enabled them to forgive.

### Wild Bill

George Ritchie, a psychiatrist for many years at the University of Virginia, wrote a profound book, *Return from Tomorrow*, in which he relates the following powerful story.

Before he became a doctor, Ritchie was part of a small medical team sent to a newly liberated Nazi concentration camp. There he met Wild Bill Cody, the nickname of one of the Jewish prisoners. His eyes were bright and he worked along with the American soldiers 15 – 16 hours a day without showing weariness. Though the soldiers showed fatigue, his strength seemed to increase. "His compassion for his fellow prisoners glowed on his face," Dr. Ritchie reported.

It seemed obvious to the Americans that Wild Bill must not have been in the concentration camp very long. When Ritchie discovered records that showed Wild Bill was imprisoned there in 1939, he was shocked. He asked Wild Bill how he had kept his vitality for six years when everyone else was barely alive. Here is what he said:

"We lived in the Jewish section of Warsaw, my wife, our two daughters, and our three little boys.…When the Germans reached our street, they lined everyone against a wall and opened up with machine guns. I begged to be allowed to die with my family, but because I spoke German they put me in a work group. I had to decide right then whether to let myself hate the soldiers who had done this. It was an easy decision, really. I was a lawyer. In my practice, I had seen too often what hate could do to peoples' minds and bodies. Hate had just killed the six people who mattered most to me in the world. I decided then that I would spend the rest of my life – whether it was a few days or many years – loving every person I came in contact with."[2]

## *Man's Search for Meaning*

This is the title of a book by a psychiatrist, Dr. Victor Frankel, who was also a Nazi death camp survivor. He survived because he was able to find meaning in his life. He noticed that those who did not have some meaning in their life often did not survive.

A new kind of therapy came out of his work helping people find meaning in their life. He felt that our primary drive in life is doing what we find meaningful. Amazon says that in the 1990s, his was considered one of the ten most influential books in America.

Finding meaning is a vital lesson not only for forgiving but also for living.

• What in your life would inspire you to forgive?

## *The Best Strategy for Dealing with Difficult Situations*

In truth, you do not know how experiences will be associated in anyone else's brain or even in your own. A new demanding situation or problem might connect to a dozen different thought patterns and experiences and twice as many different rules and judgments. This is why the best strategy for doing forgiveness work is to break down the upset (Chapter 3). If you are still having difficulty with a situation, break it down further.

## *A Technique to Make Forgiveness Go Faster*

*Look at earlier events that are similar.* Each new experience we have attaches to an *already formed* group of experiences in the brain. Thus, we see the importance of looking at earlier situations in our life that might be like the one we are dealing. I've found that forgiveness can deepen as you look at and work on the earliest occurrence of a situation that you can recall.

Remember, your appreciation of life deepens as you mend the upsets from your family, religion, and culture you were raised in.[3]

Forgiveness counseling is most effective if you look at earlier situations that are related to the current one in some way. When a person can't forgive a spouse, who is similar to a parent or sibling, drop working on the spouse for the moment, and work on the parent or sibling if the situations are alike. When you handle the earlier person first, the upset with the spouse or partner becomes much easier to handle.

If you are having difficulty forgiving someone, ask yourself:
1. Is there someone earlier in my life who has done this same or a similar thing to me?
2. Have I done this or something similar earlier in my life?
3. Have I been in this situation before?
4. Work on the earlier time and if you still have difficulty ask again if there is an even earlier situation to look at. For example, an upset with husband-2 might be like one with husband-1. If the upset doesn't change much, you might look even earlier.

## Concern for Fairness as a Block to Forgiving

A strong desire for fairness can negatively affect our willingness to forgive. Often, from our viewpoint, what another did was unfair, especially if he or she has not apologized or recognized how we were affected. There might be many reasons for the lack of apology, but often we will not consider them because we believe we are right. What's fair is tough to agree on because others see things differently. That is why we use courts of law to determine what is fair. Socially we create laws to decide fairness, and still they aren't fair. This complaint starts in childhood and never ceases: "No fair!"

Even though it is tempting to idealize how it would be if people were fair or valued you, the other person hardly ever sees it your way. You end up just causing yourself a lot of upset. Fairness is often a masquerade for personal preferences and wants. *Fair* is what I want, but what the other person wants is not as legitimate. Consequently, each person locks into his or her point of view. The result is each fighting for what is theirs and experiencing mounting resentment[4a]

With this false-fairness thinking, we often see conditional beliefs based on inner laws, as, "If he loved me, he'd make sure I had a nice car." "If he cared at all, he'd come home right after work." "If they valued my work here, they'd give me a raise." "If she loved me, she wouldn't bother me when I come home from work." As the authors of *Thoughts & Feelings: the Art of Cognitive Stress Intervention*, points out, you can undo the fallacy of fairness by recognizing that what is "fair," is often not agreed upon. It is more helpful to say what you want, need or prefer. Without the opinion of unfairness, you become honest with yourself and the other person.[4b]

## Getting Needs and Wants Met

Expressing your needs and wants, as well as having them satisfied, is difficult. Without a willingness to at least hear the other person's perspective, your needs probably will not be met. Even then, it takes excellent communication skills to express those desires to another.

Dr. Marshall Rosenberg spent his life teaching *compassionate communication*, which helped people understand themselves and others better so that they can get their needs and wants satisfied more easily. His excellent work is described in his book, *Nonviolent Communication: A Language of Compassion.*[5]

Our needs and wants often arise out of the subconscious. Doing the work in this book and the companion workbook, will enable you to look more closely at your true needs and wants from a deeper level so that forgiving can occur.

## *The Secret Attitude That Aids Forgiving*

The attitude that makes forgiving less difficult is humility. It may take a person quite awhile to understand its power. It enables us to step back from that part of us that always needs to be right, and look more objectively at the situation. Humility doesn't mean weakness, timidity, submissiveness, or groveling. It means having enough inner strength to say, "I don't know it all!"

Above any other attribute, it opens us to forgive because it enables us to let down our defenses and bring in compassion to try to understand another's situation. It quiets the reactive brain. It allows us to step back from the defensive part of us that needs to blame and attack to feel protected. Humility asks us to step away from playing God, thinking we know everything.

Humility enables us to admit that we, too, have done harmful things to others and are not so high above the other whom we cannot forgive. It also allows us to forgive ourselves by stepping down from the pedestal where we play God and can admit our shortcomings, in the admission, "There, but for the grace of God, go I." In this statement, we admit we are not that different from others except for circumstance. It helps us to let go of defense and attack, and come back to our birthright of peace, joy, and love.

## *How to See the Truth*

To see the real truth in a situation most often requires us to step back from our strong desire to always be right. Being humble is a difficult coat to put on, but when we do, it increases our joy, peace, and love. For many, humility brings the recognition of The Sacred and Divine into our life.

Anger, fear, or any expression of lack of love requires our humility to enable us to say, "I don't know what is really going on here." Then, we can step into that nobler aspect of ourselves, allowing a flow of love, life, and peace to occur. Here is the place from which forgiveness flows.

Not only does humility ask us to step away from playing God, thinking we understand everything, but it may ask us to take the hand of God. In that act, if we ask for the truth, we will see it because we will be looking through the eyes of Love.

## *Developing Your Power of Decision*

Another essential in forgiving is your ability to *decide* to forgive. In this section, decide is used as an active verb, rooted in the present, rather than a plan for later. The words *willingness* and *intention*, by contrast, focus on forgiving at some future time. The decision to forgive, therefore, may need to be continually renewed.

Early in the book, I talked about the difficulty of deciding to forgive. The decision to forgive can be powerful and comes more easily when understanding is present. As you keep reading this book, you are gaining enough understanding of your unforgiven situations and enough compassion for yourself and others to *decide* to let upsets go. It might have happened already in one situation, and you are now working on others.

The qualities of willingness and intention help in deciding of any sort. How much information you are gathering by reading this book is strongly influenced by these two qualities. Inspiration increases willingness and intention.

## *Willingness*

When we hold the highest vision (the first essential to forgiveness, Chapter 1), we are inspired to be willing to forgive. This willingness is the primary element in forgiving. All else comes from the movement of our will.

Questions to ask yourself:
1. Am I willing to work on this?
2. Am I willing to face my resistance?
3. Am I willing to let this go?
4. Am I willing to be completely honest with myself?

## *Intention*

Prepare for the *Power Forgiveness Process* with this intention: "Forgiveness has great power, and will free me." If your intention is strong, you can stay in the process until you feel an inner shift. At that point, the decision to forgive will be easier. It might take time, particularly if there are old wounds to heal, but maintaining that core intention to let the upset go is the foremost step.

At rock bottom in my own life in 1993, I tried to figure out what was going on. I read the preface to A Course in Miracles, which basically said that God is unconditional love, but to experience this love you must forgive. My highest vision, experiencing God as love, ignited. As I read the preface further, my willingness, and then my intention, to forgive increased. When I realized that to experience this unconditional love, I must forgive, I decided to sit down in my reading chair and not get up until I forgave all that I could. Many hours later, I had let go of every upset I was aware of at that time in my life.

This seems an unbelievable feat, but it was not. I had been doing inner work for thirty years and was quite familiar with psychology and spirituality. These came together to help me, and I had the experience of Divine Love for seven straight years after that deep forgiveness session.

This overall intention, along with the decision, highlights that there are always several levels of commitment to what we do. I committed to the overall process, but on individual upsets, I sometimes became stuck.

We see this same pattern in marriage. The commitment and decision to be in the marriage might remain, but there may be problems in the relationship causing conflict. If the struggle to remain together continues without inspiration to make the relationship better, the desire to be apart might become stronger than being together. Then the commitment to the marriage may fail, and the couple will decide to end the relationship.

## *Deciding to Forgive*

Sometimes you must make a conscious decision to forgive while you are in this process. This decision is an act of will made as a solid commitment to your highest self, which will carry you through the difficult emotional terrain. Openness to forgiving occurs by recognizing that anger is not working. In deciding to forgive, you are taking back the power that the offending person or situation has stolen from your life.

**Questions on Making the Decision to Forgive:** In your journal, write down your answers to these:
1. Am I willing to work on this difficult situation?
2. Why do I want to forgive this person?
3. Am I committed to freeing myself from the negative consequences in my life that this situation has caused?
4. What prevents me from deciding to let this go?

## *The Overlooked Brain Function*

The ability of the brain that we often overlook in our modern computer-focused society is the use of our *intuitive power*—a feature that is quite useful in our work in forgiving. This is often associated with the functioning of the right side of the brain.[7]

*Accessing Your Intuition* – In forgiveness work we have inner resources to help us heal. Being open to creative input and other sources of wisdom and knowledge is a key in the higher functions of the human mind. We all have a natural ability that goes by many names: intuition, hunches, inner guidance, and so on. This ability has been recognized in significant historical people through the ages. Some develop it more than others, but it is available to all.

> "The mind can proceed only so far upon what it knows
> and can prove. There comes a point where the mind takes a
> higher plane of knowledge, but can never prove how it got there.
> All great discoveries have involved such a leap."
> ALBERT EINSTEIN[8]

Thomas Edison was a firm believer in this intuitive sense and used it often. When he struggled to find a solution to a problem, he would try to sleep in a chair while he kept the area under question in his mind. In his hand, he would hold his keys. Once he fell asleep, his keys would fall, waking him. He would then remember what he was dreaming. Often in that dream, there would be an answer to his problem.[9]

Accessing intuition requires being open to trying something new. When we face an apparently unsolvable problem or dilemma, what we need is a perspective outside our normal way of thinking; this is often called "thinking outside the box."

A quiet, calm environment and mind assists in our search for this creative part of us. For me, it is most often available in the early mornings, just before waking up completely. A friend, Neal, a building contractor, would design projects or work out building problems in these early hours. (Many say that this is also the best time for meditation.) He often would become aware of mistakes he had made the day before that needed correcting.

Peace and calm keep the more reactive and emotional parts of the brain deactivated, enabling the problem-solving and intuitive parts of us to be available.

While you are working on forgiving, make sure to use this powerful source of help.

In the following passage, Patanjali, a sage scholar of the third century BC, tells us how and why our intuition works:[10]

> "When you are inspired by some great purpose, some extraordinary project, all your thoughts break their bonds; your mind transcends limitations, your consciousness expands in every direction, and you find yourself in a new, great, and wonderful world. Dormant forces, faculties, and talents become alive, and you discover yourself to be a greater person by far than you ever dreamed yourself to be."

## *Changing Old Thought Habits*

By holding resentments, we are unable to hold the thoughts of peace, much less a Higher Power. Effective thinking ability is lost under undue stress. Survival mechanisms and reactions can take over, making us incapable of those higher thoughts.

**Please note**—To assist in relieving stress, **Stop and focus your mind.**

More than thirty years ago, Dr. Herbert Benson of Harvard Medical School created *The Relaxation Response* to help people deal with stress and its negative effects, such as high blood pressure. He studied meditators from around the world to incorporate their methods into his valuable relaxation method to help people feel better and to change their negative thinking patterns.[11]

There is a great deal of data from neuroscience and cognitive studies showing the power of thoughts and beliefs. Here again, forgiveness plays an effective role. If many negative thoughts are roaming through a person's mind, he or she often will not find relief from them until they are connfronted and each put to rest. Another way is to raise the mind to a higher state through *ongoing* meditation or contemplation. Either way, forgiveness is critical.

*The Power Forgiveness Process* does this well. The person cleared of their victim and guilt thoughts will be in a more positive place to have peace, joy, and love in life. Until this happens, the deepest spiritual and life potential cannot easily be accessed.

## *How to Change Your Inner Experience:*

**Using your imagination.** Recent hypnosis research is fascinating about changing our inner experience. The New York Times reported, "What you see is not always what you get, because what you see depends on a framework built on experience that stands ready to interpret the raw information." This is a restatement of what we went over in the previous chapter. The article explained that when people who were hypnotized reviewed an event in their past and then changed it, the brain acted as though the changed event was real. When the event was recalled later, the brain responded as if the new experience from hypnosis was real.[12]

We have known this for a long time in hypnotherapy, but now science confirms it. Guided meditations also allow us to reinterpret and often change the experience of a trauma. Professor Charles Figley of Tulane University and Florida State University, a pioneer in trauma research and responsible for the establishment of the Green Cross Foundation and the Academy of Traumatology, acknowledges the Visual Kinesthetic Disassociation (VKD) hypnosis method as valid in helping relieve people of traumatic incidents.[13]

When you relax, breathe and picture yourself somewhere peaceful perhaps at a beach or in the mountains, then make the picture and feelings seem real, the mind will act as if it is true. Doing this can change your upsetting experience in minutes. It takes practice, of course, but in a short while, you will find the relaxation and the mind shift that you are seeking.

Maria was ready to quit work when she came to see me. "I hate my boss and so does everyone else," she said in tears. Her boss had been unkind to her in front of other employees. She could not forgive him. With hypnosis, I had Maria picture herself having the boss apologize. Then I had her picture forgiving her boss. I did not ask her to forgive, but only to picture it as if it had occurred. The session was 20 minutes, but at the end of it, she felt fine about her boss and felt she could be at work again. A month later, she was enthusiastic about her work and was getting along fine with the boss.

This is an example of the power of imagination in forgiving. Though this situation was done through hypnosis, you can do the method itself anytime. It is called by many names—creative visualization and self-hypnosis are the most common. It is a skill we all have; it only needs developing and practice.

**A Forgiveness Visualization:** The first step in any mental picturing is to take a break and relax.

1. Close your eyes and relax any tensions you are aware of as best you can. For just this exercise, let go of any concerns and focus on becoming calm.
2. Imagine love pouring into you in any way that you can, perhaps from a Divine Source or anyone you can think of, real or imaginary, who can send you love.
3. When you feel love filling you, imagine the person who upsets you. Send love to them (You might even hug them in your mind.) Continue until you feel a positive change in yourself.
4. You'll notice that the more you give love, the more you feel it.
5. See yourself walking in the other person's shoes and what it was like for him or her in life.
6. Imagine forgiving them. What would that feel like?

You will be surprised what this activity can do for you. We often see the negative scenarios very well—but picturing the positive can be so much better.

## *Do Positive Affirmations Work?*

Positive affirmations are optimistic statements that people repeat during the day. As you repeat these constructive assertions, you convince yourself of their truth. By taking a breath and relaxing, you help these statements go deeper into your mind. These positive statements may eventually remove the negative ones. Remember, it is similar to painting a wall that has a stain on it. The stain can often continue to seep through. Forgiveness is crucial to make sure the old stains in your mind will not destroy your positive declarations and intentions.

The secret behind positive affirmations and creative visualizations is not especially the words or what you see, but your positive emotional intention. The optimistic emotions are what carry you out of the negative brain mentality and give the confidence needed to make the words or visions happen. The words are not magic, but the uplifting emotions are. As long as you let the survival-self control your life with its negative emotions, you will not have the life you want because you are only living in the lowest part of your brain and thinking.

In psychology, Cognitive Therapy targets the negative statements you say to yourself throughout the day. Often, you are not aware of these judgments about yourself and others because they are rooted in our childhood. Nevertheless, they sit there, just under the surface of your awareness, condemning what you do. This "negative self-talk" is devastating and must be changed to achieve happiness and the ability to forgive. Distorted thinking patterns ruin lives.

Alicia came to class furious with her sister-in-law, Janet. All day she thought about how Janet hurt her. Not only did she replay the upset, but she also made statements throughout the day that kept her anger going, like "that ungrateful .." She was a wreck emotionally, and also admitted that she had made comments against herself, like "No one cares about me." Also, she started saying things to herself against her husband.

This is mind *poison*. Negative self-talk destroys. By the end of class, she could look at the unreality of what she was saying to herself, and forgive. Then she replaced the negative statements about herself and her family with positive ones.

The quest for a positive frame of mind has a four-fold action:
1. Becoming aware of the negative statements that you have been saying to yourself for years

2. Stopping each one, every chance you get.
3. Making positive emotional declarations to replace the negative ones.
4. Forgiving yourself and others.

The first three actions will enable forgiving thoughts to take hold because you are lifting yourself out of the control of the stressed brain. This brain with its survival functions is meant for crisis, not ongoing perception. If you find yourself caught in long-lasting fear or anger you are letting your reactive brain structures have too much control. Do the four steps above. Live the life you were meant to live.

## *A Summary of the Essentials*

Through the chapters, I've pointed out essentials to do in forgiveness work. Here are the key points on which to focus. Keep them in mind whenever you do this work.

1. **Hold your highest vision** – Remain inspired to forgive.
2. **Find meaning in forgiving** – Use a core value or principle in your life, as Wild Bill did in the concentration camp and Amy Biehls' parents in South Africa.
3. **Ask for help from others and The Divine.**
4. **Commit to the process** – Be willing to forgive. Intend to forgive. Decide to forgive.
5. **Feel the feelings** – Look for the feelings under the surface.
6. **Find the truth** – Be honest – The truth will set you free!

## *The Secrets of Forgiveness Work*

I've been doing a range of counseling work since 1968. Through the years of doing forgiveness work, I've found the following counseling wisdoms to be significant in helping people forgive. Because so few people, in general, are aware of these, I call them secrets. They are:

1. **Break down the situation** – Analyze it piece-by-piece, person by person.
2. **Use your intuition**
3. **Get support from others**
4. **Use your imagination**

5. **Look for earlier events** – Search for experiences in the past that are alike or similar to the one you are working on now.
6. **Let go of being right and open to humility**

## *The Fifth Hurdle*

You have now passed the fifth hurdle. You know what makes forgiving easier. You continue to gain information and skill at forgiving. You might even have reached forgiveness for your original upset by now and be working on others.

The essentials, secrets, and exercises will all come together for you as you go along. There will be a summary of the first part of the *Power Forgiveness Process* in Chapter 9, and then a full summary of the whole process in Chapter 14. With these, you will see how it all fits together so that you can use it in any situation.

Forgiveness has continued in the realm of religion because it sometimes seems to take an act of God to help us let go. Acceptance of some sort of Higher Power does help in dealing with those things that seem to have great power over us—where we seem powerless.

# CHAPTER EIGHT

# The Power behind Forgiving

"Everyone who is seriously involved in the pursuit of science becomes convinced that a spirit is manifest in the laws of the Universe—a spirit vastly superior to that of man."

ALBERT EINSTEIN[1A]

When we speak of forgiveness, we are speaking of the key to gaining happiness and love after deep hurt. It is my experience that letting go of *all* upsets, the goal of Power Forgiveness, truly can open us up to a completely different connection to love, inspiration and the creative principle of life – the Healer of woes.

## *The Core of Our Being*

Spiritual teachers from every religion have said through the ages, and my own experience has shown me that there is a center of our being that we can experience, which is beyond our ego-driven world of wants and needs or hates. In this center are our fulfillment and true peace. Out of this comes love, peace, and joy independent of our external life. This center is emphasized through the ages in all religions.

One's religion might or might not provide a framework to enable a person to experience that Center of Being. It all depends on how much a person can let go of the false self, the small personality, which pushes away or grasps life's experiences.

Complete forgiveness can take us into that spiritual experience. It is essential because it clears our mind for the experience of the Divine. Without the clear mind provided by forgiving, this experience will be minimal at best. How can love enter the heart that is filled with resentments, guilt, or grudges?

The power of forgiveness may be viewed in a myriad of ways, but is basically a heartful connection to other. Even biologically—love is built into the system. In his well-researched book on living systems, *The Self-Organizing Universe,* Scientist Eric Jantsch tells us: "Since the earliest aggregation of cells of primitive organisms is the capacity to go beyond one's self for the community." [1b] This is love in its essence.

Love, to me, is that sense in our heart of goodness, kindness, and compassion towards others and often to life itself. Love or compassion is the foremost theme in many world religions. Our love extends from us to others and the outside world, we could even say that love is a fundamental part of the uniqueness of life and seems to be at the core of the dynamic tension of life – our will to selfhood versus our will to community. This sense of going beyond one's self is integral to forgiving.

*"We must be saved by the final form of love which is forgiveness."* – Reinhold Niebuhr

Love is vital to our spiritual well-being and the most powerful and significant emotion we have. By spiritual, I mean a transcendent level of life beyond our physical, mental, and emotional survival and functioning. Focusing on this level of being not only gives our lives purpose and meaning, but also helps us rise above our bodily and emotional problems. Religion is an organized attempt to make sense of and bring about spiritual experience and perspective.[2]

## *The Principle of Life*

Even though we talk about our sense of the Divine or Higher Power, or God, the experience is in our everyday life. People with no religion still know what it means to be heartfelt, compassionate and loving.

We feel guilty when we act against the principles of love and life. This guilt seems to move us away from the highest values within and around us. It moves us out of our highest thoughts and goals to block us from feeling joy or peace. Letting go of guilt is our path back to the Principle of Life, and back to re-experiencing love, peace, and joy. This is the reason for forgiving, and gives us the ultimate power back to happiness.

"But seek first his kingdom and his righteousness, and all these things will be given to you as well." JESUS - *MATTHEW 6:33*

## Love and Forgiveness

Without love as the foundation of our life and heart, we succumb more easily to afflictions, loss, and lack—making life unpleasant and often unbearable.

Why forgiving others and ourselves works so well and heals so quickly is simple. Underneath the complexity of our emotions and reactions, and beneath our survival mechanisms is a purity of heart and honesty. I believe that is our essence, and why forgiving is so powerful in changing our life.

Forgiveness of others and gaining forgiveness for ourselves bring us back to our highest functioning. Just doing an unloving act itself sets up a reaction inside us creating guilt. This is basic to why forgiveness works. It brings us back to a more real and authentic self and state of being. It brings us back to functioning in our full neocortex.

Martin Luther King, Jr. told us: "We must develop and maintain the capacity to forgive. He who is devoid of the power to forgive is devoid of the power to love."

## My Transformative Experience

In 1993 when I hit rock bottom, I cleaned up every upset I had with others and myself. In doing this, I experienced a dynamic center of love for years. I noticed after that transformative experience that I would not feel that full loving feeling for others and life if I did not clean up upsets I had. Those upsets could be with news figures, politicians or situations that I got angry at. To keep that experience of love, every night or morning I made it a point to clean up any upset I had.

Seven years after my transformation, the first event occurred where I was not able to forgive; I lost that Love experience for four months. Finally, when I whole-heartedly forgave that person I held the resentment against, my perception of love in my life came back. Only three times in 25 years did it take more than a day or two. In those three times, depression, anger, and hopelessness returned. Each time, when I finally was able to forgive, my life immediately turned around, and the perception of Love returned. The last time, several years ago, took me over eight months to deal with it. I know now that if someone had forced me to do my own book, I'd have healed the upset much sooner, but my ego and denial got in the way.

After more than 20 years, love has become an ongoing experience in my heart. I can give you specific religious explanations about it, but that isn't necessary. In a practical sense, Love is there as a natural consequence of a life without resentment. I know that if I can experience this so can anyone else, as long as they completely clean up upsets, resentments, and judgments. This is not easy work but is fruitful, fulfilling, and worth doing.

I had a minister tell me that only a saint can do that type of work. Well, I am not a saint by a long shot, but that experience of love is far more fulfilling than anything else in the world. Ask anyone who is in love. Thus, to keep it, I must do what it takes.

It takes mindfulness to be aware of the upsets and to focus on cleaning them up. Most people I have found are not willing to do that level of inner work, but would rather be right than happy. Seriously! The skill of staying clean can be gained by following this book. By cleaning up all your upsets, when a new resentment or judgment arises, you can see it because it is not in a forest of other upsets but is standing alone to be seen. That is why I advocate remaining clean in my heart. Not only does it work to experience ongoing love, but it also enables me and you to easily find the upsets that block love.

Upsets are like trees blocking the sun's rays (love). Stepping out from behind the trees (resentments or judgments) or cutting the trees down, enables the sun's rays to be again experienced. We see this in everyday life when a couple has an upset between them. Anger, hurt and sadness often block the love that was there in previous times. Hurtful things might even be said. When the upset is cleaned up and apologies expressed, forgiveness happens, and love returns.

One of my friends, an older woman, was in a law office waiting to see one of the lawyers. She started talking to an attractive young couple in the waiting room and found that they were there to get a divorce. The marriage just wasn't working out. My friend knew her forgiveness work and did not doubt its effectiveness. She started helping them clean up some upsets right there and convinced them that forgiveness would work to heal their relationship. They walked out of the law office hand-in-hand, not seeing the divorce lawyer. Love moved them.

"There is no spiritual power quite as great as that which comes from forgiving and praying for the enemy. Forgiving our enemies and praying for them generates great spiritual power because it is love."[3]
Joel Goldsmith, Spiritual teacher (1892 – 1964)

## *Our Healthiest State of Mind*

To explain this authentic, positive state further, consider this example. Imagine your mind and heart being like a large, loose circular rubber band on a table, having no tension, but filled with thoughts of fulfillment, kindness, and love. Imagine also living your life in that state of mind. Perhaps you can feel peacefulness in your daily affairs and work at a higher level because of your clarity and heartfulness.

If you start to pull on that rubber band, you create tension. In our example, that tension could be resentment or guilt. As you know, just a little tension will remove all the space inside that rubber band, which was your true way of being. The more tension put on the rubber band, the more effort it takes to hold the tension in place. Thus, any way that you can relieve that tension allows your mind and heart to go back to its natural position—a space of fulfillment, power, clarity, and love.

Through the ages, forgiveness has been a powerful force because, in my experience, it opens us to healing through a Source far greater than our survival-self. This Source has many names: Love, Nature, God, Allah, The Great Spirit, etc. Beyond all the names is what activates our highest thoughts, goals, and our maximum potential. By letting go of any resentments, hurts, and pain of the past, we loosen the tension of our mind and heart so that we can more easily have a sense of our Highest Power, allowing us to function at a happier and more creative, fulfilling level.

**Nourish your heart with this:**
1. Put immediate concerns to the side and go through a relaxation process by letting go of tension in your body starting with your head and working down, letting tensions drain out your feet.
2. Now, be aware of a sense of love in your heart. Increase it and feel that love extending out from you into the room.

3. Feel it naturally moving outside of where you are into the neighborhood or area surrounding you.
4. Expand that love to fill your city. Fill the area surrounding your city, extending to loved ones, other people, the trees, countryside and to other towns until your whole region is touched by love.
5. Allow it to fill your nation, and then other nations.
6. Now see and feel love filling the earth and everyone on it.
7. See the love you are sending benefitting all of life.
8. Come back when you are ready.

## *Real Healing*

If you have a leg wound with dirt in it, it will not heal until you remove the dirt. Nevertheless, it may look and function okay. Before the full healing of the leg can occur, the dirt needs to be removed and time is needed for the blemish to disappear. When you remove resentment from your mind, the memory is still there, but it can now finally heal instead of festering in the poison of anger or guilt.

Likewise, if you do prayers, positive affirmations, or meditation with resentment and guilt in your heart, your positive intentions will not easily take hold. You must remove the dirt. When you remove the upset, healing takes place. Otherwise, the affirmation, prayer, or meditation will have to be redone on a continuing basis. The dirt will not allow healing or your highest vision to occur.

When I meditated before my forgiveness transformation, I could get to a "pretty good" state of mind. I even taught meditation, having meditated on and off since I was sixteen. After that forgiveness transformation, my mind was much calmer and cleaner. Thus my meditations started with a peacefulness that before forgiving would have taken much time to get to.

This experience of healing is the result of a simple principle of the mind: **Your thoughts cannot go in opposing directions at the same time and get anywhere.** Resentment, guilt, anger, and fear take the mind in the opposite direction from love, happiness, and peace. Until you are willing to let go of resentments and fears, deep change cannot occur.

If love is the essence of our being, which I believe, then by extension, it is the highest functioning of the brain. When we forgive all upsets, the mind undergoes a transformation, where there is much more love, peace, and joy. This happens, and when it does, a positive outlook naturally arises. The end goal of forgiveness work is to re-pattern your thinking, so that love, joy, peace, patience, kindness, integrity, faithfulness, gentleness, and self-control are more available each moment.

> "When you examine the lives of the most influential people who have ever walked among us, you discover one thread that winds through them all. They have been aligned first with their spiritual nature and only then with their physical selves." - ALBERT EINSTEIN[4]

The question in forgiveness work becomes: "Where are you putting your mind and do you want to keep it there?" This awareness is mindfulness at its core. Several forgiveness methods are available to assist in this:
- Put your mind on love and send that love to the offender or offenders and yourself.
- Send prayers to them and yourself.
- If you want peace, keep your mind on peace and send that to them and yourself.

These are all ways to clear the upset and have a happier outlook. Feed yourself what you need. If chaos reigns, choose peace.

> "Therefore confess your sins to each other and pray for each other so that you may be healed. The prayer of a righteous man is powerful and effective." JESUS - *JAMES 5:16*

## *The Twelve-Steps*

A Twelve-step program is a fellowship that aims at the recovery of its members from the consequences of an addiction, a compulsion, or another harmful influence on their lives, with the help of the Twelve Steps.[5] A vital component of several of the steps can be seen as forgiveness.

THE *AA BIG BOOK* says: "If you have a resentment you want to be free of, if you will pray for the person or the thing you resent, you will be free. If you will ask in prayer for everything you want for yourself to be given to them, you will be free. Ask for their health, their prosperity, their happiness, and you will be free. Even when you don't really want it for them, and your prayers are only words and you don't mean it, go ahead and do it anyway. Do it every day for two weeks and you will find you have come to mean it and want it for them, and you will realize that where you used to feel bitterness and resentment and hatred, you now feel compassionate understanding and love." [6]

We can witness the power of Twelve-step programs that work with addictions of all sorts through the first three steps:
1. We admitted we were powerless over (alcohol, drugs, or other negative influence), that our lives had become unmanageable.
2. We came to believe that a power greater than ourselves could restore us to sanity.
3. We made a decision to turn our will and our lives over to the care of God, as we understood God.

## *Being Positive*

Positive attitudes about life help you to feel better. Unforgiven situations and people perpetuate animosity in your heart. Thus, for your prayers and desires to manifest, forgiveness must occur.

If we maintain and harbor resentment, anger, and upset with anyone, we are maintaining and believing that we can split our mind in two and still be happy. Because this is impossible, we are canceling the possibility of having a joyful, peaceful, or loving life.

A clean mind and heart will more easily experience the divine nature of life. When you remove the negatives of life, you begin to maintain new and positive patterns.

> "Therefore, if you are offering your gift at the altar and there remember that your brother has something against you, leave your gift there in front of the altar. First, go and be reconciled to your brother; then come and offer your gift."  Jesus, *Matthew 5:23-24*

Enrique was an old friend who through the years was becoming more and more negative. He did not like where he lived, though it was a delightful place to most people; he was upset with his family and was not able to make friends. I convinced him to do the *Power Forgiveness Process*. He worked hard, looked deeply, and took to heart what I said. Within a month, he was in a better intimate relationship than he had been in for years, he had better communication with his family, and he was much happier with where he lived.

## *Finding the Positive in Tragedy and Trauma*

Most of us have been dealt some very hard lessons by life. Often we get trapped in those incidents because we don't see anything positive about them. Seeing the positive aids forgiveness.

But how do you gain that positive perspective about something terrible? As in the overall action of forgiving—take bite-size pieces. Start with the small things. Time heals all wounds is the old adage. But, you can speed up that healing by finding small things to be grateful for that came from that negative experience.

You might look at the book; *Thank God I...:Stories of Inspiration for Everyday Situations* edited by John Castagnini. In it are stories by people who have found the positive in their greatest and often terrible challenges.

## *Gratitude*

Gratitude is a mighty method for change. It works any time and provides the opportunity each day to feel better.

The third largest religion in Japan, Seicho-No-Ie, holds the virtue of gratitude very highly. The founder, Masaharu Taniguchi, had an enlightenment experience in the 1920s. Afterward, he started teaching that the most important virtues to develop to deepen one's spiritual experience are gratitude, forgiveness, and reconciliation. He worked with individuals to bring these into peoples' hearts. Many miracles through the decades are attributed to his gratitude work and prayers.

Positive Psychology is a movement in psychology that finally places attention on the high-quality aspects of our mind instead of our negative pathology.

One of the Positive Psychology research teams compiled more than a hundred *happiness processes*, from the Buddha to Anthony Robbins, to discover which ones actually work. One of the most effective ways to have happiness, they found, was to use gratitude daily. In the study, people wrote down three good things, big or small, that happened during the day. They did this every night for one week. Next to each entry, they answered the question, "Why did this good thing happen?" After three months, these people were still significantly happier and less depressed than the control group.[7]

## The Third Letter of the Sequence

Mediators and negotiators have used the following method to prevent revenge from starting or continuing. Since you don't always have a mediator, counselor, or another neutral person available, the sequence of letters that you started in Chapter 6 can help. You already wrote the *Letter of Hurt* and the *Response Letter*. The third is the *Gratitude letter*, which you will be composing now. If there are several people in your upset, do a separate letter sequence for each.

A portion of the Gratitude letter comes from the *Honorable Closure* work[8] of Dr. Angeles Arrien, who was a cultural anthropologist, award-winning author, educator, and business consultant. She was a friend and mentor for several years. I highly recommend her many books for anyone interested in what is common to all of us across religions and cultures.

## The Gratitude Letter

At this stage in forgiving, write a letter of appreciation to the person you wish to forgive. In the letter, tell of your thankfulness for what they have contributed to your life. Release your negative feelings, as they do not belong in this letter.

1. Thank them for the gifts you have received from them through the years.
2. Tell them, if you can, *how* you matured mentally, emotionally, or spiritually from this.
3. Thank them for what you have learned from them, and express your appreciation for who they have been in your life.
4. If there was once love, *pretend* to feel this love and remember what you once loved about the person.
5. Appreciate their positive qualities and write down what you admire in them.
6. How did they inspire you?
7. Speak of the love given and love received.
8. Notice the shift in your body. Write down your insights.

In being grateful, initially, you might have to "Fake it till you make it," but it will come. Apologize only when you recognize intentional or unintentional harm you have done.

You might acknowledge the person's skills, character, integrity, strength, appearance, and what you like about them in general.

If you can see that you might have done something similar to their offense in any way, then compassion and humility can enter into your thoughts more easily, and forgiveness might occur in a flash. Then the challenge will be self-forgiveness.

Don't send the first two letters, but consider sending the gratitude one.

- What issues does this bring to mind? Write about them.

Jeanette's gratitude letter to her abusive husband started with an appreciation of his helping her gain strength to say no and to walk away from his abuse. Then she saw how hard he had worked and even had sacrificed for her so that she could have an attractive house. It ended in tears with her seeing the love that had been there.

NOTE: I want to repeat a warning I mentioned in the first part of the book. When the love returns in an abusive relationship, the victim may go back to the abuser feeling healed and may be abused again. Forgive, take care of yourself and set limits on abuse. See Myth 11 in Chapter 3.

If it is too hard to write this letter right now, then hold off until it is appropriate. The crucial point here is to be aware of the possibility of gratitude in this or any situation, for there is a gift in it.

## *An Inner Sense of Truth*

By acknowledging that you might *not know* the whole truth in the situation, you open yourself up to look more deeply. For example, you might not know God's purpose for this situation, or the lessons to be learned. You might not know the truth behind the other person's perspective.

Besides basic intuition, most of us have an inner sense of knowing the right thing to do. I have worked with people who have felt justified in their harmful actions toward another, but when we went deeper and became more truthful, they always admitted there was a part of them that knew it was not right. Not listening to that honest part of us creates turmoil and guilt. This inner sense of rightness is conscience. This sense of truth leads us to be aware that healing can only come through honesty. Through this inner sense of rightness, we can undo much of the turmoil around unforgiven situations.

This quality within is not condemning, but wholly benevolent and wise. It might even be called the *Spirit of Compassion* within you—for you. It's available but never controls. It's subtle but feels right. If your response is not love, peace, or joy, you have listened to the pessimistic survival-self. Agitation, anxiety or fear is a sure sign that you are *not* using your inner sense of truth.

## *Journal Questions*

1. Am I prepared to be completely honest with myself and in my recollections? Can I be objective?
2. Can I be complete and not omit or add details?
3. Am I prepared to be truthful about my own participation in my unforgiven situations?

"Forgiveness is a method of giving love. It is a way of saying, 'I am going to let go of the wrong you did; I am not going to be bitter and I am going to go on loving you anyway.'"
BERNIE SIEGEL, MD, *PRESCRIPTION FOR LIVING*

# CHAPTER NINE

# Working on Upsets

In this short chapter is a summary of the steps from all the previous chapters. This is not all the steps of the *Power Forgiveness Process*, but these can carry you quite far in forgiving.

## *Vital Steps and Actions to Remember*

To deal with a person or situation:

### 1 – Make a Choice that Feels Right

Start small. Take one upset, or part of one, to work on. It might be just one of a group of people or one of many upsets with a person.

### 2 – Look at your Willingness

- Are you willing to work on this upset?

(If not, take another upset that you are willing to face.) Willingness is essential because it provides the beginning of the commitment that leads to forgiving. Your willingness to take on upsets that are more difficult will increase as you forgive. You don't have to start with the big stuff first, just take any piece you are willing to look at.

### 3 – Focus on What Inspires You to Forgive

- What inspires you to do this work?

The essential quality in doing forgiveness work is to have continual inspiration to forgive. You need to have a worthy reason to do it. This inspired reason will take you past the natural internal resistance in the mind against forgiving. This motivation can be spiritual, emotional, or even physical.

Inspiration is the most effective beginning of any endeavor—the stronger the inspiration the greater the possibility of success.

The opening stage in forgiving is the kindling or rekindling of your desire to forgive. This initial opening through inspiration carries your spirit forward to the quest for more knowledge of the subject and, later, it carries you through emotional blocks that might come up.

## 4 – Deal with Feelings Effectively
- What do you feel when you think of the situation?

Dealing with feelings is valuable to prevent false forgiveness. When your feelings change to positive ones, forgiving has occurred. You may find these questions helpful in looking at your initial mindset:

   A. What do I feel when I think of the person involved in this situation? For example, sad, depressed, angry, apathetic, guilty, hurt, anxious.
   B. Apart from my main emotion, when I think of each situation, are there other feelings underneath, or mixed up with that main one, like embarrassment, humiliation, or shame?
   C. Am I willing to engage these feelings and not avoid them?
   D. What was I afraid would happen at the time? What am I afraid of now if I forgive?

## 5 – Find Your Needs and Debt Owed
Remember, our working definition of forgiveness is letting go of what is owed – as in forgiving a financial debt.
- What do they owe you for having to feel what you have felt?
- What do you need out of the situation? What would satisfy you?

For some, having the person go to jail will bring relief. For others, watching the person die is not enough. Therefore, the initial question in any forgiveness situation is, what do they owe you?

Here are further questions to help you in this step:
   A. Am I willing to entertain the possibility of not getting what they owe me?
   B. Is it worth carrying this upset when it is unrealistic that I would ever get what I want from them?
   C. Can I let it go to gain peace of mind?

## 6 – Look at the Real Consequences of Holding on to this Upset
This step does not have to be an essay; it can be done in moments.

Payoff:
A. What do I get by keeping the upset going? Write down any benefits. Who benefits and how?
B. Is being right more important than being happy?

Negative consequences:
Sometimes you don't notice how much the upset has affected you. Here are some questions to consider:
A. What am I getting out of this upset? List the negatives.
B. What is happening to the people closest to me by my holding onto the upset?
C. Could letting go of this situation increase love, peace, and joy in my life?

Being a Victim:
A. How long has my victimization been going on?
B. How long is it okay to let others be in control of my happiness?
C. Am I a possible contributor to the problem - not just the victim?

## 7 – Handle Resistance to Forgiving

What often prevents people from letting go are misunderstandings about the nature of forgiveness.

We listed these in the Myths chapter of the book, and repeat them here to make sure misunderstandings are not inhibiting your ability to move forward.

Remember, forgiveness is: Not condoning bad behavior, justifying an offense or turning the other cheek. It's not reconciliation with the offending party; it's not the same as out of sight, out of mind; Not dependent upon an apology; Not dependent on the other person being alive or in contact with you; Not dependent on whether the offending party deserves forgiveness; Not losing, or the easy way out of a situation; Not lack of responsibility.

If any of these are affecting your forgiving, look over the Myths of Forgiveness section in Chapter 3.

## Deciding to Forgive

You can make a conscious decision to forgive. This decision is an act of the will with full intention and a solid commitment to your highest self. The decision to forgive can occur anytime.

Questions you might ask are:
1. Can I decide to forgive right now for myself?
2. Even though they don't deserve it, can I decide to forgive as an act of compassion toward the other person and myself?

As you decide to forgive, you keep going through the rest of the stages. Forgiving someone is not the end of this process; forgiving yourself is, if you want to be rid of the situation for good.

**NOTE:** The more you decide to forgive and feel the emotional relief, the easier it will be to choose to forgive at another time. Forgiveness comes more quickly as you go along because your decision to forgive becomes easier, enabling you to let go of upsets sooner. The speed of the process looks unrealistic to those who don't understand what forgiving is. The more you do it, the better you become at it. When you keep on seeing the repetitive negative patterns of your mind and how they play out in different unforgiven situations, your understanding of those situations increases and the decision to forgive becomes easy.

## Key questions

A. Have I taken the time to relax, meditate, or contemplate on the highest in myself while doing this forgiveness work?
B. Am I listening to the highest aspect of myself?
C. What is the highest goal for my life that this situation might be stopping, either in its existence or in my own attitude?

"For there is nothing either good or bad, but thinking makes it so"
SHAKESPEARE, *Hamlet*

The modern version: One man's trash is another man's treasure.

# PART III

# The Truth behind the Resistance to Forgive

Some of the significant parts of the forgiving process that we will cover in this section:
- Self-Forgiveness
- Dealing with marriage and new relationships
- Coping with stress, trauma and emotional pain.
- Effectively controlling stressed brain takeovers
- How to make forgiving permanent.

CHAPTER TEN

# Forgiving Permanently

*"Everyone complains of his memory, and nobody complains of his judgment."* Francois de la Rochefoucauld
French author (1613 – 1680)

**W**e condone revenge in our novels, films, and cultures. Our heroes do not forgive offenders; they find them and destroy them, making the world safer for people with decent values. So what's the problem if good values are upheld, and the bad guys get what they deserve? The problem is that there are always two sides to a conflict. Justice, to be fair, needs to be carried out in a controlled situation, like a legal system.

When we judge and attack people close to us based on our own opinion of what is right, we run the big risk of being wrong. This includes governments. Often, when it comes to human interaction and behavior, we do not have all the information we need to come to a reasoned conclusion, just an emotional one. Many wars have started with no better justification than revenge or humiliation.

Beneath the justification for not forgiving is the truth that can enable you to forgive. Studying your confusion and resistance can increase your quality of life and ability to forgive. Compassion enables you to be *willing* to understand a person, perhaps by walking in his or her shoes. Understanding speeds up forgiving and can make it lasting.

In the Forgiveness Therapy courses that I teach, I've found it vital to address the deep inner factors that prevent forgiving but that can, when addressed, make forgiving permanent. In the quest for understanding, we've gone over the importance of knowing why people don't act or see the world as we do, or have the values we have. In the search for truth, we must look more deeply at our reactions and their effect.

As Einstein said,[1] "A human being is a part of the whole, called by us the 'Universe,' a part limited in time and space. He experiences himself, his thoughts, and feelings, as something separate from the rest—a kind of optical delusion of his consciousness. This delusion is a kind of prison for us, restricting us to our desires and affection for a few persons nearest to us. Our task must be to free ourselves from this prison by widening our circle of compassion to embrace all living creatures and the whole of nature in its beauty. Nobody can achieve this completely, but the striving for such achievement is in itself a part of the liberation and a foundation for inner security."

To develop skill in letting go, you need to learn the deeper aspects of your mind that not only protect you but may also cause problems and affect forgiving. From this, you will gain an even better understanding of why you acted the way you did, and why others act the way they do. Fortified with this knowledge, your forgiving becomes straightforward and painless—the objective of this third part of the book.

## *How to Keep Our Stressed-Brain Reactions from Overriding Our Thinking and Creative Functions*

Being in charge of our thoughts is not easy. It takes work. We make mistakes every day, some big, some small. We need forgiveness to grease the mechanisms of social and personal interactions so that we and those around us can be happy.

The brain is programmed to react. How much influence the reactive systems have is regulated not only by how much stress is present but also by how much experience we have in controlling these strong responses.

As mentioned in Chapter 5, we need to be in a somewhat calm, non-threatening space to forgive. Meditation, prayer, contemplation, and other stress reduction methods like the *Relaxation Response* developed by Dr. Herbert Benson at Harvard, help to keep the earlier brains from gaining or holding control.

**Note**: You are not always able to control all of the stress responses in the body and mind, but with knowledge and practice, these reactions have much less power over your life.

People who have not learned how to manage their reactions will have a tough time in stressful situations. Some never learn to deal effectively with stress. It takes much practice. Putting violent people who are in prison back on the street when they have not learned to deal with these powerful reactions is a recipe for disaster. I don't advocate for punishment, but for a program of stress management and rehabilitation, along with forgiveness training. If these trainings were done, we would see a radical change for those in prison and a lowering of crime rates.

I encourage people who have been violent or abusive to learn to work with their angry reactions so that they will not be a danger to others or self. Otherwise, the violence and out-of-control responses will continue.

**Please Note:** Changing negative behavior patterns is difficult because they are often connected in some way to early pleasure and safety experiences. To change them you need to make sure that there are pleasure and safety in the new pattern. If you get angry with yourself when you are trying to put in new patterns, you defeat your purpose by putting in stress rather than pleasure.

If you go to a dance and want to learn Salsa, your old patterns of other dance steps might help or they might hinder. In any dance style, until you learn the beat and steps, you'll feel uncomfortable. That is why you learn the basics first. You start slowly so that you build on understanding and pleasure, not fear and anxiety.

Understanding our responses to stress will give insight into why forgiving is so difficult, at times passionately attacked, or equally defended.

Previously we talked about how the lower brain reactions may take away the control from our neocortex. Here are more indicators of this "takeover." When a person becomes overstressed, and their highest function is greatly dimmed, these problems may show up as:[3]

- distracted easily and/or hyperactivity
- lack of determination
- impulse control problems
- chronic lateness and poor time management
- disorganization and procrastination

If you expect yourself or another to function well when the above signs of stress are present, you are unrealistic at best.

Look at your unforgiven situation and see if you can step out of being the effect of it and move into an observer role—watching yourself. From this perspective:

1. What in your past do you think makes you react to this situation?
2. Consider why you might be having the feelings you have.

Sometimes you will quickly get an insight into what is under the surface; sometimes it will come days later when you least expect it. The goal is to gain the ability to separate yourself from your reactions by gaining a deeper insight into the cause of your reactions in this situation.

## The Defenses that Prevent Forgiving

*"Why do you look at the speck of sawdust in your brother's eye and pay no attention to the plank in your own eye? ... You hypocrite, first take the plank out of your own eye, and then you will see clearly to remove the speck from your brother's eye."*

JESUS, *MATTHEW 7:3,5*

What we most loudly condemn in others might be what we are suffering from ourselves. Shakespeare implied this, centuries ago in *Hamlet*: "The lady doth protest too much, methinks." Jesus' teaching of removing the plank from our own eye before removing the speck of sawdust from our neighbor's eye is a lesson in a major obstacle to forgiveness—our defense mechanisms.

When something is too uncomfortable for us to deal with, our mind will protect us through a set of defenses. We are not aware of these defensive responses. Like our stressed-brain responses, these too are below our conscious awareness, which is how they can continue causing terrible trouble for us.

We often use defensiveness to respond when we are in a stress reaction or when we have made a mistake. The part of us that is concerned with our moral sense and tries to contend with reality has a tough time with the struggle to keep the stressed brain satisfied, but not let it get out of hand. Often, we make decisions and act in ways that we regret. To preserve the sense of who we are morally and to feel better about our self, we adopt mechanisms to defend and justify our desires, mistakes, and behaviors.

I have seen very effective forgiveness work done through becoming aware of the subconscious mechanisms that hold us back. Some of these *ego defense mechanisms*, as they are called, point to a truth that enables forgiving to be permanent. Though they are usually below our conscious awareness, with attentiveness/mindfulness, some can be seen and worked with. The key to working with them is not the awareness of them alone, but using self-forgiveness to undo them.

By understanding the basics of ego defenses, we:
- Gain a deeper understanding of the resistance to forgiving
- Find strategies that make forgiving permanent.

## *The Defenses*

Defending are what we do to make us feel better and often justify our negative responses to stress. Instead of dealing with our reactions directly and quieting them before we make a mistake or react, we create an elaborate system to justify our actions and then hide it from our selves so that we feel better. If we just quieted the stress system and made effective decisions, we would feel better and not continue to put trash in our subconscious. However, this can be very difficult because often these defenses occur in tough situations and usually begin in childhood.

Two primary defenses seem to have a great deal to do with the inability to forgive. One defense is to hide upsetting or intolerable thoughts, events, or desires deeply below our conscious perception. There are many subtleties and names for this hiding defense: denial, repression, suppression, dissociation. For our work, I will use the word *denial* for this general category of *hiding the upsets inside us*.

The other defense, called projection or displacement, is to put the upsetting thought outside us onto others. Here, we hide it in another person, then deny it has anything to do with us. Blaming and scapegoating are the typical result. I will use the term *projection* for this act of placing responsibility for our negative beliefs or actions onto others, and then we deny our own involvement.

Jesus' scolding of taking the plank out of your own eye before taking the speck of sawdust out of your neighbor's eye, points to these two subconscious methods of defense. In projection, we deny a failing in ourselves, but readily see it in others.

Ted prided himself on his honesty, and part of his identity. Sometimes, however, he lied to his wife about their bank balance because he did not always make as much money as he thought he should. Because he could not admit to that dishonest behavior, he accused the bank of dishonesty when he received the monthly statement. Sadly, he believed it!

With projection, we accept these distortions as true. Hitler blamed the Jews for the trouble Germany was having after World War I and millions agreed with him. It is easier to blame than accept responsibility. The whole idea of the scapegoat is behind this mental mechanism and comes directly from the more primitive stressed brain reaction.

## *Making Forgiveness Permanent*

Projection and denial cannot easily coexist with self-forgiveness, which is a courageous and effective alternative. Instead of defending against emotional pain, forgiveness begins by confronting it and the circumstances surrounding it with scrupulous honesty. It is completed by transforming it into something positive, even inspiring, focused on preventing rather than perpetuating harm. Psychology has overlooked forgiveness for over a century by relegating it to religion.

With clients who have held anger for years, I often search for how they have projected upsets with themselves onto others. Looking at projection and doing self-forgiveness on that self-upset, removes the reason to put it on others. Looking at projection and gaining self-forgiveness is one of the fastest ways of getting out of an upset with another.

What we will go over now is for long-held resentments, not, I repeat NOT traumas that were out of your control, e.g., rapes and other acts of violence or terrorism.

This is an advanced model. I offer it because I have seen it work. (If you are doing this work with friends or clients, don't use it if the person doesn't get the point. If it works, great, if not there are plenty of other methods.)

To help another forgive permanently:
1. Help the person look at the situation to see if, in any way, they have been guilty of the same or a similar behavior for which they are trying to forgive the other person. If so, then,

2. Have them forgive the other person, since they have done the same thing themselves. Then,
3. Get them to forgive themselves, if possible, or find a way that they can gain forgiveness for what they have done.

With self-forgiveness, they may not have done the offending act to the same degree, but I have seen the upset released when people see how they have done a similar thing in some way, known only to themselves.

Remember that the mind works in metaphor, which is the comparison of two unlike things that have something in common,[3a] for example, Jesus says, "you are Peter, and upon this rock, I will build My church." Peter is not a rock, but the rock symbolizes Peter's strength. Or, the verse in a song, "You are the wind beneath my wings." The person doesn't have wings but the wind and the wings symbolize the person's relationship to the other. That commonality is what we are looking for in the projection. It is not literal, but might be; normally it points in a direction.

The next example shows this shared meaning. Even though I addressed a violent situation, which normally I would not, I did so because of the awareness, sincerity, and intelligence this woman had shown previously in class. Riva, a great-grandmother, could not forgive Hitler for what he had done to the Jews and her family. She was an angry, unhappy woman. Because nothing seemed to work to move her toward forgiveness, we started talking about projection centered on Hitler. She was willing to look at this.

It was obvious that she had not killed any Jews, but when asked how many times she had killed Hitler and the Nazis in her mind, and through the years killed herself inside for surviving, she became quiet. She found the courage to look at this aspect of herself. With great honesty, she admitted that the anger and hate she carried all those years had negatively affected her family and those around her. Her children did not see her often, nor did she have many friends.

I did not ask her to condone or justify what Hitler did, or even forgive him. I asked her to forgive herself for the hate, anger, and negativity she had indirectly put on others for so many years. When she finally did that, the tears flowed for her family, and she said she felt a peace she had not felt for decades.

Janet, a friend, shared the following event with me. She and her husband were going to a lovely resort. Her husband had arranged to pick her up from her work at a certain time, but he was delayed by a phone call from his brother, whom he had not spoken with for several months. She waited for forty-five minutes in the hot sun and was quite angry with him when she heard that he had put a phone call ahead of their meeting.

Her anger ruined that night for both of them. Luckily, her forgiveness training enabled her to gain insight into why her anger was so strong and persistent. "Finally, in the middle of the next day, I saw that I had done the same thing to my children."

She admitted that she had left her kids "waiting" so that she could get her Ph.D. She left them home at night and sometimes had them get their meals—all because she felt she had something more important to do. She had *left them waiting*, just as her husband had left her. This brought up her guilt and ire because it is something in her, not his action. She did her forgiveness work right there. The rest of their stay at the resort went wonderfully.

Charlotte's situation is an example of denial. Her mother told her that her father had severely beaten her when she was 18 months old. Her mother was in tears relating this incident. Several years later, her mother denied the story completely: "I don't know what you're talking about. Your father would never do something like that."

Charlotte, an older psychotherapist, understood the protective function of defense mechanisms. She understood that her mother's denial was not a lie, but simply an attempt to protect her illusions about the man she had married and the mother she was. What kind of mother would allow her child to be beaten like that? People will naturally defend against being bad. It is built into the system. Eventually they will believe the defense, in this case, the defense is denial.

## *Working with Projection*

Here is an example of how you can work with projection. Suppose you are angry at a foreign dictatorship. You might have a picture of the leader in your mind. Ask yourself, "What is it I don't like about what he's doing?" There might be a whole list. Let's say one of your answers is, "Taking freedom away from people." Remembering the previous section on defense mechanisms, to see a possible projection ask yourself:

1. How do I behave as that dictator in my own life?
2. Do I take away the freedom of others, or let others take away the freedom of another?
3. Do I take my own freedom away? (This is usually the essential question.)
4. Do I tie myself to the grindstone and never take a break or vacation?
5. Do I feel imprisoned in my own life?
6. Have I imprisoned myself and feel unable to get out?

These are all questions that look at this projection from different angles. Situations that cause strong emotions may often point right back to our own mistakes and failure to forgive ourselves.

> Bo Diddley, Creedence Clearwater Revival, and Eric Clapton remind us of this in the song *Before You Accuse Me*,
> *(take a look at yourself)*.

Gil was a tough guy. He was big and had been in many fights through the years, often taking on several men at a time. But life had crushed him. He was angry, depressed, but wanted to change. During a counseling session, he admitted for the first time to anyone that he was the victim of incest. He had always hated his father but had never talked about him as a perpetrator of incest. He cried for five minutes in deep sobs.

Later, he could see how being sexually abused caused his reckless driving and his desire to fight. He saw that his fights were to punish *tough* men like his father. He also saw that he was punishing himself for feeling so degraded. As he worked with the results of his resentment, he realized that he was continuing the original injury in his own life, bringing himself alienation, humiliation, and powerlessness. Two years later his lifestyle had changed. He was working to help other men who were violent and had stopped his drinking, reckless driving, and fighting.

**Journal Activity:**
1. Look at the list that you have been making. Take one offense that seems appropriate.
2. Write down any time that you have done the same or a similar thing.
3. At this point, you may notice resistance. Write down what comes up for you. Our defense mechanisms may be keeping us from the truth of the situation because they are too hard to face. Be honest with yourself and know that truth will set you free from the old patterns.
4. Look at where you feel resistance. Try not to defend yourself or attack with a denial. Pay attention to your emotions.
5. If you can see that you have done a similar thing, forgive the offender. (It shouldn't be hard since you've done the same thing.)
6. Now forgive yourself for that. This might be much harder. But find a way to gain forgiveness.

**Note**: Byron Katie has done excellent training on looking deeply at how we prevent our healing. I highly recommend her method, which she calls "The Work." I have used this method and her book *Loving What Is: Four Questions That Can Change Your Life* with wonderful success in forgiveness groups I've led.[4]

## *Awareness of Defense Mechanisms Is Not Enough*

Awareness of projection is not sufficient to change your life. Forgiving what the projection reveals is also necessary.

Riva, the great-grandmother I mentioned earlier, had to forgive herself for the damage she did to her own family because of her hatred of the Nazis. She saw how she continued the work of Hitler and Goebbels by clinging to her hatred. She could see why her son did not like to be around her and how her daughter had developed the same negativity.

Psychiatrists have been aware of defense mechanisms for 70-plus years, yet their suicide rate is extraordinarily high. Lack of forgiveness of self or others is a major factor in the depression or hopelessness that causes suicide.

**How to Unearth Your Defense Mechanisms:** To reveal your projections and denials, examine those situations that always leave you feeling offended. Your touchiness is the evidence and guide.

Write down what you frequently find fault with in other people. This can provide you with clues to your defenses, particularly denial and projection. Take particular note of faults of those closest to you.

Go to a quiet place where you will be undisturbed for at least an hour. Write down what people do that sets you off, or that you find intolerable. Try to be as honest with yourself as you can and simply record those events. Keep this list for later chapters.

Now with that list turn the situation around. Ask:

1. Have I done the same thing to another? Or to myself?
2. Is this similar in any way to something I've done to another or myself?
3. Is this similar to a family pattern or the actions of someone else in my family?

My forgiveness transformation came out of going down my extensive list of upsets with people and seeing how I had, in some way, done a similar thing to people. For me, forgiving the offender was easy. I needed help on forgiving myself for all my offenses to others.

## *Stressed Thinking That Sabotages Forgiving*

There are three main ways that we sabotage our thinking and happiness.

### *A. Focusing on the Negative & Rejecting the Positive*

For survival under immediate threat, the brain focuses sharply on danger. This tunnel vision toward only the negative qualities of a person or situation does reveal dangers, but it also exaggerates fears, failures, and frustrations, leaving us agitated and unhappy.

Roberta could only see the negative aspects of her marriage. She could not forgive herself for being in such a dire situation. She couldn't see anything positive until she did an exercise to specifically notice and write down what was positive in her home and family when she saw them. For a week, she did this by carrying a pad with her all the time. To her surprise, her list of positives was longer than the list of negatives.

**Try this:** In a negative area of your life, look for and write down the positives in it. As much as possible try saying, "What is positive in this?" and "What have I gained from this?" Do this even when you think you can't. Also, see if you can forgive the negatives in that person directly, remembering that the other person might be doing the very best she or he can do.

### B. *Black and White Thinking*

In this kind of reactive thinking, there is good or bad with no in-between - no shades of gray. One day a person is wonderful, the next he's horrible. For the much earlier reactive brain, which activates in stress, the simple way to sort through a great deal of input from the environment is to see only danger or safety. This kind of thinking affects relationships quite adversely. For example, daughter one is wonderful, daughter two, terrible. People, however, are not either–or, smart or stupid, good or bad, beautiful or ugly, but are somewhere along a scale.[5]

We are too multifaceted to be reduced to the black-or-white judgments of the stressed brain. In this thinking, the greatest pitfall is how you judge yourself. If you aren't perfect, you're a failure – no room for mistakes. This is a major issue in self-forgiveness.

I knew an especially bright person who had been caught up in a cult when she was younger. Even though she was competent and had held quite responsible jobs, she continued to berate herself for being stupid for falling for the lies of the cult leader. Because of this mistake, she would only hold menial jobs. Her statement to herself was, "I used to be smart, now I'm stupid." It is quite common for women coming out of abusive relationships to consider only jobs that are below their level of competence, even though they know they had excelled before.

To overcome black and white thinking, Dr. McKay, Dr. Davis and P. Fanning, the authors of *Thoughts and Feelings*, tell us to think in terms of percentages.[6] Here are examples: "25% of her work is unsatisfactory, but 75% is quite good." Another is, "About 60% of the time he seems terribly preoccupied with himself, but there is the 40% when he can be quite generous," or "15% of the time I'm a jerk, the rest of the time I do all right."

By catching yourself in this *either-or* thinking, and by using percentages, you are more forgiving, because you are stepping out of the judgment you have made. Self-forgiveness is essential here, as is forgiveness of imperfections in others.

**Remember**: When we forgive other's imperfections, we exercise the muscle of forgiving ourselves. **Try this:** Make a list of all the behaviors or qualities for which you condemn yourself, and look at it realistically, using percentages. Then forgive yourself for each thing.

C.   *Catastrophe Thinking (Catastrophizing)* --

This thinking sees disaster in anything negative that happens. It is like #1 but more out of control. Both are common with people who have lived with tragedy and trauma. It may also be a learned response from parents. It's the movement of fear and hopelessness into a situation with the complete loss of rationality, faith, and positive thinking. Your job loss = loss of your house = your wife and children, will leave you. These thoughts occur within seconds. Then the emotional response occurs with the brain going into a range of reactions from hiding and no movement to rage and killing others.

When this perspective becomes chronic, there is no trust that life will get better. The future is bleak, and there is rage over minor events or ongoing fear. Jim's father, who was raised in Brooklyn, NY, couldn't play on the street when he was young because his mother was concerned that he would be "hit by a car." This was when there weren't many cars. All his buddies were out there except him. In fact, he owned the ball and bat they played with! No wonder he left home at the age of fifteen.

This type of thinking can create bad situations, not because of the stressing incident but because of the reaction to it. Man loses a job and kills coworker is obvious. Subtler is that a mistake at work means they will fire me, so I may as well not work as hard because they are going to fire me anyway. Or a prevalent one for people trying to forgive the termination of a relationship: I will never find another person to love me again. With this attitude, they probably won't, which is why forgiving is so worthwhile. With it, you are relieved of the pain and attitude of being a victim.

This kind of thinking shows a lack of trust in others and in self and contains no forgiveness. What it needs is patience and some rational control so that the person can look at other options and possibilities other than the first one presented by our stress reactions.

To step out of an immediate catastrophe response, first, you need to quiet the stress-reacting system. Take a walk, call a friend, do the Relaxation Response, etc. Once you are calm and somewhat rational, do the exercise below.

**Try this**: As you re-look at these three negative thinking styles. In your situation, observe what is happening from an objective perspective, one that is separate from your reactions, as if you were your friend perhaps.

For catastrophizing, make a list of what you think will happen because of what happened.
1. With each item, ask, "Is it true?" and then "How do I know it will happen?"
2. Look for positive possibilities that could occur for each one.
3. Note any behaviors or qualities for which you condemn others or yourself. Then see if you can forgive yourself or the others for each thing. Save this list as you will use it again soon.

If you can't do these right now, carry on reading the chapters and doing the exercises.

Catastrophe/disaster thinking takes more than forgiveness to resolve. Though forgiving helps a lot, it takes trust and faith in Life and yourself, which are beyond the scope of this book. Trust and faith take connecting with the truest part of us. That journey, to me, is our main one. Self-forgiveness especially helps to clear the way.

> "As a goal commonly advocated by all the world's religions, forgiveness can be a truly transforming experience that allows us to move beyond our often selfish desires and needs."
> HUSTON SMITH -- *THE WORLD'S RELIGIONS*, 1989 ED

# CHAPTER ELEVEN

# Self-Forgiveness and Empowerment

*"Misfortunes one can endure – they come from outside; they are accidents. But to suffer for one's own faults – ah, there is the sting of life."* OSCAR WILDE

## The Keys to Self-Forgiveness

In the previous chapter, we looked at making your forgiveness permanent by viewing your defense mechanisms and doing self-forgiveness. That is not easy. Now we will look even more deeply at gaining forgiveness for yourself.

Researchers have stated that self-forgiveness entails not only facing your wrongs but also letting go of the negative thoughts, feelings, and actions against yourself and "replacing them with compassion, generosity and love." You know you have forgiven yourself when you have positive feelings, actions, and thoughts, for yourself.

## Guilt, Pain, and Punishment

People's values, rules, and moral code set the standard by which they live. When they act against their values and standards, they feel bad, knowing that what they did was not right. At those times, they will often experience guilt in some way.

Our perceived *lack of worthiness* keeps us from our inner strength. This lack often comes from guilt, which is anger directed at ourselves. Because of guilt, we feel we deserve punishment and have often concluded that we are unworthy because of some shameful behavior. If we hold onto these negative feelings, keeping them alive with judgments and self-attack, we set up a destructive loop. When you let go of all the guilt that you can, you restore the highest qualities within you, just as you restore your personal relationships when you forgive others. This often restores our sense of worthiness.

In his book, *Big Prisons, Big Dreams: Crime and the Failure of America's Penal System*, Michael J. Lynch shows that of the three methods for changing behavior: positive reinforcement, negative reinforcement, and punishment, **punishment is the least effective on humans**. Positive reinforcement is the most successful. Please take this to heart when dealing with yourself.

Punishing yourself is not effective to change behavior for the better.[1] Punishment has been used for eons in cultures to change behavior. Through habit, we will usually do what was done to us. Nevertheless, you need to resist this temptation because punishment only brings fear by activating the lower brains and increasing resentment, which you are trying to get rid of. Thus, it defeats your purpose in self-forgiving.

Letting go of guilt is not easy. You might have to use *many* methods to assist you. I recommend working with someone else as opposed to doing it by yourself if you aren't noticing much change in your life.

Carl felt terrible that he hadn't cleaned up a big upset with his father who had died suddenly. He used one of the oldest methods known for help. He went for regular long walks in nature and in his own way prayed for release from his guilt. Finally, on one of those long prayerful walks, he felt the forgiveness he sought.

Guilt should only be a call to action. When you see that you "missed the mark," (the meaning of *sin* in the original biblical Greek) you only need to correct your aim and try again.

Repeated self-blame does not improve behavior or skill; practice and confidence do.

## *Dealing with Inner Conflict*

Matthew was raised as a strict Christian and was vehemently opposed to the enormous profits in capitalistic ventures. A favorite teaching for him was: "it is easier for a camel to pass through the eye of a needle than for one who is rich to enter the kingdom of God" – *Matthew 19:24 (NAB)*.

But as an adult, he made plenty of money in his business and lived quite a comfortable lifestyle. Because of this inner conflict, guilt and depression tortured him.

Through his sister, he eventually did a forgiveness method of listing the positives in his life and the culture he lived in. That action led him to a deeper appreciation of the value of providing for his family and teaching his children important principles in a system that had much good. With this new perspective, he saw that he could use his money to help others who were not as fortunate as himself. In helping others, his guilt evaporated. As an added benefit, he was less judgmental of others. To many, his solution was obvious, but because he felt trapped in such self-criticism, he hadn't seen it.

Juliette hated her father for his violence and felt terrible guilt because she could not protect her sisters or mother when she was young. Adults around her told her, "You shouldn't feel this way," and "You could do nothing being so young." That did not change her guilt because she had to have these realizations for herself. The forgiveness process helped her see the irrational aspect of her guilt and let go of her self-anger.

Agnes was raped on a date. She felt many emotions, among them shame. In therapy, she took all of these emotions apart and examined what was behind them. She saw that she felt ashamed and guilty that she had let this happen to her. Although this response was not rational because she was blameless in the attack, she nonetheless experienced guilt. When Agnes forgave herself for getting into the situation, even though she could not have helped it, not only did she feel a great weight lift from her mind, she also saw that it was her rapist who must bear the *full* responsibility for the rape.

## *Differing Values*

We can observe that most people have values and a sense of ethical behavior. Though we might not agree with others' morals, we see that they do have values and standards. By understanding that the unforgiven person's life was quite different and dominated by different values, humbleness can enter that says, "I don't know everything." Forgiveness may then be a gift of the heart, creating a new and refreshing dynamic for them and you.

One hot summer afternoon, Lucy's life changed when she had the insight that her father was a decent father compared to his father. She always resented how strict and emotionless he was, and how distant he kept himself. But she said, "When I talked with my aunt, his sister, I could see he has come a long way from his childhood, where he had been beaten often and mercilessly. He was a good father compared to the father he had." Hearing this gave her a newfound appreciation of her father, which enabled her to let go of much of her resentment for his seeming lack-of-love parenting. And she could see that it was not her fault.

How people deal with their early childhood training may be different even among family members. In an interview with two brothers, one said, "My parents were alcoholics; they got drunk all the time. So, of course, I became an alcoholic." The other said: "I saw what alcoholism did to my parents and how it ruined their lives, so of course, I never drank."

We should note however that self-forgiveness is not the whole answer. In the article "Unforgiveness, depression, and health in later life: the protective factor of forgivingness," researcher, Drs. Ashley E. Ermer & Christine M. Proulx in a study found that especially for women it was not necessarily self-forgiveness, but forgiveness of others that was a protector against depression.[2]

## *Giving and Receiving*

We would all like to be happy. However, we can only be happy to the level that we can experience it. The person who can bring happiness to others has attained a skill, which often translates into his or her own life. Likewise, to get love, you give it. How can you encourage people to love you if you do not allow that love into your own perspective of yourself? It seems that if you can find out what prevents you from having love, you could have more of it. This is also true of joy, peace, and other positive feelings.

Don't ask the questions "Why can't I find an intimate partner or someone who will love me?" or "Where did the love go?" if you are unforgiving toward yourself or others. Love disappears in the choice to resent, to be angry, or to hate. In some way, you receive what you give. If you are angry, realistically that is what you are giving, and you get the result.

Anger gets results, but, are they worth the cost? One of my early students, Glen, was a building contractor. He was able to get a lot done through his anger. People jumped when he showed it, giving him a sense of power that he liked. However, after a few years, he disliked anger's other results, such as high blood pressure, a failed marriage, little happiness, temper tantrums from a short fuse, poor sleep and depression. When he started looking for another way to live his life, he finally started to forgive and enjoyed his life more.

The Beatles said it very nicely in the song *The End*:
"The love you take is equal to the love you make."

Forgiveness, love, and peace are choices. They cannot be forced or demanded. We have seen this for the past two thousand years. Priests and clergy counsel forgiveness without teaching effective methods on how to achieve it, and often without modeling it. Or, they tell a person they are forgiven without the person believing or feeling it. Forgiveness will only take place when the desire for love, peace of mind, and joy becomes more important than the desire for attack, anger, and getting even. What you receive might be the result of what you give. If you give no respect, love or positive regard for yourself, don't complain about your life, change your attitude toward yourself, and watch change happen in your life.

**Try this:** If you feel you are not getting the positives from life that you deserve, look more deeply at your worthiness, which is in your own eyes only. Self-forgiveness is the key to your inner riches and worth. Search out your unworthy feelings. Find the guilt associated with the unworthiness. It's there. Take care of it by forgiving.

## *The Cycle of Victimhood and Guilt*

Many people do not know they are caught in a cycle of being a victim that keeps them feeling guiltier and at the effect of others. Here is how it goes:
1. We do something against our moral codes, rules, or values.
2. This leads to guilt, shame, regret.
3. We condemn ourselves, and thus, we will accept punishment from our self or others because we feel we deserve it. In addition, there is often fear of attack from a higher being.

4. Our self-protective defenses kick in and then we blame others for what happened, and thus
5. We will attack the other, subtly or overtly, creating more guilt for ourselves. We will also fear attack from them, which justifies attacking them more, which keeps the whole cycle going.

This cycle gets worse and worse the more we attack others or ourselves, making us more depressed and unhappy. The attack, whether external or internal, doesn't have to be terrible, though sometimes it may be. It can be as simple as talking behind a person's back to try to ruin their standing with others

*Forgiveness can enter this cycle at any point and change it.*

If you feel you are giving love and get anger back, you need to sort out deeper issues. Margaret was a loving, religious person whose husband beat her regularly. She always forgave him and went back to him after having left him. It seems that her forgiving caused her to be harmed. This is like saying that people who have more than three car accidents should not drive. Rather, it is a matter of finding out what they are doing wrong and correcting it.

If someone loves and gets anger in return, a deeper issue might be the inability to set limits. The ongoing victim usually does not have this ability. We often see this in domestic violence. Healthy people on the outside ask the victim, "Why do you stay in the relationship?" or "Why don't you get rid of that bum?" These are legitimate questions.

The *victim effect* is a result of the emotional programming of "less than," "not good enough," and "lacking." This usually comes from childhood. In victimhood, there is often complaining and whining; the person sees only the negative, and mainly feels regret, guilt, and resentment. Victims usually attack themselves or are attacked from the outside because in some way they feel they deserve it. This is what needs to be changed. Women fall into this more easily than men because of their long history of abuse and denigration.

On the other side of the same coin is the attacker. The perpetrator also experiences victimhood but acts it out differently. It was standard in the domestic violence groups I ran, to ask the angry man what he feared. If he could answer that honestly, the anger would immediately shift.

Chuck, a wiry, tough guy, was deliberately cut off on the freeway. He intentionally damaged the car that cut him off while driving down the freeway. When he saw how crazy he was acting, he pulled back into the traffic and exited the freeway. In the counseling session, when I asked what was going on, he said no one was ever going to take advantage of him again. In questioning further, he talked about how his father beat him in drunken rages from ages five to twelve. At twelve, he fought back and had been fighting ever since.

Continuing to listen to these victim ideas and thoughts is like letting a child run your life. It is letting an egocentric, weak sense of you run the show. With this happening, you become your worst enemy. Forgiving all abuses and finding self-forgiveness is essential. Forgiveness is the choice to regain peace of mind and love. It brings joy. Some therapists will disagree with me and say the anger is good, but that has never been my experience of ongoing anger.

Meredith, an abused wife, started going to Co-Dependents Anonymous meetings every week, and eventually three times a week until she started feeling better. Co-Dependents Anonymous (CoDA) is a twelve-step program for people who share a common desire to develop functional and healthy relationships. It's adapted from Alcoholics Anonymous but not limited to alcohol. In this program, she learned why she kept going back to abuse and even why it kept happening.

She started rehabilitating herself with the 12-steps, which has strong spiritual and forgiveness components. Meredith saw how the pattern of returning to the abuse was an old pattern of her mother's and reflected her mother's lack of self-worth.

In Meredith's case, because her husband would not quit drinking and was becoming more abusive, she escaped and never went back. When I talked with her in class, she said she still loved him but knew she deserved more. Now she was with a man who loved her and treated her well. She was actually in class to work on forgiveness in her family of origin.

Because her husband was an alcoholic, she could have gone to Al-Anon[4], but she chose CoDA because she had a friend in it. Al-Anon, which includes Alateen for younger members has been offering hope, understanding, and support to familylies and friends of alcoholics. It is also adapted from Alcoholics Anonymous.

Feeling persecuted may come from habitual perceptions of being externally controlled and helpless—a victim of fate. These thoughts may keep people stuck because they don't believe they can create positive results in their life, let alone make any difference in the world. Someone or something is responsible for their pain, loss, and failure; "They did it to me!" is their cry. It's hard to find solutions with this attitude in place because "they probably won't work anyway."[6]

The truth about our seeming lack of control is:[7]

1. We are constantly making decisions.
2. Every decision affects our lives.
3. In general, we have a responsibility for what happens to us.

You undo the lie of helplessness by taking more control of your brain responses. You are largely responsible for what happens in your inner world because you make your own life happen by your choices. You have to take responsibility to deal with that hopeless/helpless victim perspective. The most important step is to realize you are possessed by negative responses, then take control and seek help.

Of course, events happen in your outer world over which you have no control, but overall, your choices also affect your outer world. Contentment and joy also come from specific choices you made and continue to make. These facts the victim does not understand,[8] and suffers for it. Compassion helps in forgiving someone, like a parent, who has regularly chosen the role of victim in life.

In forgiving others, remember that people choose what they think is most valuable to them. They believe it will bring happiness, even though it won't necessarily.

Gabrielle thought that being secure in her life was more fundamental than anything else. Thus, she remained married for 30 years to a man who provided her money, but *nothing* else. She paid for her security at the expense of passion and joy. In looking deeply, she saw that her husband had provided what was crucial to her, security. That changed her whole perspective of their marriage.

## *Looking Deeper*

To forgive constant victimization in your own life or that of another, try to find the overriding desires—what was most important for you or them? There is usually a conflict. The victim gets something from the situation, which keeps him or her in it, but feels lack of control or hopelessness because something else significant is not provided. We all have free will and make choices.

If you don't appreciate the choices you or another made, bring in a compassionate perspective and find what was behind the choices. What was most important? In unforgiven situations, for many, being right is often more important than being happy.

> "We cannot love unless we have accepted forgiveness, and the deeper our experience of forgiveness is, the greater is our love." – PAUL TILLICH - Theologian

I've counseled several cult members. All admit that even though being in the cult was terrible, it provided something at the time that they felt gave meaning to their life—enough to put up with the abuse. Often, for people to forgive oppressive situations that they chose to remain in, they will have to see that they made choices to be there. Then it becomes a matter of self-forgiving.

"What if you were lied to?" LoriAnne, one of my students, asked. "We were all lied to about what the church did and its success. You can't justify that. I would have never stayed in it if I knew it was all lies." I agreed with her and asked, "How do you forgive the church's lying to you so that you can get on with your life?" Each person could work on that question differently. That is why I have provided this book.

In her final paper for a forgiveness therapy class, LoriAnne dealt with it by seeing that we are lied to all the time, by parents, media, politicians, advertisements, etc. "It seems to be common for people in organizations to do this. Yes, and I lied to my family and friends about how well I was doing and how wonderful the church was when I knew it wasn't true."

**Questions:** Here are insight-provoking questions concerning a perceived lack of control:
1. What choices did I make that resulted in this situation?
2. What decisions did I make?
3. What decisions can I make now to change it?

## *Help in Gaining Self-forgiveness*

Researchers have shown that our survival mechanisms are fully engaged right after birth.[9] As we get older, we continue to use them for our protection and well-being.

Also available to us is something else—an experience that takes us above our daily familiarity. It inspires us toward the best within us as opposed to mere survival. It is the source of our inspiration and love. This experience, in general, remains the domain of religion. There you will find some of the methods to help connect with this spiritual experience and thought.

As psychology developed in the late 19th century, it labeled this spiritual experience as abnormal. The struggle at the time was between church and science, and between Freud's rising popularity and his dislike of religion. This unfortunate split also shows the divide between our spiritual experience and everyday survival modes.

Transpersonal Psychology helps people incorporate these seeming separate experiences. In general, though, the schism between religion and psychology remains. This is unfortunate for the field of forgiveness. However, it isn't an accident that religions have used the power of forgiveness for ages—it transforms.

If you are unable to attain forgiveness for yourself, many people can help, including a priest or clergyperson. I certainly have had benefit from church rituals in helping me find forgiveness when I was having difficulty. Through the centuries, rituals have been powerful vehicles to assist in depossessing from ongoing stressed brain reactions that prevent self-forgiveness.

Unforgiven situations take tremendous power away. You gain strength when you show compassion for another's situation, as well as your own, and forgive them and yourself.

There is an irony here—this work may be intense and require personal power. But, that power is tied up in the unforgiven. Thus, there is limited energy available in the beginning to do the work of forgiving. This is why forgiveness may be such hard work initially. But, only initially.

# CHAPTER TWELVE

# Dealing with Stress and Trauma

*"Chronic stress is like slow poison."* Dr. Jean King,
University of Massachusetts Medical School

Because unforgiven situations create stress for us, we need to look even further at how to alleviate our reactions to stress so that we can forgive more easily. This chapter is about dealing with our tensions, whether it be from family or work burnout, or trauma and its consequences.

In the previous chapters, we went over why we react as we do. In this one, we'll address some of the serious problems that arise from these reactions and how to deal with them effectively to keep them from overwhelming you. Of course, forgiveness is necessary, but to get there, often you must calm down first.

Stress can be useful. Under stress, we will come up with new ways to respond when the old ways no longer work. However, too much stress overloads the system and shuts it down—then your behavior becomes less rational. Life's pressures often evoke habitual responses of fear or anger because flight and fight are activated pretty easily. Flight comes from fear, which produces anxiety and panic attacks. At its emotional extreme, we have hopelessness, apathy and even suicide. Fight in its extreme brings murderous responses. We are seeing more of these extreme responses in schools and workplaces.

It's vital for you to catch the early signs of stress in yourself, and to see those symptoms in the people you are trying to forgive.

*Psychology Today* tells us that the experience of stress in the past magnifies your reaction to stress in the present.[1]

We know that traumatic incidents can have devastating effects, but many people get over them in time. However, these painful incidents may have harmful long-term consequences if they are not dealt with appropriately. Because trauma heavily activates the body's stress response, I find forgiving benefits people suffering from the long-term consequences of traumatic incidents. Often a person's inability to cope with chronic stress comes from earlier trauma in his/her life.

Traumatic or catastrophic events are sudden, overwhelming, and often dangerous, such as a car accident, combat, rape, natural disasters, robbery at gunpoint, living in a war zone, or near drowning, to name a few. The victim usually feels intense fear, helplessness, or horror at the time or afterward. While many survivors can deal with the memories of the trauma and cope well, some develop strong anxiety reactions later. When this happens, it's called Post-Traumatic Stress Disorder or PTSD.[2]

**Please note**: Family, close friends, and professionals who help survivors of these intense incidents can also be affected by the event because of their empathy for the person or people involved.[2a] It's called compassion fatigue, which we'll address this later in the chapter.

I've emphasized trauma and its effects in the second part of this chapter for two reasons:
1. Trauma often causes seemingly unforgivable situations, especially if there was major loss, death or serious injury.
2. In this time of terrorism, new traumatic events close to us may be quite possible. Thus, we need to be aware of their effects, especially when those effects might be happening in us, someone close to us, or someone we need to forgive.

You can do something about stress by changing your habitual thought and behavior patterns. Cognitive Therapy helps, as does meditation and prayer. Likewise, Eye Movement Desensitization and Reprocessing (EMDR) and Visual Kinesthetic Disassociation (VKD) have been effective in relieving people's trauma experiences. EMDR works to decrease the emotional charge of specific traumatic events; VKD is a hypnosis method that does the same.[3] For my own trauma and resulting PTSD, forgiveness worked the best.

In stressful situations, a variety of methods help. A wife who expects a beating might finally decide to protect herself and leave, instead of living in fear. Courage brings new behavior. Finding a different way to respond helps remove the habitual emotion tied to the action. Anything done to change any part of the response will change the whole reaction.

We know from psychology and brain studies that shining the light of logic onto emotional distress will help alleviate it. Why? Because the linear thinking, analytical part of the brain is set up to work with our emotional system to calm it down.

The unforgiving person keeps him or herself in a constant state of tension by often thinking about the situation and people involved or suppressing it so that it is still there subconsciously. When you add old stress reactions to the normal stress that occurs in our environment, you may become overloaded. Therapy can help.

Stress research has shown that failing to adapt to what stresses us, affects the body causing symptoms: from tiredness to a cold or flu, to more serious disease. In earlier times, after a stressful event occurred, for example, a brush with a wild animal, the body could relax and recover later. Today we rarely have recovery time.

In the stress response, there is a surge of hormones and chemicals in the body, creating changes. If these changes are not allowed to revert to normal through relaxation, trouble will occur.[4] Of course, we can take more vitamins and energy drinks, but remember, if the high power additives and fuel are used all the time in an engine for more speed, it will eventually burn up. It is the same with the body.

If this stress phase continues for too long and becomes a normal state, stress exhaustion and burnout take place, causing problems including heart disease, chronic degenerative diseases, and eventually death.

## *The Signs of Stress Overload and Exhaustion*

Please take note of the signs and symptoms of chronic stress and burnout to see if they are or were present in the person you are trying to forgive, or in yourself.

Research shows that the chemicals and hormones the body releases during stress have these effects on us: [5]
1. Opens us up to cancer, and chronic infection and disease;
2. Encourages ulcers, swelling, pain, tenderness in the joints, and asthma;
3. May weaken the circulatory system, leading to strokes, heart disease and attack, and high blood pressure;
4. Affects the emotional system causing depression or aggression.

There is even evidence that intense psychological stress can change the brain's makeup, perhaps permanently.[5a]

When stress is chronic, it may easily lead to burnout, which has these physical conditions: [6]

- Emotional, mental and physical exhaustion
- Sleep disruptions
- Headaches, stomachaches, body aches
- Susceptibility to colds or flu

A person may feel many of the following attitudes and emotions when burnt out: [7,b]

- Powerless, hopeless, helpless
- Drained, exhausted, sad, bored, cynical
- Frustrated, irritable, anxious, resentful
- Little satisfaction from work, so productivity is low. Sometimes the sufferer doesn't go to work
- Feels trapped in a situation and cannot free him or her self
- Withdrawn and cut off from coworkers, family, and friends
- Insecure about capability, feeling like a failure

All of these are signs that something is drastically wrong. A person with the above feelings needs immediate help. If your unforgiven situation has resulted in these symptoms in you or another, you must understand that you or they were unable to function rationally or compassionately. When I experienced these symptoms, I also felt that life was not worth living. The *Power Forgiveness Process* helped me.

In these situations, alcohol and drug abuse often increase. Many times, people use alcohol or drugs to relax and get away from it all. This also includes prescription drugs, nicotine, and coffee. These substances become addictive because they are the only things that relieve the pain or suffering people feel. The problem, however, is not the substance, but the stress responses that the person is unable to deal with. Around the world, Alcoholics Anonymous, Narcotics Anonymous, and 12-step recovery programs, in general, have revealed that addiction is a spiritual and emotional problem. The disease is not the addictive substance or action, but the mind that creates the addition.

## *Pain*

People with chronic pain often exhibit the above symptoms. Those living with unending pain are frequently not in their right mind, often making poor decisions for themselves or others. If you know someone like this, or you are this way, compassion and understanding are needed tools.

Barbara married a disabled veteran after WWII. He was often in pain and alienated people at work with his impatience. Then, he would quit for some reason. He had many jobs—always looking for a better place, and never finding it. His anger and rage scared her. She stayed with him because she knew he was a decent man who had to cope with too much pain. But, she added, his pain didn't justify the pain he inflicted on her.

She was never prepared for the next outrage, dropping of friends, or decision to move. Sometimes they separated. Her religion enabled her to forgive. Sometimes, she forgave only to keep the family together for the kids. His pain took its toll on her too, making her fearful and bitter.

People who have debilitating diseases or chronic pain have a difficult time and are often on painkillers or other drugs. These medicines affect their quality of life and personality. They struggle continually to control the pain and side effects of the medicine. Alcohol and drugs, illegal and prescription, are often used to handle the pain.

Children raised by someone in chronic pain, whether on painkillers or not, may show all the symptoms of those raised by alcoholics.

Max was a great guy; everyone loved him. He was successful at his work. At a party, people would always be around him telling jokes, laughing and drinking. At home, though, he had another face. The pain from an injury years before still tortured him. The kids had to keep quiet, couldn't have friends over, and were often verbally abused. No one outside the household realized what his family endured because "he was a great guy."

You need to keep continuing inner work to come to forgiveness with these people. You may be confused because the drugs, alcohol, or medicines can also have their positive effects of relieving the pain so that the person will show a pleasant and even lovable side. If you are forgiving someone in your past who was like this, the work is worth the effort. I recommend help, though.

Many times, the pain is camouflaged by alcohol or drugs, and you miss it, and blame the addiction. This may get even more confusing and difficult when the pain is emotional. The sequence can often happen like this: original injury > pain > drugs or alcohol > their children injured emotionally > their children use drugs or alcohol > their children injured emotionally > on it continues down the generations.

Do everything you can to understand this cycle in your own family and work on it. Forgiving is the best thing you can do for your whole family, people around you, and generations to come.

## *What You Can Do*

In burnout and chronic stress, a person never sees a good way out of the miserable situation. The unrelenting demands and pressures cause him or her to give up searching for solutions.

If you get to that point of hopelessness or know someone who has, please remember that this is the effect of the lower brain reactions. As I've said before, it is like being possessed. This is not you or the other person but a survival/non-survival reaction. There are ways out. Please find help for yourself or the other person.

There are many reasons why a person may react to stress this way, for example, poor belief systems, distorted thinking patterns, or early trauma. Nevertheless, the way out requires active self-examination, often with professional help or with people who can hold a loving and objective perspective for you.

The worst part of chronic stress is that people get used to it and see no way out. When stress is at this unremitting, chronic level, it can kill through suicide, violence, heart attack, stroke, and cancer, because it wears people down. Chronic stress is difficult to treat and may require extended medical treatment, psychotherapy and stress management.[9]

If you have seen a friend, family member, or yourself having the above symptoms, please be aware that there are many ways to assist. Although I won't go over all of them here, I will say that doing *Power Forgiveness* allows you to come back more easily from the edge of overwhelm. In years of teaching stress management methods, I can also say that stress reduction methods take much longer to be effective when someone has resentments and anger at self or others.

Removing upsets that have bothered a person for years, perhaps from childhood, has an obvious positive outcome. My grandmother-in-law did not hold upsets with people. I first met her when she was 96 years old. She was still sharp mentally and talked wistfully of the newspaper route she had had in her 80s. She still looked attractive and held herself well. Her presence, smile, and loving eyes told me that she had found a secret to life – she had stopped holding onto the upsets of her early years and found peace.

## *What Do Trauma Survivors Need to Know?*

Drs. Eve Carlson and Josef Ruzek have written a careful synopsis for the National Center for PTSD on what survivors of trauma need to know. These are: [10]

- You can't protect yourself or others completely from trauma: it happens to many competent, healthy, strong, good people.
- There may be long-lasting problems following a trauma. Up to 8% of people will have PTSD some time in their life.
- After a trauma, sometimes people think they are going crazy or are personally weak. This isn't true. They are just experiencing the symptoms connected to a trauma reaction.
- Well-adjusted, physically healthy people can develop PTSD.

Understanding the symptoms of trauma enables a person to manage them better and hopefully get help. Even if a person does not have long-term effects from the trauma, reactions still occur close to the time of the incident.

Facing trauma is often too hard to do alone. You might find a therapist to help. Some agencies give trauma support. However, psychiatrists, psychologists, psychotherapists, and social workers, though licensed, are not necessarily trained in trauma work.

## *Trauma's Long-Term Consequences – PTSD*

As noted earlier, a small percentage of people develop and maintain strong responses to a trauma. When a person has intense reactions to a trauma for more than a month, it is called Post Traumatic Stress Disorder or PTSD. In families of American veterans, rates may be high. In countries that experience current or recent violent conflict, rates of PTSD for the general population may be high.[13] In 2007, the PTSD rate for children in the Gaza Strip was 70%.[14]

PTSD is complex and intense. I've studied, worked with it, and had it myself for several years, which eventually forced me into forgiving. I am addressing it here because I've found forgiveness to be essential in dealing with situations that were unbearable. Why? Because there is always someone we judge responsible for the disaster. This can often include themselves. Research has shown that forgiveness decreases PTSD symptoms.[15]

PTSD was first identified during the Vietnam War. Doctors noticed that returning soldiers were incapacitated by nightmares and persistent flashbacks to the stresses they had experienced. This condition in World War II was called "battle fatigue." In the 1980s, psychologists started using PTSD as a term. Later, they acknowledged it could occur in anyone suffering from prolonged trauma, such as child abuse.[15a]

Dr. Charles Figley, one of the foremost authorities on the effects of trauma and PTSD, notes the following characteristics in the person with PTSD:[16]

- Re-experiences the most traumatic aspects of the event many times, in flashbacks, memory, or dreams
- Makes efforts to avoid exposure to reminders.
- Is on edge, unable to relax.
- Is unable to think about the event without being obsessed.
- Experiences symptoms for more than a month.

He or she can also exhibit the following symptoms:[16a]

- Phobia and general anxiety (especially among former POWs and hostages and natural disaster survivors),
- Substance abuse,
- Depression and/or intense guilt,
- Psychosomatic complaints, increased hospitalization,
- An altered sense of time (especially among children),
- Grief reactions and obsessions with death (especially among those who survived a trauma in which someone else died or could have died),
- Increased interpersonal conflicts and outbursts of anger,
- Absenteeism, criminal behavior, and truancy.

If there has been family trauma, one or more family members may exhibit these symptoms. If you have PTSD, get help. If you are assisting another - get them help - and especially get them to help themselves.

Brain imaging studies done by Bessel A. Van der Kolk, MD, noted international trauma specialist, tells us that during a traumatic event, the part of the brain that does not have language shows the most activity. The front part of the brain associated with speech and being able to talk about events literally shuts off during trauma.[17]

When a trauma victim does eventually "speak" it may be with the "voice" of rage, substance abuse, or even physical violence. This means that people don't necessarily need to talk about trauma to resolve it. Dr. Van der Kolk emphasizes the power of qigong, tai chi, yoga, dancing, and breathing to quiet the body down.[18] At his Trauma Center, they teach people self-regulation through biofeedback and use EMDR[19] which is a powerful method to help people resolve fear and problems through the use of eye movement. It is only done by licensed therapists. A similar approach done by everyday folks is called EFT – Emotional Freedom Technique. It is easy to use and learn, has no negative side effects and is empowering.

## *Complex Post-Traumatic Stress Disorder*

C-PTSD, as it is called, is a more intense and difficult psychological disorder, which occurs as a result of repetitive, prolonged trauma involving sustained abuse or abandonment by a caregiver or other interpersonal relationships. It is associated with sexual, emotional or physical abuse or neglect in childhood, domestic violence, victims of kidnapping and hostage situations, victims of slavery and human trafficking, prisoners of war, victims of bullying, concentration camp survivors, residential school survivors, and cult survivors to name a few of the tragic situations that cause it. It includes situations involving captivity and entrapment that can lead to prolonged feelings of terror, worthlessness, helplessness, and deformation of one's identity and sense of self.

## *Forgiving and PTSD*

Trauma or its aftermath often occurs because of the actions of others. With the continuing lack of acceptance of what happened, resentment builds. Forgiveness can stop the continuing inner dialogue and replaying of abuses or trauma. *The Power Forgiveness Process* works well because it deals with the whole situation in a complete and methodical way. Because of the intensity of the trauma and its long-term effects, I recommend doing the Power Forgiveness work with an experienced counselor.[20] As with any work with deep hurt, safety is extremely important. The person being worked with must know they are safe. Kindness goes a long way.

## *Veterans, PTSD, and Unforgivable Experiences*

"A group of mental health experts is giving a name to the guilt and remorse troops feel when they see or do bad things during war—moral injury. They say failure to recognize and acknowledge exposure to military or civilian carnage in Iraq and Afghanistan sets up troops for post-traumatic stress, a severe and often debilitating anxiety disorder that affects 1 in 5 combat troops." This begins Mark Walker's article on *"Moral injury as a Wound of War - Conference to Examine Consequence of Battlefield Transgressions, Exposure to Carnage."* [21]

This group of psychologists from the Department of Veterans Affairs, lead by Dr. Brett Litz, says that the *moral injury* comes from "perpetrating, failing to prevent, bearing witness to, or learning about acts that transgress deeply held moral beliefs and expectations." [22] This experience, they say, can have bad long-term effects, emotionally, psychologically, behaviorally, spiritually, and socially plus can, they believe, leads to the symptoms of PTSD—withdrawal, self-condemnation, and avoidance. [22a]

If there was ever a place for forgiveness it is in military experience of PTSD. In fact, a study of vets being treated for PTSD found that lack of forgiveness was associated with worse PTSD and depression symptoms.[23] Also, National Center For PTSD of the US Department of Veterans Affairs in their Spirituality and Trauma webpage points out four times the importance of forgiveness in the recovery process following trauma. [24]

But who knows how to help people forgive effectively? Sadly even though there is a forgiveness therapy, pastors, priests, psychiatrists, and therapist are only barely aware of it, so it is not used. It's like knowing about penicillin when it was first around and seeing doctors still chopping off limbs because of infection. I had PTSD for years. A spiritual and psychological forgiveness process pulled me out of my PTSD and deep depression. It works.

So please let others know that there is help and that there is a forgiveness therapy that works. Tell your pastor, priest or therapist. Give them this book. The tragedy of moral injury and PTSD harming our vets does not have to go on. Working with vets is a skill and learning about the military culture is essential. See the National Center for PTSD website, which is part of the US Department of Veterans Affairs for much more information on working with vets.

Remember though, as with anyone with PTSD, first of all, the vet needs to get to the point of seeing the value of forgiving.

## *Compassion Fatigue*

Another disturbing aspect of trauma is the secondary trauma that may occur from indirect exposure to trauma through hearing an account, firsthand, of a traumatic event. Repeatedly watching a shocking incident on television can bring this about. The clinician or any person listening to the vivid description of a trauma by the survivor creates thoughts or emotional response to that event which may sometimes result in a set of symptoms and responses that parallel PTSD, such as re-experiencing, avoidance and being constantly on edge. This secondary result of the trauma is called *compassion fatigue*.

Clergy, social workers, and anyone counseling others need to deal with the impact that the client's trauma has had on them. Those who often listen to people's traumas need to regularly renew a sense of satisfaction, inspiration, and support for their work.[26]

## How and Why Self-Forgiveness Helps

We can often feel that we are responsible for traumatic events that occur in our lives. You can prevent those incidents from harming you further by finding forgiveness for your mistakes (whether they are rational or not), especially if you have guilt around a trauma and are saying negative things against yourselves. Everything changes by dealing with your *"If only"* and *"I should have"* statements through finding forgiveness for yourself for what happened.

In relationships that have had trauma, forgiveness of self wipes out the guilt and regret so that people can learn from their errors and establish a new way of dealing with future mistakes. Relationships built on love rather than condemnation are more satisfying, and allow us to proceed from our highest self. This is true in all of our relationships.

When people react improperly to a highly stressed situation, they often have regret, shame, guilt, and blame. How badly they acted may seem unforgivable. Forgiveness enters with the understanding that *Reaction happens!* By remembering that the reactive brain is not who the person is, you can step out of blame and away from your own guilt.

Remember, you are not that reaction. It was only a powerful survival mechanism that inconveniently entered into a situation.

## Trauma and Forgiveness

Remember that forgiveness has its timing. If a person is in the middle of a reaction to a terrible event, forcing forgiveness will not work, and will probably upset the person more. Initially, a person who is still reacting might need to use other methods including meditation relaxation, massage, walks, and psychotherapy. For the person willing to look at forgiving, Power Forgiveness therapy may be quite helpful when used along with the other accepted treatments.

I appreciate this comic statement because it hits so close to the craziness of self-condemnation:

**From The Management:**
   **The beatings will continue until morale improves!**

# Part IV

# Doing the Work

- Successful Preparations for Power Forgiveness
- The Power Forgiveness Process

# CHAPTER THIRTEEN

# Successful Preparations for Power Forgiveness

## *An Overview of Power Forgiveness*

As I mentioned in the first part of the book, forgiving has different stages and steps. You will go through these different levels with each situation you address. Sometimes you will go through them quickly while with other situations, you'll take more time.

It takes time. How long is entirely up to you. Once I made the decision to forgive and committed myself to the process, I worked on it in one long sitting until I felt it was complete. Others find that it works better to take many sessions over a longer period. It does not matter as long as you follow the *Power Forgiveness Process* outlined here.

Here are the major areas of *The Power Forgiveness Process*:
Part 1 – Identifying all your upsets
Part 2 – Forgiving all your upsets (this has several stages)
- Stage 1 - opening to the upset.
- Stage 2 - expanding your understanding and compassion.
- Stage 3 - realizing your attitude toward that person has changed.
- Stage 4 - self-forgiving on what you just forgave in the other.
- Stage 5 - giving thanks for the healing, then repeating stages 1-4 until all is forgiven.

Part 3 – Feeling the transformation

Forgiveness is a process—a series of actions, each having a set of steps, which brings about viewing a bad situation in a different, more flexible way. Forgiveness is the art form of moving the mind toward being more open, happy, and accepting of others and self. Often forgiving will not be effective until there is understanding and compassion. Once these enter, forgiveness might be automatic, or the decision to forgive becomes easier so that healing can occur.

Making the decision is difficult without digging deeply into the situation and without understanding how the mind is set up to prevent forgiving.

## *Power Forgiveness*

In the book, we follow the different areas of forgiving through many questions, exercises, and suggestions. I've found that the process speeds up as you become familiar with it. Forgiveness for most people is not simple and quick. While it can become faster with practice, initially it takes work. If you have reached this place in the book, you understand this and probably still have more work to do. The initial preparations to help you do this work more effectively follows.

In forgiving, you need to look more deeply at your past with the wisdom of the present. If you can add humility to the equation through the insight that, in some way, you have done a similar thing, and you forgive yourself, then your forgiving is permanent. This is the basic process and its goal. It brings transformation.

I had a therapist say, "This Power Forgiveness Process can't be effective. This is a lifetime of hurt. You can't let go of it just like that." This perspective comes from schools of thought that do not acknowledge the truth of who we are, at our essence is Love, and the power of a Divine Source, which assists in all of this. Einstein's statement is relevant here: "No problem can be solved from the same level of consciousness that created it."

If you are in the position of supporting this work for another person, as a facilitator, friend or counselor, you will assist them best by remaining in touch with your own Higher Power and by having full positive regard for their effort as you witness them releasing resentment. It is far more difficult to do this work alone. The positive regard of the forgiveness facilitator for the person forgiving makes a great deal of difference.

Often, the facilitator/counselor needs to look at the same issues. In my psychotherapy training, we were told that the client would bring the therapist's issues into the room. Perhaps, the client cannot or will not forgive, but in the process, the counselor sees something in his own life that is affected. In many ways, the support person or forgiveness facilitator is a participant in the forgiveness process. His or her role is extremely valuable.

## *Review of Secrets & Essentials of Forgiving*
## *The Small Shifts of Heart and Attitude*

The most important discovery in doing forgiveness as a process is how quickly it can occur. This is because there are many small transformational shifts of the heart and thoughts that bring about major changes. With each of these shifts, we regain the life energy that was tied up in the mental and emotional upset.

Pay attention to your body during this work:
- Watch for that feeling of "ahhh" and relief.
- Notice shifts inside your body and in your major muscle groups.
- Notice changes in your body temperature and your breathing.
- Pay attention to your energy level and take breaks as you feel you need them.
- Notice shifts in perspective and understanding, which is the Aha! response.

**Felt shift questions:** Ask these questions to test for the felt shift:
1. Have I felt relief or release while working on this?
2. Is it time to take a break?
3. Have I felt a little love or understanding come into this?
4. Is it done with for now?

## *Keep the Essentials in Mind*

Here are the key points to focus on during the process.
- **Safety** – Take care of yourself – In all counseling and conflict work, all parties need to feel safe. That includes you when you are doing work on yourself. If you feel overwhelmed, take a break and do some stress relief work or send lovingkindness.
- **Hold the highest vision** – Focusing on your highest purpose or vision will allow forgiveness to take place. Focus on what inspires you to forgive.

- **Find meaning in forgiving** – Use a core value or principle in your life – as Wild Bill did in the concentration camp and Amy Biehls' parents in South Africa. Find a deeper meaning in the situation.
- **Commit to the process** – Be willing to forgive. Intend to forgive. Decide to forgive.
- **Feel the feelings** – Keep feelings in view while forgiving. Look for the feelings under the surface. Avoiding difficult feelings is normal but not helpful in this work. You cannot let go of something that is hidden.
- **Find the truth** – Be honest – *When the truth is known, healing occurs. Honesty with our self is of paramount importance to our health and well-being. Defensiveness will prevent the truth of the situation from being seen and felt.*
- **Ask for inner help** when you are not sure what to do or how to understand something you are working on. Be silent, and offer it to the Divine Help you have. Turn it over and listen. Have faith in Divine Love.
- **Be Grateful**—Anytime that you can be thankful to a person or about the situation, you change it. At the end of any forgiving, find gratitude. What did you gain from the situation? For what can you be grateful to that person?

## *The Secrets*

The following counseling wisdoms are significant in helping people forgive. I call them secrets because few counselors use them.

The Secrets in doing this work:
- **Use your intuition.** Most of us have an inner sense of knowing the right thing to do.
- **Get support.** Help from others in forgiving moves you through it more quickly and easily.
- **Break down the situation** – Analyze it piece by piece, person by person. Break down big upsets by listing everything the person has done. Break down any upsets with an organization by listing all of the people who represent that organization. As you think of one, others will come to mind.

- **Look for earlier events** – Search for experiences in the past that are alike or similar to the one you are working on now. *Deal with the earliest people and situations in your life.* Appreciation of life deepens as we mend the upsets with our family, religion, and culture of origin.
- **Access humility** – Humility enables us to bring in our compassion to try to understand another's situation. It quiets our stress reactions and allows us to step away from the defensive part of us that needs to blame and attack to feel protected.
- **Use your imagination** – To truly understand the worldview of the person you are forgiving, walk in their shoes.
- **Find forgiveness for yourself** – *Forgiveness becomes permanent when you forgive yourself, because y*ou will no longer need to project your upset with yourself onto others to protect and feel good about yourself.

## *The Principles for Doing Power Forgiveness*

*I.* **The experience of healing is the result of a simple principle of the mind:** *Your thoughts cannot go in opposing directions at the same time and get anywhere.* Resentment, guilt, anger, and fear take the mind in the opposite direction from love, joy, and peace. Until you are willing to let go of these resentments and fears, you won't have the deep change you'd like.

*II.* **The intention** of Power Forgiveness is to "let it all go." That means all resentments and upsets with anyone and everyone. This is central to coming into one's own full potential of life – spiritually, mentally, emotionally and physically.

*III.* **Willingness is essential** because it provides the beginning of the commitment that leads to forgiving. Sometimes a person needs to manage resistance and objections to forgiving by ensuring that none of the Myths of Forgiveness are standing in the way.

*IV.* **Put yourself in a comfortable, non-threatening environment for this work.** The brain does its magic best when we feel safe.

*V.* **Calm down or stop and your stress reactions** anytime that you find they are running you. We are a complex mixture of mind, body, and spirit, not a primitive stress reaction. It's normal for people to misidentify these reactions as themselves. They are not us!

*VI.* **Forgiveness is a movement of heart that opens us to more compassion and love.** Performing acts of kindness or charity toward our self and others is healing and transformative. This is how forgiveness gets its power, for the essence of our being is love.

*VII.* **Find the metaphor or symbol of the upset.** The mind works in metaphors and symbols. In looking at difficult situations and people, find how they may symbolize something else in your life that is similar, i.e., a boss might be like dad.

*VIII.* **Self-forgiveness relieves guilt, shame and the need to blame.** In our own healing, self-forgiveness is as important as forgiving others. Guilt and shame hold us back from living a full and happy life.

*IX.* **Know your values and beware of judgments.** We condemn others when they do not adhere to our morals, values, and rules. Guilt and shame arise from not adhering to our own highest morals, values, and rules.

*X.* **Forgiveness is a re-examination of our self and others in a different light.** Re-evaluating the standards by which we judge others, and our selves is an ongoing practice.

*XI.* **Our reaction to our outer world is a reflection of our inner one.** As you become familiar with this work, you will recognize that the world you see outside of you is a reflection of what is going on inside you. That is why finding the projection is so crucial. Often, people are just showing you things about yourself and your judgments and rules. When you see this, all forgiveness becomes self-forgiveness.

*XII.* **Love is the key. Love is for giving.**

## *Preparing for the Process*

A. *Have a pen and plenty of paper available.*

B. *Allow yourself adequate uninterrupted time* for this process. Depending on the stage on which you are working, you will need blocks of time of at least thirty minutes to two hours, or more. In my process, I worked many hours straight. However, I was quite familiar with inner processing.

C. *Eat, but don't allow food to be a distraction.* Be aware that when you are dealing with a difficult situation, you will feel an urge to avoid the tough areas. Pay attention to cravings for food, cigarettes, or caffeine. Sometimes the desire to find distractions can provide a clue to the presence of defenses that are preventing forgiving.

D. *Work with other people.* Groups of people working together on their forgiveness processes have achieved excellent results.

E. *Have no drugs or alcohol* in your system. I'm not talking about medicines, but recreational drugs. These temporarily deaden the consequence of stress. In any kind of inner work, they will often prevent going more deeply into a situation.

F. *Meditate, retreat, and relax.* Start with the easy ones first.

Angeles Arrien, Ph.D., my mentor for many years, said, "You cannot go further on your spiritual path until you do rectification work on your family of origin, your country of origin and your religion of origin."

Rectify means to make right. My forgiveness work with my first religion brought back experiences of a deep connection to God that I had as a young person. I would not have regained that experience if I hadn't made things right and moved back into a realigned relationship with my past.

I was once asked, "If you know your life is not going well but can't think of any bad stuff done to you, what do you do?" I recommended that he make a list of everything that upset him in the world. Once he wrote down the upsets, he gained a strong inroad into forgotten situations. You have to be ready and willing to deal with what is going on inside yourself to forgive effectively.

## *A Review of the Basics*

- Keep your motivation high through the inspiration of your highest vision.

- Write what is going on with you now or about a specific subject; this might be your most frequently used tool. Writing down all of your upsets, guilts, and hatreds will provide you with the raw material for your *Power Forgiveness Process.*

- Don't take the most difficult situations first. Look at what you are *willing* to work on and release what you can. That will bring you the energy and the feel for what to work on next.

- Once you progress through some of the major upsets and can let them go, you will find that you have more energy, which will move you quickly through the list. In all of this work, *you regain the emotional and spiritual energy* previously tied up in holding the unforgiven offenses in place.

- With each act of forgiving, you should feel a change inside—*the felt shift*. When you allow each of the forgiven people to pass through your mind, be aware of your body tensions and your heart. With many people on your list, you will know immediately that you have forgiven them because you'll feel great; with others, you will sense there is more to forgive. As you progress, you will forgive more easily, yet still get the same joyful, peaceful, or loving result.

- With true forgiveness, there will be no animosity at all. You will have a neutral or positive experience of the person in your mind. When you feel relief, joy, love or peace with each person you forgive, there should be no upset left.

- Do the same thing for each person or situation on your list.

- Sometimes a release occurs by simply acknowledging that you have done a similar thing to another.

- Use the Secrets, Essentials, and Principles if you are stuck.

- Break down the upset as far as you can.

- As you go along, you will find that the process will speed up. You will forgive more easily but still get the same joyful, peaceful, loving result—sometimes even more so. Toward the end, if you are doing the whole *Power Forgiveness Process*, you will just think of the person and be able to forgive because you have regained your personal power and Love.

# CHAPTER FOURTEEN

# The Power Forgiveness Process

*The Power Forgiveness Process* has three parts or phases.

>Part 1 – Facing the unforgiven in our lives
>Part 2 – Working on the incidents
>Part 3 – Being aware of the transformation

In the first part, you are looking at all of the unforgiven people and situations in your life. You write up lists instead of letting them fester under the surface.

In the second part, you work on one person at a time or one specific incident. This part deals with the basics in forgiving which we went over in the first chapters. When you forgive all of the people and no upset is in your life, a transformation happens, which is the third part.

**Please Note:** Because this is *The Power Forgiveness Process*, we are talking about dealing with ALL of your upsetting people instead of letting them fester under the surface.

If you are starting out, I recommend not writing down all of your upsets at once unless you are on a retreat, supervised intensive, or close supervision where you are in a contained space and routine so that you can focus on the process and not be distracted by all of your upsets.

If you have read the book completely and have had some success with letting go of your upsets and feel ready, then write down ALL of your upsets. But, you **must** immediately follow through with the forgiving. Don't wait.

If you do not feel comfortable with the process, then just take one upsetting person and work on him or her. Make sure that person is not your most upsetting one. You will get to the most "charged" person but not yet. Get familiar with the process and have some success at doing it first.

## Part 1 – *Facing the Unforgiven In Your Life*

Write down the people, organizations, situations, or places with which you have resentment, hate, anger, fear, or critical judgment. You might find there are many negative acts connected to one person or just one incident. At this stage, you are simply writing down the situations that you **want** to deal with. (If some are too upsetting, you can address them when you feel more confident with the process. For now, do the forgiving that you can; that will bring you the energy to face the more the upsetting situations.)

The main questions of this step are:
   A. Who or what upsets me?
   B. What are **all** the things that each person did?

**Note:** It is necessary to break down their offenses. Make sure you break down each offense into all of its pieces. One situation might have twenty little different situations that need forgiving. Likewise, a person in a big event might have twenty different offenses. Take care of each of those offenses before you work on someone else. It is easier to forgive the 20 separate acts than try to do it all at once.

   C. After you have broken the situation down to its smallest parts, work on each piece until you've handled them all.

Here are questions to help look more deeply at A and B.
1. When I look at my home, what do I need to release?
2. Who am I having problems forgiving?
3. Is there something I want to forgive myself for?
4. Are there any situations I just don't have the strength or willingness to let go of and forgive?
5. Are there acts that are completely unforgivable?
6. Are there situations that I am inclined to respond to negatively on a regular basis?

7. Are there situations where I am being ill-treated presently?

Write just enough to jar your memory. One sentence or a phrase can be enough for the whole thing. This is for you to read, not someone else. I had 30 pages of one-liners. They weren't funny, but they were all down on paper.

It is important to write all of your upsets down. Doing it all at once may mean staying agitated and upset. That may be too difficult. I wanted to feel all my victimhood to get it all down on paper so that I could release it all completely. It might be easier for you to take sections of your life.

After you have written your upset and broken it down, the next step is to choose what to work on first. Because this may be overwhelming, I recommend taking the smaller upsets first and get those out of the way. Some people like to jump into the hard stuff first. We all have our different styles and comfort levels. Once you have chosen what to work on, try in one sitting work on it until you have forgiven. Spend at least an hour on each sitting. When I work with people, I like to do several hours at a time, but that depends on you and the person working with you.

Remember to review and use the essentials and secrets.

## *Part 2 – Working on an Incident*
## *Stage 1 – The Opening Stage – Unlocking an Upset*

This is the preliminary stage for working on an upset. We went over this in Chapters 1 through 8 of the book. A full summary is at the end of Part II in Chapter 9. With the knowledge of the first chapters, this opening stage can go quickly.

Please note that this whole first stage can occur in moments. Once you understand each step, it becomes a checklist to make sure you cover each.

Here is a summary of the first stage (See Chapter 9 to go into these more deeply):

**1 – Make the choice that feels right.**
Break down the upset and select one offense.
**2 – Look at your willingness.**
Make sure you are willing to face that upset.
**3 – Focus on what inspires you to forgive.**

The stronger the inspiration, the greater the success.

**4 – Deal with feelings effectively.**

When you think of each situation, are there other feelings underneath, or mixed up with the main emotion, like hopelessness, humiliation, or guilt? What were you afraid would happen at the time?

**5 – Find your needs and the debt owed.**

Figuring out what the offender owes you is basic, along with the reality of what you want. What do they owe you?

See the needs, wants, and debts summary in Chapter 2.

**6 – Look at the real result of holding on to this upset.**
- What is the payoff for keeping the upset?
- What are the negative consequences of holding on to it?

**7 – Handle resistance and objections to forgiving.**

Make sure no Myths of Forgiveness are active. If you need to, look over the Myths of Forgiveness section in Chapter 3 to make sure none are in the way.

**8 – See if you can forgive it.**
- Can you forgive right now for yourself?
- Even though it is not deserved, can you forgive as an act of compassion toward the other person and yourself?

## *Taking the First Stage Deeper*

The first stage of *The Power Forgiveness Process* deals with the basics in forgiving. Many people can get relief with those first eight steps, which basically follow the first chapters in this book.

The next stages take the process deeper to completion by:
- Delving further into the situation
- Changing our perspective about the person
- Looking at the inner mechanisms that tend to keep the real reason for the upset hidden
- Finding the positive in what happened
- Doing self-forgiving

Continue until you complete all upsets.

## Stage 2 – The Understanding Stage – Expanding Understanding and Compassion

Understanding is a basic key to unlocking feelings and a closed heart when you are doing forgiving. After the opening stage where you start looking at the upsetting situation, the second stage is where you go over methods and guides to aid in deepening your understanding and compassion for another and yourself. Any one of the following "Skills" can bring the forgiveness you want. Just keep going down the list until you feel the felt shift of success.

By understanding how the brain works and how we use it, forgiveness students gain compassion for our humanness. Compassion quells the emotional fires of anger and resentment.

In human physiological growth, the emotional (limbic) system develops before the intellectual. Even teenagers' nerve cell development is not complete in the brain governing intellect. Because of the earlier development of the emotional system, the emotions are quite capable of shutting down our logical thinking side. We know from psychology and brain studies, however, that shining the light of logical analysis onto emotional upsets can help to alleviate the upset. This is because the linear thinking, analytical part of the brain, which is the left frontal lobe of the neocortex, is set up to manage our emotional system.

### Ways for Increasing Understanding and Compassion

We can take many avenues to deepen our understanding of one another. This deepening often results in changing our perspective of situations. Changing viewpoints is really the art of counseling, whether it is with a friend, minister, forgiveness counselor, or psychotherapist. The methods that follow will enable you to be your own forgiveness facilitator. However, I recommend you work with someone familiar with this work so that he or she can carry you through the process, instead of your being both client and facilitator.

Here are helpful skills you have been reading about to aid in deepening your understanding of the situation, another person, and yourself:

## Skill 1 – Look for Your Rules for Conduct

In our discussion of justice, we saw that it is necessary to be aware of our principles, values, and rules for behavior and conduct.
- Which of your principles did the offender or you not follow?
- Which of your values were rejected or disregarded?
- What rules were broken?

Now with each rule, principle and value ask:
1. Though we feel that others should observe our principles, values, and rules, given the life experience of this person, is my expectation realistic?
2. Have I always been able to follow these principles and rules myself?
3. Have I done the same thing in any way to others or myself?

## Skill 2 – Change your Perspective

Shifting the way you see the person or situation is where you can begin to separate the person from his/her actions. As Terry Hargrave, Ph.D., points out, "When you, as the victim, can begin to understand the limitations of your victimizer, you can also begin to recognize his humanity." [1]

Sometimes, to shift our perspective sufficiently, we need a God's-eye-view. In situations that are seemingly unforgivable, we must hold to our highest vision for ourselves. In this way, we can accomplish the necessary shift in perspective that will lead us to let the upset go.
- Ask yourself: "Is it possible there are perspectives other than my own?" Again, initially, just the willingness to look at other perspectives is significant. Our desire to be right often overpowers our desire for the truth of the situation and blinds us from taking other perspectives.

One of my students complained vehemently throughout class about a building contractor who had cheated him and caused his family trouble. He was right from his perspective, and I agreed that what the guy had done was not decent. Nevertheless, I know that when I see a great deal of anger, there is more to look at than being right, if a person truly wants to feel better and heal.

It was not until he wrote his paper for that class that he saw how the contractor had also lost time and money. That shift in perspective, about the situation in general, and specifically about the other person's perspective, helped him to feel better. The change in view does not justify what happened, but it does bring an understanding of why the contractor acted as he did.

## A. Walking in the Other's Shoes

In your journal, write down the circumstances that surround the event from the point of view of the person who hurt you. Using what you know about their background and early life, write down their version of this situation. Try to understand what it is like to walk in their shoes. This may be difficult to do, particularly for seriously upsetting situations.

Make use of meditation and possibly prayer to complete these exercises if you notice a great deal of resistance. Note in your journal where you feel stuck.

1. Write down what you believe to be the governing moral code that this person lives by, and that should have influenced their behavior in this situation.
2. Write down what you believe were their fears and hopes, likes and dislikes.
3. What was it like growing up in their family?
4. What was it like to come from their culture or time?
5. What are their issues?
6. What is their emotional intelligence?
7. What was their expectation of you, of others?

If you don't have enough information about the person to do this exercise, ask someone who might know. For example, Lucy forgave her father when her aunt told her that, as a child, his father had suffered vicious treatment at the hands of his father, Lucy's grandfather.

As you write their version of the situation, look for the felt shift. Notice any difference in your understanding of the situation. Write any insights about the person that you may have experienced in this. After you get familiar with the process, this need only take moments.

### B. What is the Big Picture?

1. Write down how this situation might fit into your idea of Karma or a Divine Plan.
2. Was this person in your life to teach you a valuable lesson?

### C. Other Shifting Perspectives Questions

1. What other ways could I see this situation?
2. Can I listen to others who might have a different viewpoint?
3. Can I get help from others?
4. How would an impartial observer look at this?
5. What have I left out? Have I skipped over anything where I may have contributed to the bad outcome?
6. What have I added that I should not have?
7. Am I holding onto this resentment out of loyalty to someone else?

For Completing this Skill:
- Make sure you have written down all the ways that the offender is correct and justified from his or her perspective.
- Be sure to pay attention to the felt shifts in your perspective and your feelings during this stage.

## Skill 3 – Face Your Defenses

Now that you have looked at the situation from what you believe is the offender's point of view, it's time to go deeper.

Remember, the mind is set up to defend our goodness and rightness. Thus, as I discussed in Chapter 10, we often push wrongs we have done out of our mind and onto others. Then, we deny we have done that wrong action. One way in which we defend ourselves is by being hurt or indignant. By blaming what happens in our world on others, we seem to maintain our ideal self-image. It takes courage to consider that our reactions may have their source in the specific defense mechanism of projection – blaming another to avoid feeling the pain of being at fault in some way.

If you can see that you have done a similar thing to the upset you are working on, forgiveness becomes easier because humility has entered your perspective, enabling understanding and compassion to occur. For the moment, our defense about that wrong is undone. It will come back again if self-forgiveness for that action is not complete, which is why there is a self-forgiveness stage in this work.

Here are other questions to help you look for signs of projecting:
1. How would an impartial observer view this?
2. What have I added that I should not have?

**Facing Defenses Summary Questions**
- A. Detach from it all by asking, "How would an impartial observer view this?"
- B. See if you have done something similar yourself – perhaps not in magnitude, but in context – maybe not to others, but to yourself.
- C. If you have, ask yourself:
    - a. Can I forgive this person for doing the same thing I've done? Or for breaking an unrealistic value, moral code, or rule that I have?
    - b. Can I forgive myself for doing the same thing?

So far, in this situation, you have:
- Examined your responsibility in maintaining your hurt and resentment,
- Shifted your perspective sufficiently that you can see the offender's humanity,
- Looked at your unrealistic expectations,
- Found unenforceable values and unrealistic rules,
- Gained more compassion and understanding for another's viewpoints.

# Skill 4 – Work with Ways to Feel More Positive
## *A. Find a Deeper Meaning in the Event*

Forgiveness will increase your capacity to love because it requires a shift in your vision of the world. With this new perspective, it's possible to look for a deeper meaning in the situations that you have released through forgiveness.

Questions to ask yourself:
1. What has this hurtful experience taught me about myself, the world, or other people?
2. How have I matured from this experience?

3. What have I learned about love and compassion, as a result of this experience?
4. How have my values changed?

## B. *Appreciate What You Gained – Be grateful*

Gratitude is a powerful method for change that works at any time. In forgiveness work, look for and acknowledge ways that the person has helped you. There are different possibilities and perspectives on this. Even a negative role model could have taught you something positive. For example, Ron was in a particularly unkind and vicious cult whose leader opposed the concept of love. Seeing how terribly people treated each other in this unkind cult, he decided to live his life as much as he could with loving kindness as his goal.

When you extend thanks to those who have taught you a major life lesson, you send love, the greatest healer. That love, oddly enough, heals you as you give to another.

Being thankful makes it easier. A powerful contemplation is to ask yourself, "What am I thankful for from this situation?" You ask this over and over until you are feeling grateful. I've seen people start this inquiry seemingly having nothing to be thankful for. They had to search their mind for anything to be thankful for. In the end, they realized that they were appreciative of many things because of this situation.

## C. *Give love*

Can you imagine holding the person you are trying to forgive and just love them no matter what? Hold them as a mother or father would their child, perhaps not agreeing, but still loving. You might still disagree, but not with anger, or resentment.

Remember: At any time as you work on this, you might feel a <u>shift</u> inside yourself. This could be all you need to change it for good. You will be quite surprised at what a small shift in perspective can do!!

▶ **If** you forgave, go to the next piece in the situation you have already broken down.

▶ **If** you could not forgive the piece you were working on:
- See if it will break down further. Then do the opening steps on the newly broken-down upset.

**OR**
Look back further. Ask these questions:
1. What in my past reminds me of this?
2. Is there an earlier situation in my life that might be similar to this one?
3. What do I need to let go about my past, including my family of origin, to help me in this?

Then go back and do the above "Understanding steps" on these new items.

▶ **If** no change – take another incident from Stage 1 and work on it, and come back to this later.

Remember:
- If you find that it has not lifted, ask:
  1. What other ways could I see this situation?
  2. Can I get help from others? Are there others I might talk with who have a different perspective?
- Be silent, and give it to the Divine Help you have. Turn it over and listen. Have faith in Divine Love. You have done all you can do. Remember to ask for Divine help in seeing this a different way!

## *Stage 3 – Realization Stage*

During your work on this person, you will feel a shift in your perspective and attitude. When this happens, take time to feel the change within and think of the person again to see if there is any resentment or hurt left. If there is, go back to where you left off in the Understanding Stage.

When you forgive the person or a specific action they did, the first level of forgiving is complete. Sometimes your work in forgiving will go fast. You might go through each stage in minutes. As long as you feel a definite emotional shift on each person's unpleasant action, you are doing fine. Eventually, you will be able to forgive the person completely as long as you keep doing the steps on all their offending deeds.

When you feel forgiveness has occurred with this specific incident move onto the Self-Forgiveness Stage.

## *End Result of the Realization stage*

Somewhere along the way by using these skills for expanding understanding and compassion, you will:
- shift positively in your perspective about the situation or the person,
- and realize forgiveness for the person

When that occurs, go to the Self-Forgiveness Stage to carry the forgiveness work to completion on that specific offense.

## *Stage 4 – Gaining Self-Forgiveness*

Because the world you see reflects your mind and thinking, it is always useful to see that what you are dealing with pertains to yourself. Thus, for forgiving to be permanent, you need to address the second level of forgiveness, which is dealing with your own similar deeds.

The first part of this stage is personal responsibility. Here, you look at what the person did in the situation you have just forgiven to see if it has something to do with you. Here are questions that might help:
1. Is this unforgiven situation mirroring something about me?
2. Have I done anything similar to others? Or myself? (The magnitude might not be the same but is there a similarity?)

**Note**: Without self-forgiveness, there is the possibility that the upset will continue in other ways with other people.

The second part is to forgive yourself for the similar action you might have done to others or yourself.

I don't know what it will take for you to gain self-forgiveness. Many people finally just decide to let go of the burden they have been carrying. Peter said to me after he did the process, "I saw that I have been in pain for enough years. That pain was my amends. I just decided enough is enough and was able to let go of the upset I had with myself on each thing that came up. As I did, I felt more compassion for myself and could see how much I had been torturing myself. Each act of forgiveness was a relief for my heart."

**Self-forgiveness questions:** Use the following questions on yourself in the situation you are dealing with.

1. Am I prepared to forgive myself for the same transgressions I am willing to forgive in another?
2. Can I forgive myself for the same offense I've forgiven in others?
3. Do I feel any guilt around my own transgression for which I need to forgive myself?
4. What will it take me to forgive myself for this? Do I need to make amends to anyone?
5. For those with a Christian orientation, this question might help: Can I accept God's forgiveness of me on this?

When you feel you have forgiven yourself, you naturally go to the next stage to finish off this situation.

## Stage 5 – The Healing Stage – Thanksgiving

With the completion of that incident, you have forgiven the other and then yourself. You experience a break in the intensity and a natural movement toward giving thanks occurs. Here are questions to aid in the conclusion of the offense from that person. In this stage, you look at what you have learned and how it helped you.

Is there something you gained from having this person in your life? Here you appreciate how far you have come in your life, and change your perspective of what happened with that person. Other questions from the gratitude section to assist are:

1. What can you be grateful for in this situation?
2. What did it teach you?
3. Did it influence your life making you stronger, more capable, or successful?
4. What did you learn?
5. How did the person or people help you?
6. How have they helped others?
7. How did they affect a positive change in your life?

When you have forgiven the situation and yourself, feel the successful completion of that situation. You should not feel animosity, and normally, there will be a sense of loving-kindness toward the person involved.

In non-threatening situations, you might even want to extend appreciation to the person. For example, when Mary Lou dealt with an upset with a mentor, she sent her a letter of appreciation for the help the mentor had given her through the years.

Any of these ways might be appropriate to give appreciation:
- Thank you letter
- Flowers
- A letter of acknowledgment
- Acknowledging them in person

There may even be a desire for reconciliation. For now, just keep doing the process and go to the next part of this step, which is clearing up the next upset.

**The Second Section of this Healing Stage is to** take another situation that is bothering you. Go through the same process to success in forgiving that person and you by returning to the Healing stage until eventually there is nothing left to forgive. Repeat the stages until *all is forgiven*.

When you let go of all of your upsets, a peace, love, and joy will be there for you that you haven't felt for a long time. This takes you to the next part.

## *Part 3 – Transformation*

Initially, you might not notice all the changes that have happened in your life. Some will be subtle; some will be big. They will not only affect you but will spread to others around you. This is similar to the Christian concept of Grace. Of course, this experience is not restricted to Christianity but is experienced in every religion, because it is a letting go of our conscious upsets and moving into our heart.

This transformation allows you to view situations differently than before and functions more capably. Power Forgiveness is not the ultimate life process, but it does give you effective tools to let upsets go more easily, allowing faster recovery and renewal.

## *The Shorter and Original Power Forgiveness Process*

When you find things are moving quickly for yourself, and you
1) understand projection and 2) can see it in your life, you might try this shorter form of the *Power Forgiveness Process*.

If you don't feel the joy and increased energy from doing the following steps, then go back to the complete process in this chapter and use it. Begin this process after you have:

    A. Found all the upsetting situations and people in your life and written them down, and

    B. Chosen one person you are willing to work on.

With one of the offenses the person has done, ask:
1. What am I feeling about what they did?
2. What was I afraid of?
3. What value, law, rule or moral code of mine did they break?
4. Do I have an unreal expectation for them or myself to hold that law, value or rule?
5. Have I done the same thing in any way to others or myself?
6. Can I forgive them for doing the same thing I've done? Or for breaking an unreal value, moral code or rule that I have?
7. Can I forgive myself for doing the same thing? (An essential step.)
8. What are all the things I can be grateful to them for?

Then choose something else the person has done that you are willing to work on and do steps 1 – 8.

"If we could read the secret history of our enemies, we would find in each person's life sorrow and suffering enough to disarm all hostility."
    HENRY WADSWORTH LONGFELLOW - AMERICAN POET, 1807 –1882

# Part V - After the Process

This section deals with maintaining and strengthening the benefits of the Power Forgiveness process.

There are several key actions to remember:
- Keeping a regular practice
- Staying inspired
- Finding inner and outer support
- Using in-depth tools for further forgiveness

# CHAPTER FIFTEEN

# Continued Healing

## *After Deep Change*

The transformation I have been speaking of is a spiritual rebirth. Through it, the potential of life opens to us. The sense of much deeper spirituality is often apparent. Dr. Herbert Benson has an excellent book on the effects of this peak experience called *The Break-out Principle*.

After you have done your forgiveness work, you'll find your life has improved in many ways. These include:
- Release from emotional prison
- Living from the heart
- Finding a deeper meaning for your life

Without a way to channel this joy, love and deepening of life, a crisis of meaning may occur in one's life. People often become active in their churches, and/or help and do activities to make a difference in their community. Having a positive effect in the world satisfies us. As social beings, we need to feel we are moving in a direction that is noteworthy–not only to us, but also to the greater whole–socially, spiritually or even nationally.

## *Release from Emotional Prison*

At this point in your inner work, you have let go of old hurts that have been holding you hostage. Once you release them, you free yourself from the destructive cycle of reliving the injury every time you think about it. Being free of those wounds brings back ample positive emotional energy.

When you release yourself from the emotional prison of resentment, joy is the natural by-product. Joy is your best guidepost in aligning with the truth of who you really are, your authenticity.

"Love is the victor in every case. Love breaks down the iron bars of thought, shatters the walls of material belief, severs the chain of bondage which thought has imposed, and sets the captive free."[1] — ERNEST HOLMES,
THEOLOGIAN, AUTHOR AND SPIRITUAL TEACHER

## *Living from the Heart*

Any action motivated by resentment will lead you away from expansion, love, and joy. This includes servitude, which may sometimes masquerade as service to others; the difference is that the underlying motivation is resentment at feeling trapped. True service to others carries a surge of positive energy and love.

Forgiveness, particularly when done as a regular practice, allows you to live from the heart in joy and peace. Whether it is in your work or your close relationships, be mindful of the movement of
the heart. To live from love requires a way to release these negative emotions once we have heard what they have to tell us.

## *Deeper Meaning*

Forgiveness will increase your capacity to love and shift your vision of the world, yourself, and other people. With this new perspective, you will discover a deeper meaning in your life because of what has happened to you. You might even have a God's-eye-view of your life instead of the restricted self-centered view you had before.

An example of this perspective is from a local police officer's dream that had this kind of effect on me. Jack has 20 years in law enforcement and has led an intense life. One night in a dream, he was surfing, which was his favorite sport. As he was going down an enormous wave, an angel flew next to him and said, "This is it!" He understood in the dream that it meant that this was the end of his life, and he said, "Well, this has been a great life, thank you very much. I have lived this life to its fullest. Thank you."

When I have relayed this story to others, they all have had the same reaction as he did. They felt much better about their life, and about what they had gone through and who they had become.

## *Reconciliation Possibilities*

Reconciling, if it occurs in a relationship, can feel like a blessing, but forgiveness does not always lead there. The person with whom you have the upset may be deceased, no longer in your life, or simply not open to a relationship with you. In such cases, reconciliation will not be possible, but forgiveness does not depend on it. You let your upset go whether you reconcile with that person or not.

After doing your forgiveness work, if you desire reconciliation, I recommend the following books:

- *Forgive for Love: The Missing Ingredient for a Healthy and Lasting Relationship,* by Fredric Luskin, Ph.D.;
- For Christians, Part Three of *Forgiving and Reconciling: Bridges to Wholeness and Hope*, by Dr. Worthington.

Besides helping you feel better, sometimes reconciliation is possible for the benefit of the person you have forgiven. After Kirk and Nate had entered into a financial arrangement, Kirk did not keep the agreement, and Nate came out the loser. Nate, however, had forgiven Kirk and let the matter go but had nothing more to do with him. Later, a friend told Nate that Kirk was devastated by the situation and regretted losing their friendship. Nate called Kirk and apologized for not remaining in touch. Then, Kirk said, "I've been stuck for six months. I just cannot move in my life, and I can't change anything about that situation. I'm sorry." For Nate, the matter was over when he forgave Kirk. For Kirk, it was important for them to be reconciled. Nate said later, "If I had not wanted to reconcile, Kirk would not have come back into my life and enriched it, and he would have remained stuck with the loss of our friendship, and I would have too."

This ability to let go and reconcile is not solely human. In the book, *Natural Conflict Resolution*, Filippo Aureli, and Frans de Waal document reconciliation in no less than 27 species of primates, as well as bottlenose dolphins and goats.[3]

The ideal of the spiritual movement in Japan, Seicho-NO-IE, is to be reconciled with everyone. As the founder said:

"True reconciliation cannot be achieved by patience or forbearance with one another. To be patient or forbearing is not to be reconciled from the bottom of your heart. When you are grateful to one another, true reconciliation is achieved."[4]

This also applies to self-forgiveness. Even further, we are really talking about reconciliation with life itself – to be grateful for everything and everyone in our life. When I can see the situation or person with gratitude, I feel reconciled. I can then more easily come up with an effective solution to the problem that I perceive.

## Giving a Meaningful Apology

When we see the importance of forgiving there is a desire to help people forgive, especially when we have been hurtful to another. An apology is an especially effective way to help clean up the situation. Beverly Engel's book, *The Power of Apology: Healing Steps to Transform All Your Relationships*, is a useful resource.

## Maintaining Regular Practice

Keeping up a regular practice of forgiveness is the most effective way to maintain your success in this work *and* to quickly release upsets that arise. Although you might get surprisingly upset about something, you will be able to regain your balance and peace of mind more readily and handle upsets with greater ease.

The best way I've found to maintain a regular practice is through an *evening review*. At the end of each day, make it a practice to forgive the upsets that occurred that day.

1. Mentally go over your day and clean up any upsets that have accumulated – those that you did not let go of at the time.
2. Release them.

If you find that you are having a repeated upset, you can be sure that forgiveness is necessary.

## Re-Forgiving?

Just because you've rid yourself of all the upsets you can think of doesn't mean that more will not come up. You have the tools now to sort them out. If you maintain a regular forgiveness practice, you won't be overwhelmed with what might come up.

If a major situation arises that you thought you forgave, know that there is just more work to do. When you look closely, you will see that what has come up now is a different aspect of that situation. Likewise, people you thought you forgave might again come up. This different aspect of them was not forgiven originally.

**Please note:** Your processing does not guarantee upsets will not occur again. They will! This is because our defense mechanisms and stressed brain reactions are still there. Sometimes we forget our commitment to our highest potential, and sometimes we go on automatic and get surprised. You will find, however, that you will sort out what happened faster and forgive more easily.

## *Humor*

You might find that you will laugh more at your reactions as opposed to condemning yourself. With that laughter, all aspects of forgiveness will come. As Victor Borge said, "Laughter is the shortest distance between two people."

Indian physician, Dr. M. Kataria, started a new phenomenon called Laughter Clubs. Today, the laughter movement has become a global phenomenon with over 6000 clubs in 60 countries. Because Laughter Clubs realize the great power of laughter and its efficacy as the best prescription for wellness, they have brought laughter to the lives of many people suffering from upsets that are physical, mental and emotional. They even have a laughter for forgiveness![5]

## *Beware of Old Habits of the Mind*

Even though you have transformed your mind, old neural brain patterns may still show their face. You are still human. Reactions will occur but will dissipate more quickly.

The day after my transformation, I woke up with the same early morning reaction to the day that I had had for months, "Oh no, not another day!" Then I came to my senses, remembering that the day before had been incredible. I understood that my reaction was just an old habit. It went away immediately. I heard that *Oh no!* reaction upon waking up for another couple of weeks with its strength diminishing each morning. In the end, I laughed at it. The laughter and joy remained for years upon awakening.

## *Feed Yourself the Good and Positive*

In religion, as in traditional psychology, there is the question of how to deal with upsets. In psychology, we analyze what is happening and has happened in the past. We might try to change our present behaviors or get a better understanding of past events. We have done a great deal of that in this book.

It is most efficient to take care of the problem from the spiritual state of mind. From this level, changes occur more easily. To get to this level of mind, the question becomes, "Where are you putting your attention, your conscious mind?" The approach is to move toward the positive aspects of life and towards the Divine. The only problem with this placement of mind is that a mind in turmoil has difficulty finding the positive. Unforgiven situations will always continue to create turmoil until you work with them.

Even after forgiveness, there can be the question of how we find a positive state of mind. This is a question of desire. To feel better more often, *feed* your mind more of what it needs. If you want peace, then feel peace, be more peaceful. It is not always what is in your mind that is the problem, but the negative thoughts you keep feeding your mind.

Gene, a client and cult survivor, spent years in recovery from the atrocities of being mind-controlled by a particularly abusive cult. Every day he replayed the upsets, hurts, and betrayals. "Eventually, I became so depressed that I saw no reason to keep on," he confided. Through the help of friends, he started letting go and forgiving. However, that was not the only thing he did. He started going to a church that was loving. He meditated. He read inspirational books regularly. He stopped watching the news and commentators on TV. He started hanging out with people who provided a more positive influence on him. He started feeding himself better mind, soul, and heart food. His depression went away, and he could maintain feeling good by keeping inspired and positive.

## Stay Inspired

Make it part of your practice daily to read inspirational materials that keep you aligned with your highest vision for yourself. Associate with like-minded people.

With the forgiving mind active in your life, spiritual understanding deepens. In contrast, those who cannot forgive condemn themselves to constricted lives of fear and anger requiring them to develop protection and defenses.

So look now and see if there are inspirational writings, a church, or organization that can help you to continue with forgiveness.

## Give Support—Help People Forgive

The most powerful way to maintain your forgiving attitude is to teach it. Some people have also formed Power Forgiveness groups to help others forgive. This is the original vision that I had of the earth becoming more harmonious and peaceful – people helping others forgive. It went on like that spreading around the world. We have the tools to do it. The Forgiveness Foundation is here to help.

Give forgiveness workshops at your church, community center, or local college. Use this book as a guide.

> One cannot arrive at true nobility of spirit if one is not prepared to forgive the imperfections of human nature. For all men, whether worthy or unworthy, require forgiveness."
> INAYAT KHAN, 1882 – 1927 INDIAN SUFI TEACHER[6]

CHAPTER SIXTEEN

# The Ultimate Result

Forgiveness is an act of inclusion—that is what love is. It includes. That is what The Divine is. Our joy at the deepest level of ourselves is to go beyond our small stimulus-response self. At the highest level, we want alignment with integrity—God in Its many aspects.

## *Final Statement*

Neither the field of psychology nor religion understands mental and emotional health very well. Continuing use of forgiveness can change the face of mental health because it puts our mind's well-being into our own hands, opening us up to a potential far greater than that provided by our survival mechanisms alone.

The field of mental health must change. Though there are good methods in psychology that help a person let go of upsets and heal relationships, I believe that psychology is not effective enough in bringing mental and emotional health to our society because of the rejection of the concept of forgiveness and the importance of letting go of all upsets. T

For the health of our society and communities around the world, we can no longer allow this maligning of forgiveness to occur. We cannot afford declining mental health and increasing acts of violence. The legal and prison systems in many countries around the world and especially in the United States are operated mainly on retribution, revenge, and punishment with little mediation and rehabilitation involved. This can change. We can start using forgiveness in our lives for taking care of our mental health and setting limits on harm to others and ourselves.

As I've shown throughout this book, there is a reason for the unacceptability of forgiving even beyond the rift between psychology and religion, which is the rift in our own minds. It is the split between our highest and true-self versus our basic survival-self. Both are part of us. One gives us our highest vision and goal of community, peace, and kindness. The other protects us by seeing limitations and problems, but can also keep us small, fearful, and seeking revenge.

Forgiveness raises our ability to remain in control of our thinking, pointing it toward the highest within us to bring joy, peace, and love far greater than we have had before.

Forgiving is critical to our mental health, emotional well-being, and spiritual fulfillment.

## *The Ultimate Result*

I've met people through the years who don't understand the emphasis on forgiveness that many people have. It is not that they are unforgiving, just the opposite. They don't hold upsets with people. They have the humility within them not to take offense at people or God when bad things happen. They retain a love of life and Spirit. This requires a state of mind that has great compassion and understanding for neighbor and self. I believe this capacity is in each of us because The Divine is available to each of us.

The ultimate result of this work is the deepening of our connection to others, to life, and to the Divine Presence and sacredness in our lives. With the tools of forgiveness:

- We can have love, peace, and kindness among us;
- We can be our genuine selves, living the joy we deserve; and
- We can have a knowing bond to the Source of life and love.

## *A Vision for Forgiveness*

- ◆ We have sufficient forgiveness methods right now to transform our lives to ones of love, peace and joy.
- ◆ We will promote forgiveness sufficiently so that people will not doubt the power of forgiveness.

- We will choose to be happy instead of being right.
- We will chose to be loving in relationships for we know that is more rewarding than being resentful.
- We will recognize that we are the first to be healed by forgiving. We never know how it will affect someone else.
- We will understand that without forgiveness first, there is no true reconciliation.
- We will teach our children how to forgive and to grow up willing to forgive so that they will have happier lives with less conflict.
- Our hearts will allow differences with other people without blame for those differences.
- Friends will counsel friends to forgive instead of just agreeing with them on how bad things are.
- Individual and couples counseling will use the many methods of forgiveness to help people to let go of their upsets with themselves and others.
- Schools will expect social proficiency through teaching communication skills, forgiveness, and conflict and anger management so that students' minds will be open to creative win-win solutions to a conflict.
- Clergy will not only preach that forgiveness is important but will teach people how to do it. They will put on forgiveness intensives and workshops to enable their congregants to clear their minds and hearts in order to live deeper spiritual lives by experiencing God.
- Conflict resolution programs throughout the world will use forgiveness regularly because there is no true conflict resolution without the movement of heart that forgiveness brings. Plus, forgiveness brings the capacity to hear what the other person is really saying or wanting.
- Conferences on healing will prominently address forgiveness as a powerful agent for health instead of barely mentioning it at all.
- Psychology will hold the torch of forgiveness as a precursor to mental health.
- All psychology students will study Forgiveness Therapy.
- Anger control groups will use forgiveness as a valuable tool for healing.
- Conferences on healing will address forgiveness as a powerful agent for health instead of barely mentioning it.

- PTSD will no longer be so incapacitating because self-forgiveness will be part of the healing process.
- Law students and medical students will be taught the power of forgiveness as a regular course of study in their schools.
- Judges will require defendants to go to forgiveness counselors.
- Nations will ensure their representatives and most valued negotiators are also accomplished in forgiveness in their own lives.
- Nations will establish and promote their own Truth and Reconciliation programs to bring about healing among races, ethnic groups and religions. Our hearts will allow differences with other people without blame.
- The Forgiveness Foundation will no longer be necessary because churches, schools, universities, governments and households will have taken up the cause of forgiveness.
- The healing among religions and nations will bring us to a new era of non-violent compassionate communication and interaction.

Thank you for developing the skills to forgive.

The following pages give:

APPENDIX

NOTES

BIBLIOGRAPHY

And

INDEX

# Appendix

## How We Are Likely to Feel When Our Needs Are Not Being Met

| | | | |
|---|---|---|---|
| afraid | dislike | horrible | passive |
| aggravated | displeased | hostile | perplexed |
| agitated | distressed | hot | puzzled |
| angry | disturbed | hurt | reluctant |
| anxious | downhearted | impatient | resentful |
| apathetic | dread | indifferent | restless |
| bad | embarrassed | infuriated | sad |
| bitter | embittered | insecure | scared |
| blue | exhausted | irate | shaky |
| bored | fatigued | irritated | shocked |
| brokenhearted | fear | jealous | skeptical |
| cold | frightened | let-down | sorry |
| confused | frustrated | lethargy | spiritless |
| dejected | furious | listless | surprised |
| depressed | grief | lonely | suspicion |
| despair | guilty | mad | terrified |
| disappointed | hate | mean | troubled |
| discouraged | heavy | miserable | unhappy |
| disgusted | helpless | nervous | upset |
| disheartened | horrified | overwhelmed | worried |

## Feelings Likely to Be Present When Your Needs Are Being Satisfied

| | | | |
|---|---|---|---|
| affection | elated | glorious | quiet |
| amazed | electrified | glowing | radiant |
| appreciation | encouraged | grateful | satisfied |
| astonished | energetic | happy | secure |
| blissful | enjoyment | helpful | sensitive |
| calm | enthusiastic | hopeful | splendid |
| carefree | exhilarated | inspired | surprised |
| cheerful | expansive | joyful | tenderness |
| confident | exuberant | loving | thankful |
| contented | free | optimism | thrilled |
| delighted | friendly | peaceful | tranquil |
| eager | fulfilled | pleasant | trust |
| ecstatic | glad | proud | wonderful |

---

**From** *Nonviolent Communication: A Language of Life* by Dr. Marshall Rosenberg, www.NonviolentCommunication.com

# Notes

## Introduction
1. See Coelho 1996
2. See Guyton
3. Ibid

## Chapter 1
A. *NIH* is one of the world's foremost medical research centers
1. See Legaree 2007
2. See Sevrens
2a. McCullough, et al. (2000)
3. Legaree2007
4. See CBS News
4a. Willson 1999
5. See MacLean
6. See Dubruc 2002
6a McCullough-Beyond Revenge
7. See MacLean
9. See Pert 1997
10. Healy 2007
11. Bio-medicine 2003
12. Potenza 1996
13. Abagayle 2009

## Chapter 2
Note A -Type A individuals can be described as impatient, excessively time-conscious, insecure about their status, highly competitive, hostile and aggressive, and incapable of relaxation. They are often high achieving workaholics who multitask, drive themselves with deadlines, and are unhappy about the smallest of delays. Because of these characteristics, Type A individuals are often described as "stress junkies." – From Wikipedia.
1. See Legaree 2007
2. McGinnis 2006
3. See Wohl 2008, 3a. ibid
4. See Wilson, A. 2014
4a. See Carlsmith et al.,
4b. See Mccullough(2008),
4c. See De Quervain, D.
4d. See Mccullough(2008),
4e Carlsmith 4f De Quervain
4g Carlsmith 4h 4j 4i Jaffee
5. See Science Daily 2007
6. See Brehm
7. See Smalley p 91
8. Research by Dr. Redford Williams, See Goodier
9. See Rosenberg 1999
10. Gendlin, 1981
11. See Reid, 2000
12. See Wikipedia-TRC, 2006

## Chapter 3
2. See Toussaint et al., 2008
3. See Luskin, 2000
3a. Ibid   3b. Ibid
I. Harvard Health Publications.
II. Silton, Nava, et al
III. Witvliet, C. et al
IV. Ibid
V. Friedberg, J., et al
VI. Waltman, Martina A., et al.
VII., VIIb Larsen, Britta A., et al.
VIII. Ermer A, Proulx C., 2015
IX. Kiecolt-Glaser, J. K., et al.
X-XIV. Ibid
XV. Thornton, L. & Andersen, B.
XVI. Yu, Ting, et al
XVII. Ibid
XVIII. Healing Cancer Naturally
4. See Enright et al., 2000
5. Luskin 2007
6a. Personal communication
6b. Ibid
7a. Kiecolt-Glaser, et al., 2005
7b. See Real Age, 2006
8a. See Loukas 1995
8b. *Univ. Of Michigan 2000*
9. See Allen 2009 *Judy Allen wrote a book about her experience with cancer, entitled, The Five Stages of Getting Well.*
10. See Smedes 1988   11. the word heart was changed to reactions

# Notes

## Chapter 4
A. Jerry's book on Attitudinal Healing is *Teach only Love*.
1a. See Gordon et al. 2000
1b See Warren 2006
2. See Luskin 2007
2b. See Clottey 1999
3. See Tutu 1999 p271
4. See Warren 2006
5. Siegel 1999
6. This comes from the title of a little inspirational book, popular in the 70s & 80s written by Dr. Jerry Jampolsky
7. See Arbinger 2006
8. See McInnis, N. 2006
9. Coelho 1996
9a. Engel 2001
10. Berg 87

## Chapter 5
A. Maclean 1990
1. Wikipedia-Triune brain, (2018)
2. Healy 2007
3. See Amen, D. G. 2006a
4. See Do Amaral 2003
5. See Frantz_2005
6. See Wikipedia- Frontal Lobe, (2006)
7. See Miller 2002
8. See Amen, D.G. (2006)a.
9. See Do Amaral 2003
10. See Le Doux 2000
11. See Lewis P37
12. See Christison 2002
13. See Wikipedia - amygdala
14. See Do Amaral (2000) limbic
15. See Amen, D.G. (2006)a.
16. See Amen, D.G. (2006)b
17. See Lewis et al
18. See Facts for the Family (2016)
19. See Amen, D.G. (2006)a.
20. See Cory (2002)
21. Van der Dennen, 2005
22. Ibid
23. See Do Amaral
24. See Prettyman 1997
25. Maclean 1990
26. Ledoux 2000
26b. Conforti 2011
27. See Amen, D.G. (2006)a.
28. Do Amaral
29 & 29b. De Beauport 1996
30. Conforti 2011
31. Maclean 1990
32. Ledoux 2000
33. See Khan

## Chapter 6
1. See Hall 2005  2. Ibid
3. See Caine
4. See Begley 2007  5. Ibid
6. Lewis, et al. 2000
7. Ibid  8. Ibid
8a. Rosemergy 2009
9. Ibid p.118
10. Bob received his version of the letters from Dr. John Gray of *Men are from Mars, Women are from Venus* fame.
11. See ho'o pono pono
12. Quoted in Forgiveness Web

## Chapter 7
1. See Reid 2000
2. See Ritchie 1978
3. See Arrien 1991
4a. See McKay et al., 1981
4b. Ibid
5. Rosenberg See p. 88
7. For an excellent series of articles on intuition, see Dr. Daniel Benor's website at www.healthy.net.
8. See Clark 1971
9. Benor 2002  10. Ibid
11. See Benson 1976
12. See Blakeslee 2005
13. See Figley 2000

## Notes

### Chapter 8
1a. See Einstein (2) from a letter in 1936 to a child who asked if scientists pray.
1b. See Jantsch 1980
2. See Young 2004, chap 10
3. Goldsmith
4. See Einstein
5. Wikipedia-12 Steps 2006
6. See AA 1976
7. See Seligman 2004
8. See Arrien 1991

### Chapter 10
1. See Einstein 1972
2. Quoted in Heartquotes
3. See Amen, D.G. (2006)a.
3a. About.com 2009
4. Katie 2003
5. See McKay et al., 1981
6. Ibid

### Chapter 11
1. See Lynch 2007, p101
2. See Merton
4. See http://www.alanon. Alateen. org/ for more information on alanon.
5. Berg 1987
6. Mckay
7. Ibid
8. Ibid
9. See Lewis et al., 2000

### Chapter 12
1. Capri 1996
2. Figley 2002 2a. Ibid
3. Figley 2000
4. Capri 1996
5. Ibid 5a. Ibid
6. Young 2004
7b. Helpguide.com 2006
8. Peeples, 2000
9. APA 2004
10. Carlson, 2005
12. Flannery 1999
13a. Friedman (2006)
14. ROTA (2008)
15. Witvliet, et al. (2004)
15a Friedman (2006)
16. Figley 2000, 2002
16a. Figley, 2002
16b. Figley 2000, 2002
17. Van der Kolk 2009
18. Starnes 2005
19. Van der Kolk 2009
20. Wikipedia- complex ptsd
21. Walker 2010
22. Litz, et al. 2010 22a ibid
23. Witvliet, et al. 2004
24. NCPTSD 2010
26. Peeples 2000

### Chapter 13
1. See Khan

### Chapter 14
1. Foltz-Gray, 2002

### Chapter 15
A. You can answer a free questionnaire at www.authentichappiness.com to find your main character strengths.
1. Ernest Holmes 1984 p331
3. Dugatkin 2005
4. SNI
5. Kataria, M. 2009
6. Khan

# BIBLIOGRAPHY

- AA (1976) *The Big Book*, Alcoholics Anonymous World Services, Inc.
- APA (2004). *The Different Kinds of Stress,* Retrieved 6/2006 from the American Psychological Association Help Center webpage: apahelpcenter.org/articles/article.php?id=21
- Aba Gayle, (1995) Personal correspondence.
- Aba Gayle, (2009) retrieved 2/4/09 from www.catherineblountfdn.org/rsof.htm
- Allen, J. *Judy tells her moving story of using the Course to find healing for cancer,* Retrieved 2-16-09 from the Circle of Atonement: circleofa.org/articles/HealingJudyAllen.php
- Amen, D.G. (2006)a. Retrieved 6-4-06 from amenclinics.com/bp/systems/limbic
- Amen, D.G. (2006)b. Retrieved 6-4-06: amenclinics.com/bp/articles.php?articleID=10
- Arbinger Institute, (2006). *The Anatomy of Peace: Resolving the Heart of Conflict,* San Francisco: Berrett-Kohler.
- Arrien, A. (1991). Personal notes from lectures in 1991
- Begley, S. (2007) "In Our Messy Reptilian Brains," *Newsweek Web Exclusive* April 09, 2007, Retrieved 1/16/09: www.newsweek.com/id/35728
- Berg, C. (1987). "The Art of Return," *Parabola* - Volume XII, Number 3, Aug.1987 Society for the Study of Myth and Tradition
- Benor, D.J. (2002). Intuition, *The International Journal of Healing and Caring,* Volume 2, No. 2, Retrieved 11 Aug06 www.healthy.net/scr/column.asp?ColumnId=34&ID=728
- Benson, H. (1976). *The Relaxation Response*, NY: HarperTorch.
- Bio-Medicine (2003) "New scientific study finds women more forgiving than men" Retrieved 1/17/09 from http://news.bio-medicine.org/biology-news-2/New-scientific-study-finds-women-more-forgiving-than-men-3496-1/
- Blakeslee, Sandra (2005). Hypnosis can profoundly change the brain, *New York Times,* Published on 11/22/05, Retrieved 12/15/05 from http://www.ajc.com/news/content/health/1105/22hypnosis.html
- Brehm, B.A. (1994). Type A revisited: Is Type A behavior OK?, *Fitness Management Magazine*, September 1994, Vol. 10, No. 10, p. 24, Los Angeles, Calif. Retrieved 8/19/06 from www.fitnessmanagement.com/FM/tmpl/genPage.asp?p=/information/
- articles/library/labnotes/labnotes0994.html
- Brinkley, D., Perry, P., Moody, R. A. (1994). *Saved by the Light*, NY: Villard Books.
- Brock, R. & Lettini, G. (2010) "The moral injuries of war," On Faith section of the Washington Post, Nov. 17, 2010, retrieved 5/26/2011. http://onfaith. washingtonpost.com/ onfaith/ guestvoices/2010/11/the_moral_injuries_ of_war.html
- Bushak, L, Mental Health Benefits Of Forgiveness: Forgiving Others Can Protect You From Depression (2015) http://www.medicaldaily.com/mental-health-benefits-forgiveness-forgiving-others-can-protect-you-depression-350888
- Caine, R & Caine, G. (2006) "The Brain/Mind Learning Principles", Retrieved 7/6/2006 www.cainelearning.com/pwheel/expand/
- Carlson, E.B., & Ruzek, J. (2005). *Effects of Traumatic Experiences*, A Fact Sheet for the National Center for PTSD of the Department of Veteran Affairs, Retrieved 4/26/2006 from http://www.ncptsd.va.gov/facts/general/fs_effects.html
- Carlsmith, K. M., Wilson, T. D., & Gilbert, D. T. (2008). The paradoxical consequences of revenge. *Journal of Personality and Social Psychology*, 95, 1316–1324.
- CBS News (2007) "Suicide Epidemic Among Veterans," November. 13, 2007 Retrieved 1-21-08:cbsnews.com/stories/2007/11/13/cbsnews_investigates/main3496471.shtml
- Castagnini, J. editor (2008) *Thank God I...: Stories of Inspiration for Everyday Situations*, Las Vegas, NV: Inspried Authors, LLC.

# Bibliography

- Christison, MaryAnn (2002). *Brain-Based Research and Language Teaching,* English Teaching Forum Online, Volume 40, Number 2, Bureau of Educational and Cultural Affairs, Retrieved- http://exchanges.state.gov/forum/vols/vol40/no2/p02.htm
- Clark, Ronald W. (1971). *Einstein: The Life and Times, p 622,* World Pub. Co., New York, Retrieved 8-10-06 from "Einstein's Last Thoughts" www.einsteinandreligion.com/lastthoughts.html
- Clottey, K., Abadio-Clottey, A. (1999). *Beyond Fear – Twelve Spiritual Keys to Racial Healing,* H.J. Kramer, Tiburon, CA
- Coelho, P. (1996) *By The River Piedra I Sat Down and Wept: A Novel Of Forgiveness,* From the "About the book" section, Harper Perennial; Translation edition
- Conforti, Michael, workshop -*Forgiveness and Redemption,* April 29, 2011 Chapel Hill, NC
- Cory, G.A.. (2002). Reappraising MacLean's triune brain concept. The Evolutionary Neuroethology of Paul MacLean: Convergences and Frontiers.
- De Beauport, E. (1996) "Crossing the Threshold of the Unconscious: Into The Basic Brain," Retrieved 7-13-06 from www.motley-focus.com/crossing.html Taken from her book with Aura Sofia Diaz:
- *The Three Faces of the Mind: Developing Your Mental, Emotional, and Behavioral Intelligences.* Quest Books. (1996) Wheaton: The Theosophical Publishing House.
- De Quervain, D. J., Fischbacher, U, Treyer, V., Schellhammer, M., Schnyder, U., Buck, A., & Fehr, E. (2004). The neural basis of altruistic punishment. *Science,* 305, 1254–1258.
- Do Amaral, J.& de Oliveira, J. (2003). *Limbic System: The Center of Emotions,* Retrieved 7-12-2006 from http://www.healing-arts.org/n-r-limbic.htm
- Dossey, L. (1993). *Healing Words- The Power of Prayer and the Practice of Medicine,* NY: Harper Collins
- Dubuc, B. (2002). "The Brain from Top to Bottom," *The Evolutionary Layers Of The Human Brain,* Retrieved http://www.thebrain.mcgill.ca
- Dugatkin, L.(2005. "Why don't we just kiss and make up?," *New Scientist,* 5/7/05
- Einstein, Albert (1972). *New York Post, November 28, 1972.* Retrieved 8-9-06 from www.ivu.org/history/northam20a/einstein.html
- Einstein (1)Retrieved 2-7-08 from http://thinkexist.com/quotation/
- a-person-experiences-life-as-something-separated/411055.html
- Einstein (2) Retrieved 08- 11-06 from "Quotes by Albert Einstein," http://quotes.zaadz.com/Albert_Einstein
- Engel, B. (2001) The Power of Apology: Healing Steps to Transform All Your Relationships, NY: John Wiley & Sons, Inc.
- Enright, R.D., Fitzgibbons, R.P. (2000). *Helping Clients Forgive: An Empirical Guide For Resolving Anger And Restoring Hope,* Washington DC: American Psychological Assoc.
- Ermer A, Proulx C. Unforgiveness, depression, and health in later life: the protective factor of forgivingness. Aging & Mental Health. 2015.
- Facts For the Family (2016) Teen Brain: Behavior, Problem Solving, and Decision Making; No. 95; September 2016; The American Academy of Child and Adolescent Psychiatry -www.aacap.org retrieved March 18, 2018
- Friedberg, Jennifer P., Sonica Suchday, and Danielle V. Shelov. "The impact of forgiveness on cardiovascular reactivity and recovery." *International Journal of Psychophysiology* 65.2 (2007): 87-94.
- Figley, C. R. (2000). *Post-Traumatic Stress Disorder,* American Association for Marriage and Family Therapy -AAMFT -Clinical Update Volume 2, Issue 5, Sept. 2000,

## Bibliography

- Retrieved 12/29/05 from www.aamft.org/families/Consumer_Updates /PTSD_AAMFT _Clinical_Update.htm
- Figley, C. R. (2002). *AAMFT Consumer Update on Post-Traumatic Stress Disorder*, American Association for Marriage and Family Therapy, Retrieved 5/15/06 www.aamft.org/families/Consumer_Updates/PTSD.asp
- Flannery, R.B. Jr. (1999). Psychological Trauma and Posttraumatic Stress Disorder: A Review, *International Journal of Emergency Mental Health*, 1999, 2, 135-140. Retrieved from www.icisf.org/Acrobat%20Documents/TerrorismIncident /PsyTrauPTSD.pdf
- Foltz-Gray, D. (2002). "Start Forgiving," *Arthritis Today*, 9-10/2002. Retrieved from http://www.drrandijones.com/newsltr4.htm
- Foundation for Inner Peace (1975) *A Course In Miracles,* Sausalito, CA
- Frantz, R. (2005). "Introduction To Intuition," *Two Minds: Intuition and Analysis in the History of Economic Thought,* Berlin: Springer. Retrieved 5-03-07 from http://www-rohan.sdsu.edu/~frantz/docs/Chapter1.pdf
- Friedman, M. J. (2005). *Posttraumatic Stress Disorder: An Overview*, A National Center for PTSD Fact Sheet, *Dept. of Veteran Affairs.* Retrieved from http://www.ncptsd.va.gov/facts/general /fs_overview.html
- Guyton, R.(1995) *The Forgiving Place,* Waco: WRS Publishing.
- Gendlin, E. (1981). *Focusing,* NY: Bantam.
- Goldsmith, J. (1984). *Living by Grace,* NY: HarperCollins.
- Goodier, S. "A Life That Makes A Difference," retrieved 11/2/02 from http://lifesupportsystem.com/
- Gordon, K. C., Baucom, D. H., & Snyder, D.K. (2000). "The Use Of Forgiveness In Marital Therapy." In M. C. McCullough, K. I. Pargament, & C. E. Thoresen (Eds.), *Forgiveness: Theory, Research, and Practice,* pp. 203–227, NY: Guilford Press.
- Hall. D. (2005). "Social Support," Health Plus – Vanderbilt Faculty and Staff Wellness Program, Wellsource, Inc. Retrieved 1/10/06 http://vanderbiltowc.wellsource.com/dh/content. asp?ID=563
- Harvard Health Publications (2004)"Power of Forgiveness - Forgive Others." October 08, 2013 http://www.health.harvard.edu/press_releases/power_of_forgiveness
- Healing Cancer Naturally. "DNA experiments prove the direct influence of feelings on DNA activity." *Healing Cancer Naturally.* 2013.Web. October 02, 2013 <http://www.healingcancernaturally.com/emotions-and-cancer-healing.html>.
- Healy, M (2007) "Humans may be hard-wired to have a soft spot: The predisposition to forgive appears genetic and may have been selected through evolution" *Los Angeles Times*, Dec. 31, 2007, Retrieved 1/17/09 www.psy.miami.edu/faculty/mmccullough /Media%20Coverage/Humans%20may%20be%20hard%20wired_la_times.pdf
- Heartquotes, retrieved 5-18-07 http://www.heartquotes.net/ Anger.html
- Helpguide.org (2006) "Emotional and Psychological Trauma: Causes, Symptoms, Effects, and Treatment," retrieved 5/11/2006 from www.helpguide.org/mental/emotionalpsychological_trauma.htm
- Holmes, E. 1984. *Living the Science of Mind*, Marina del Rey: DeVorss and Co.
- Ho'oponopono, From classes with Keoki Sousa, Sept-Oct 1999, Maui Community College, Maui, HI and Kapi'ioho Lyons Naone, June 1999, Bailey House, Maui, HI
- Jampolsky, G.(1990). *Out of the Darkness into the Light* NY: Bantam.
- Jaffe, E. (October 2011.) The Complicated Psychology of Revenge. *Observer* Vol.24, No.8
- Jampolsky. G. (2000) *Teach Only Love: The Twelve Principles of Attitudinal Healing*, Beyond Words Publishing, Inc, Hillsborough, Oregon

## Bibliography

- Jantsch, E. (1980). *The Self-Organizing Universe: Scientific and Human Implication of the Emerging Paradigm of Evolution,* Pergamon, NY, NY
- Kataria, M. (2009) "Laughter Clubs" retrieved 2/6/2009 from
- http://www.laughteryoga.org
- Katie, Byron, (2003) *Loving What Is: Four Questions That Can Change Your Life,* NY: Three Rivers Press.
- Khan, H.I., *The Sufi Message of Hazrat Inayat Khan* - Volume VII – IX, Retrieved 6/2005 http://wahiduddin.net/mv2/IX/IX_9.htm
- Kiecolt-Glaser, Janice K., et al. "Psychoneuroimmunology and psychosomatic medicine: back to the future." *Psychosomatic Medicine* 64.1 (2002): 15-28.
- Kiecolt-Glaser, J.K., Loving, T.J., Stowell, J.R., Malarkey, W.B., Lemeshow, S., Dickinson, S.L., Glaser, R. (2005). Hostile marital interactions, proinflammatory cytokine production, and wound healing. *Archives of General Psychiatry* 62(12):1377-1384. 4/19/06 http://archpsyc.amaassn.org/cgi/content/abstract/62/12/1377
- Larsen, Britta A., et al. "The immediate and delayed cardiovascular benefits of forgiving." *Psychosomatic Medicine* 74.7 (2012): 745-750.
- Le Doux, J. (1996) *The Emotional Brain: The Mysterious Underpinnings of Emotional Life,* New York: Simon& Schuster
- LeDoux, J. (2000) Emotion Circuits in the Brain, *Annual Reviews Neuroscience* 23:155–184 www.csmn.uio.no/events/2008/machamer_docs/ledoux.pdf
- Legaree, T., Turner, J., Lollis, S. (2007) "Forgiveness and Therapy: A Critical Review of Conceptualizations, Practices, and Values Found In the Literature." *Journal of Marital and Family Therapy*. The American Association for Marriage & Family Therapy. Gotten 2/02/09 from www.highbeam.com/doc/1P3-1270855471.html
- Lewis, T., Amini, & Landon, (2000).*A General Theory of Love*, NY: Random House.
- Litz, B. T., Stein, N., Delaney, E., Lebowitz, L., Nash, W. P., Silva, C. et al. (2009). Moral injury and moral repair in war veterans: A preliminary model and intervention strategy. Clinical Psychology Review, 29 (8)
- Loukas, Chris (1995). Faith, forgiveness help crash victim heal, *The Press Democrat,* December 25, 1995, Santa Rosa, CA.
- Luskin, F. (2000). *Forgive For Good: A Proven Prescription for Health and Happiness,* pp 77-93, San Francisco: Harper.
- Luskin, F. (2007) *Forgive for Love: The Missing Ingredient for a Healthy and Lasting Relationship,* NY: HarperOne.
- Lynch, M.J. (2007) *Big Prisons, Big Dreams: Crime and the Failure of America's Penal System* NJ: Rutgers University Press.
- MacLean, P. D. (1990). *The Triune Brain in Evolution,* NY: Plenum
- McCullough, M. C., Pargament, K. I., & Thoresen, C., (Eds), (2000) *Forgiveness: Theory, Research, and Practice,* NY: Guilford Press, p.3,
- McCullough, M.E. (2008). *Beyond Revenge: The evolution of the forgiveness instinct.* San Francisco: Jossey-Bass.
- McInnis, N. (2006). Retrieved June 5, 2006, http://www.mediamessage.com /archive/forgivenesspractice.htm#Staying%20in%20the%20Grace
- McKay, M., Davis, M., & Fanning, P. (1981). *Thoughts & Feelings: The Art Of Cognitive Stress Intervention,* Oakland: New Harbinger.
- Miller, J. (2002). Science searches the brain for mystical experience: Newberg, Delio and the mystery of the brain, *Science & Theology News,* July 1, 2002, Retrieved July 19, 2006 http://www.stnews.org/print.php?article_id=1696
- Myss, C., (1996) *Anatomy of the Spirit: The Seven Stages of Power and Healing,* NY: Three Rivers Press

# Bibliography

- NCPTSD (2011) National Center For PTSD, "Spirituality and Trauma: Professionals Working Together," US Department of Veterans Affairs, retrieved 5/26/2011 www.ptsd.va.gov/professional/pages/fs-spirituality.asp
- Potenza, (1996) a talk on forgiveness given July 1996
- Peeples, K.A. (2000). Interview with Charles R. Figley: Burnout In Families and Implications for the Profession, *The Family Journal*, 8: 203-206. Retrieved 11/17/2004 from http://mailer.fsu.edu/~cfigley/burnout.htm
- Pert, C.B. (1997). *Molecules of Emotion: Why You Feel the Way You Do*. New York: Scribner.
- Prettyman, J.W. (1997). *Deep And Deeper: Deep Blue vs. The Triune Brain*, Retrieved 7-12-06 www.americanreview.us/deepblue.htm
- Real Age, Inc., (2006). April 21-Tip of the Day-A Case for Peace, Retrieved 4/19/2006 http://www.realage.com/news_features/tip.aspx?v=1&cid=16586
- Reid, F., Hoffmann, D. (2000). *Long Night's Journey Into Day: South Africa's Search for Truth & Reconciliation*, Iris Films, Retrieved 2/25/2008 from www.irisfilms.org/longnight/
- Ritchie, George G., M.D. (1978). *Return From Tomorrow*, Old Tappan, N.J, Fleming, H. Revell, of Baker Book House Company.
- Rosemergy, J. (2009) Email of 2 March 09
- Rosenberg, M. (1999). *Nonviolent Communication- A Language of Compassion*, PuddleDancer Press, Del Mar, Ca.
- ROTA (2008). "ROTA (Reach Out To Asia) and Save the Children Collaborate to Support Children in Gaza Strip." Retrieved 4-15-09 from http://www.reachouttoasia.org/output/page275.asp
- ScienceDaily (2007). Outwardly Expressed Anger Affects Some Women's Heart Arteries, Source: Cedars-Sinai Medical Center, 1/15/07 Retrieved 6-8-07 from www.sciencedaily.com/releases/2007/01/070114185909.htm
- Siegel, B. (1999). *Prescriptions for Living: Inspirational Lessons for a Joyful, Loving Life,* NY: Harper Paperbacks.
- Seligman, M. E. (2004). Happiness Interventions That Work: The First Results, *Authentic Happiness Coaching News*, Vol 2, Number 10 5/3/2004, Retrieved 7/13/2004 from www.AuthenticHappinessCoaching.com
- Sevrens, J. (1999) *Learning to Forgive*, San Jose Mercury News, 9/6/99
- Smalley, G. (2001). *Food and Love: The Amazing Connection*, Tyndale House Publishers, Wheaton, IL, p. 91
- Smedes, L. (1988). *Forgive and Forget: Healing the Hurts, We Don't Deserve*, NY: Pocket Books.
- Starnes, G. (2005) "The Psychophysiology of Trauma" Returning Warriors Blog, 5/16/05 Retrieved 1-17-09 www.returningwarriors.org/2005_05_01_archive.html
- Steiner, C. *Transactional Analysis, and the Triune Brain* Retrieved 7-9-06 from http://www.emotional-literacy.com/triune.htm
- Silton, Nava R., Kevin J. Flannelly, and Laura J. Lutjen. "It Pays to Forgive! Aging, Forgiveness, Hostility, and Health." *Journal of Adult Development* (2013): 1-10.
- Thornton, Lisa M., and Barbara L. Andersen. "Psychoneuroimmunology examined: the role of subjective stress." *Cellscience* 2.4 (2006): 66.
- Toussaint, L., Williams, D., Musick, & Everson-Rose, (2008). "Why forgiveness may protect against depression: Hopelessness as an explanatory mechanism," *Personality and Mental Health*, 2, 89-103.
- Tutu, D.M. (1999). *No Future without Forgiveness*, NY: Doubleday.

# Bibliography

- The University Of Michigan, (2000) "New Study Shows Link Between Hopelessness And Hypertension," *ScienceDaily*, 2/18/00 Retrieved January 31, 2009, from www.sciencedaily.com/releases/2000/02/000217100606.htm
- Van der Dennen, J.M.G. (2005). "Ritualized 'Primitive' Warfare And Rituals In War: Phenocopy, Homology, Or..?" Retrieved 6-12-06: WWW.irs.ub.rug.nl/ppn/280499396
- Van der Kolk, B., (2009) "Specialized Treatment Approaches" *The Trauma Center at Justice Resource Institute* Website, retrieved 1/21/09 http://www.traumacenter.org/clients/spec_svcs_treatment.php
- Warren, R. (2006) Some excerpts from a Rick Warren article on forgiveness from the Spring 2006 issue of "The Worshipper" Magazine. Retrieved 6/05/09 http://exubfjc.wordpress.com/2006/12/18/rick-warren-on-forgiveness/
- Walker, M.(2010) 'Moral injury' as a wound of war -Conference To Examine Consequence Of Battlefield Transgressions, Exposure To Carnage www.nctimes.com/news/local/military/article_79c6d17-ebb5-5e26-9aa4-8dc4c8f721cd.html Retrieved 8/5/10
- Waltman, Martina A., et al. "The effects of a forgiveness intervention on patients with coronary artery disease." *Psychology and Health* 24.1 (2009): 11-27.
- Wikipedia- Amygdala (2006) The Amygdala, Retrieved 7/09/06 from http://en.wikipedia.org/wiki/Amygdala 7-9-06 Wikipedia-12Steps, (2006*). The Twelve Steps,* en.wikipedia.org/wiki/12step_program#The_Twelve_Steps
- Wikipedia – Complex PTSD (2018) retrieved 5/22/18, https://en.wikipedia.org/wiki/Complex_post-traumatic_stress_disorder
- Wikipedia –TRC (2006). *List of truth and reconciliation commissions*, from Wikipedia, http://en.wikipedia.org/wiki/List_of_truth_and_reconciliation_commissions
- Wikipedia-Triune brain, (2018*).* Retrieved 3/22/18: https://en.wikipedia.org/wiki/Triune_brain
- Wikipedia-Frontal Lobe, (2006*).* Retrieved 7/9/06: en.wikipedia.org/wiki/Frontal_lobe
- Wilson, A., (2014) "Loving-Kindness Meditation and Change," Huffington Post, retrieved 12/15/2017, https://www.huffingtonpost.com/kripalu/loving-kindness-meditation_b_3961300.html
- Willson, B., (1999) "Memorandum: Accelerated Mortality Rates of Vietnam Veterans," retrieved 3/8/09: www.brianwillson.com/awolvetmemo.html
- Witvliet, C.V.O., Phillipps, K.A., Feldman, M.E., & Beckham, J.C. (2004). Posttraumatic Mental and Physical Health Correlates of Forgiveness and Religious Coping in Military Veterans. *Journal of Traumatic Stress*, 17, 269-273.
- Witvliet, C.V.O, Ludwig T.E., and Vander Laan, K.L. "Granting forgiveness or harboring grudges: Implications for emotion, physiology, and health." *Psychological Science* 12.2 (2001): 117-123.
- Wohl, M. J A; DeShea, Wahkinney, (2008) "Looking Within: Measuring State Self-Forgiveness and Its Relationship to Psychological Well-Being." *Canadian Journal of Behavioural Science*. Canadian Psychological Association
- Worthington, E. (2001) *Five Steps to Forgiveness*, NY: Crown Publishers.
- Worthington, E. (2003). *Forgiving and Reconciling: Bridges to Wholeness and Hope,* Downers Grove, IL: InterVarsity Press; Revised Edition
- Young, M. A. (2004). *The Community Crisis Response Team Training Manual-2$^{nd}$ edition,* National Organization for Victim Assistance, U.S. Department of Justice, Wash., DC. Retrieved 3/5/03 from http://ojp.usdoj.gov/ovc/publications/infores/crt/
- Yu, Ting, Hui Ling Tsai, and Ming Liang Hwang. "Suppressing tumor progression of in vitro prostate cancer cells by emitted psychosomatic power through Zen meditation." *The American journal of Chinese medicine* 31.03 (2003): 499-507.

# INDEX

A General Theory of Love, 78, 81, 214
AA, 123, 210, 211
abusers, 67, *See* domestic violence
abusive, 60, 66, 67, 93, 127, 136, 145, 154, 200, *See* domestic violence
affirmations, 114, 122
aggression, 83, 84, 87, 161
alcohol, 19, 28, 54, 82, 124, 151, 154, 161, 163, 177
Amini, 78, 81, 214
Amy Biehls, 103, 115, 174
anger, 18, 19, 20, 21, 27, 30, 31, 35, 38, 39, 42, 47, 48, 50, 55, 59, 60, 61, 62, 67, 70, 71, 72, 79, 89, 97, 102, 109, 114, 115, 122, 124, 139, 140, 141, 148, 150, 152, 153, 154, 158, 162, 164, 166, 175, 180, 183, 184, 188, 201
anger control, 62
apology, 23, 34, 38, 41, 64, 68, 70, 101, 106, 131, 198
Appendix, 72, 207
Arrien, Angeles, 9, 126, 177, 209, 210, 211
attitudes, 15, 20, 35, 71, 80, 85, 96, 97, 124, 161
BERG, 73, 209, 210, 211
Black and White Thinking, 145
blaming, 33, 52, 102, 138186
Blocks to Forgiving, 42, 59
brain, 16, 19, 24, 25, 26, 27, 28, 29, 38, 55, 58, 59, 61, 67, 70, 73, 75-88, 89, 91, 92, 93, 94, 97, 100, 105, 107, 110, 111, 112, 114, 115, 122, 135, 136, 139, 144, 145, 146, 157, 160, 161, 163, 166, 169, 175, 183, 199, 211, 214
  structures, 26
Brain research, 25, 26
brain structures, 27, 87
Breaking it down, 43
Catastrophe Thinking, 146
catastrophizing, 147
church, 22, 34, 86, 89, 140, 156, 157, 200, 201
**CHURCHILL**, 19
CIRINCIONE, 63
Clottey, 62, 209, 212
Co-Dependents Anonymous, 154
Coelho, 10, 18, 32, 69, 208, 209, 212
Coles, 65
comfort zone, 90
compassion, - 2 -, 14, 16, 17, 25, 36, 48, 51, 57, 59, 63, 69, 71, 80, 88, 104, 107, 108, 118, 127, 132, 135, 148, 157, 159, 162, 168, 171, 172, 175, 176, 182, 183, 186, 187, 188, 190, 203
*Compassion*, vii, 10, 72, 102, 107, 128, 134, 155, 183, 215
compassion fatigue, 159, 168
*Compassion Fatigue*, 168

condoning, - 4 -, 15, 60, 63, 68, 131
Conforti, 84, 87
consequences, 60, 78, 88, 110, 123, 131, 158, 159, 182
contemplation, 61, 112, 135, 188
cults, 86
Davis, 145, 214
De Beauport, 87, 209, 212
**debt**, 33, 34, 42, 130, 182
Deciding to Forgive, 109, 132
defenses, 19, 29, 91, 107, 137, 138, 144, 153, 177, 201
demons, 28, 30
denial, 19, 63, 138, 139, 141, 143, 144
depression, 19, 24, 28, 47, 48, 50, 66, 69, 77, 80, 91, 100, 126, 130, 142, 143, 150, 152, 153, 161, 168, 200, 207, 215
Divine, 18, 22, 41, 54, 56, 58, 68, 107, 109, 113, 115, 117, 118, 172, 174, 186, 189, 200, 202, 203
Divine Love, 18, 41, 56, 109, 174, 189
domestic violence, 61, 67
domination, 82
drugs, 19, 28, 124, 161, 162, 163, 177
Edison, 110
EINSTEIN, 55, 135, 172, 210, 212
EINSTEIN[8], 110
EMDR, 159, 166

emotional intelligence, 102, 185
Engel, 70, 198, 209, 212
Enright, 35, 50, 212
essentials, 115, 116, 181
Essentials, vi, 41
*Evil*, 16
expectations, - 1 -, 34, 58, 93, 95, 96, 97, 167, 187
fair. *See* fairness
fairness, 106
Fanning, 145, 214
fear, 19, 26, 27, 28, 42, 45, 58, 60, 62, 66, 67, 72, 78, 79, 83, 85, 86, 87, 88, 90, 92, 93, 101, 107, 115, 122, 136, 146, 149, 152, 153, 158, 159, 160, 166, 175, 180, 201, 207
feelings, 17, 20, 35, 36, 51, 60, 61, 65, 69, 71, 72, 78, 79, 99, 100, 112, 115, 126, 130, 135, 137, 148, 149, 151, 152, 161, 174, 182, 183, 186
    avoiding, 27, 61, 71, 72, 79, 106, 130, 145, 207, 214
felt shift, 39, 40, 173, 178, 183, 185
Figley, 112, 165, 209, 210, 212, 214
Finding the who, 64
*forgiveness*
    false, 22
    success, 42, 64
    true, 23
Forgiveness 8, 10, 11, 12, 15, 16, 18-23, 25, 27, 28, 30, 31, 39, 45, 47, 48, 50, 52, 54, 57, 58, 59, 60, 61, 63, 65, 67, 68,

69, 71, 72, 86, 95, 96, 97, 99, 100, 102, 105, 109, 113-116, 119, 128, 131, 132, 139, 147, 148, 150, 152-154, 167, 169, 171, 172, 175, 176, 182, 187, 189, 190, 196, 201, 202, 203,
   controversy, 23, 24
   definition, 33, 35
   myths, 23
   *Stages and Phases of*, 16
   types, 22
Forgiveness
   definition, 33
*Forgiving Big Issues*, 44
Forgiving Permanently, 134
Frankel, 104
freedom, 20, 93, 142
Freud, 22, 157
Gandhi, 31, 34
Gendlin, 39, 208, 213
generosity, 36, 148
**God**, 33, 41, 45, 46, 54, 65, 68, 69, 70, 86, 107-109, 116, 118, 121, 124, 125, 127, 149, 177, 184, 191, 196, 202, 203, 211
Goldsmith, 121, 210, 213
**Grateful**. *See* gratitude
gratitude, vii, 125, 126, 188
Gray, 99, 209, 210, 213
grudges, - 4 -, 15, 20, 35, 47, 55
guilt, 11, 17, 20, 22, 44, 57, 60, 64, 69, 100, 112, 118, 119, 121, 122, 127, 130, 139, 141, 148, 149, 150, 152, 153, 166, 167, 169, 175, 176, 182, 191, 207
habits, 65, 75, 76, 149, 200
**Hall**, 89

happiness, 18, 26, 30, 39, 52, 56, 64, 114, 117, 118, 122, 123, 125, 131, 144, 151, 152, 155
Hay, 17
healing, - 1 -, - 4 -, vi, vii, 8, 10, 16, 17, 18, 19, 35, 41, 42, 52, 55, 60, 63, 67, 80, 100, 121, 122, 125, 128, 143, 171, 172, 174, 175, 176, 191, 192, 195, 198, 209, 211- 215
Herbert, 53, 103, 111, 135, 195
Hitler, 139, 140, 143
honesty, 106, 108, 115, 127, 128, 143, 144, 174
*Ho'o Pono Pono*, 100
humiliation, 100, 130, 134, 142, 182
humility, 46, 95, 107, 108, 116, 127, 172, 175, 186, 203
humor, 199
Huntley, 35
*Hurdles*, 46, 58, 72, 102, 116
imagination,112, 113, 115, 175
injustice, 33, 37, 44
inner guidance, 110
intention, 22, 57, 58, 108, 109, 114, 132, 175
intuition, 110, 111, 115, 127, 174, 209
Jampolsky, 10, 63, 209, 213
Jantsch, 118, 210, 213
Jesus, 66, 118, 123, 124, 137, 138, 140
journal, 30, 98, 110, 185

joy, - 1 -, 16, 20, 21, 28, 38, 41, 56, 71, 78, 86, 93, 107, 112, 117, 118, 123, 128, 131, 151, 152, 154, 155, 175, 178, 192, 193, 195, 196, 200, 202, 203
judgments, 95, 96, 97, 105, 114, 145, 149, 176
justice, 37, 38, 42, 63, 184
*Justice*, 37, 134, 215, 216
Kataria, 199, 210, 213
Katie, 143, 210, 213
KEMPIS, 102
KHAN, 201, 209, 213
Landon, 78, 81, 214
laughter, 78, 199, 200
legal system, 38, 45, 79, 134
Letters, 99-102,126
Letting go, 30, 65, 117, 118, 149, 195
Lewis, 15, 35, 54, 78, 81, 209, 210, 214
love 15, 16, 20, 21, 26, 32, 35, 36, 38, 40, 41, 51, 54, 55, 56, 60, 62, 66, 69, 70, 71, 78, 81, 82, 86, 88, 93, 101, 103, 107, 108, 109, 112, 113, 117-119, 121-124, 126, 127, 128, 131, 146, 148, 151-154, 156, 157, 169, 173,175, 176, 178, 187, 188, 192, 195, 196, 202, 203
lovingkindness, 36, 173
Luskin, 10, 12, 47, 60, 95, 197, 208, 209, 214
Luskin, F., 9
Lynch, 149, 210, 214
MacLean, 27, 208, 214

Martin Luther King, Jr, 33, 119
MCGRAW, 32
McKay, 145, 214
meaning, 58, 66, 69, 78, 96, 103, 104, 115, 118, 140, 149, 156, 174, 187, 195, 196
meditation, 61, 66, 135
moral code, 101, 148, 185, 187, 193
Moral injury, 167, 214, 215
MYSS, 10, 88, 214
Myth, 59, 60, 61, 62, 63, 64, 65, 66, 68, 71, 127, 211
Myths, vi, 23, 59, 68, 69, 131, 175, 182
Summary, 68
Negative self-talk, 114
neocortex, 26, 77, 78, 79, 82, 87, 91, 92, 97, 136, 183
*Nonviolent Communication*, 72, 107, 215
**Note**, 27, 29, 30, 35, 39, 51, 56, 85, 88, 97, 111, 127, 132, 135, 136, 143, 144, 147, 159, 160, 165, 179-181, 185, 190, 199,
NOTES 208-210
Obama, 60
Ornish, 39, 90
pain, 20, 24, 32, 33, 35, 37, 38, 41, 53, 58, 59, 67, 71, 79, 80, 88, 121, 139, 146, 155, 161, 162, 163, 181, 186, 190
panic, 50, 84, 90, 158
Patanjali, 111
*Payoff*, 131
peace, 15

peace of mind, 20, 25, 34, 54, 64, 130, 152, 154, 198
Pert, 29, 208, 214
Plath, 99
Post Traumatic Stress Disorder. *See* PTSD
Power Forgiveness, - 1 -, vii, 17, 19, 42, 45, 52, 55, 109, 112, 116, 117, 124, 129, 161, 164, 167, 169, 171, 172, 175, 177-179, 182, 192, 193, 194, 201
*Power Forgiveness Process*, 19, 52, 179-193
prayer, 29, 31, 41, 45, 56, 57, 61, 66, 78, 95, 122, 123, 135, 159, 185
*Prayer*, 33, 56, 212
projection, 11, 138, 139, 140, 141-144, 176, 186, 193
psychology, 8, 15, 18, 19, 21, 22, 109, 114, 125, 157, 160, 183, 200, 202, 203
PTSD, vii, 50, 79, 86, 159, 160, 164, 165, 166, 167, 168, 211, 212, 213, 214
*Punishment*, 37, 96, 148, 149
*questions*, 17, 20, 21, 29, 46, 55, 56, 57, 64, 86, 96, 99, 100, 102, 130, 131, 132, 142, 151, 153, 156, 172, 173, 180, 187, 189, 190, 191
**Questions**, 41, 64, 108, 110, 128, 132, 143, 156, 186, 187,
reconciliation, 35, 38, 59, 60, 68, 125, 131, 192, 197, 198, 216

relationship, 38, 51, 52, 60, 66, 67, 77, 80, 82, 93, 94, 100, 109, 124, 127, 140, 146, 153, 177, 197
religion, 15, 22, 93, 96, 105, 116, 117, 118, 125, 139, 157, 162, 175, 177, 192, 200, 202, 203
repentance, 37, 60
**repression**, 138
Reptilian Brain, 82
resentment, - 4 -, 15, 17, 18, 19, 22, 30, 35, 54, 59, 60, 61, 72, 76, 102, 121-124, 142, 149, 151, 153, 167, 172, 180, 183, 186, 187-189, 195, 196
Resistance to Forgiving, 131
revenge, 30, 38, 55, 79, 126, 134, 202, 203
Ritchie, 10, 103, 104, 209, 214
ritual behavior, 83
Rosenberg, 10, 72, 95, 106, 208, 209, 215
rules, 37, 38, 93, 95, 96, 97, 98, 105, 148, 152, 176, 184, 187
**Safety**, 173
*Secret*, vi, vii, 21, 107
self-blame, 17, 149
self-forgiveness, - 1 -, 11, 36, 65, 69, 70, 127, 138, 139, 140, 145, 148, 154, 157, 176, 186, 190, 198
Self-forgiveness, vii, 17, 25, 57, 146, 152, 157, 176, 190
*Self-Forgiveness*, 216

settting limits, 35, 61, 66, 67, 97, 153
shame, 17, 100, 130, 150, 152, 169, 176
Siegel, 65, 128, 209, 215
sin, 57, 84, 96, 149
SMEDES, 15, 35, 54, 208
SMITH, 10, 147
snake brain. *See* Reptilian brain
**social support**, 89
*Stress*, vi, vii, 24, 50, 79, 106, 158, 159, 160, 165, 211-214,
submission, 83, 87
*Success*, 30
suicide, 24, 28, 143, 158, 163
Taniguchi, 125
Thoresen, 21, 213, 214
TILLICH, 156
transformation, vii, 17, 192
trauma, 18, 21, 24, 28, 30, 53, 71, 79, 85, 92, 112, 146, 158, 159, 163, 164, 165, 166, 167, 168, 169, 213
*Trauma*, vi, vii, 24, 125, 158, 159, 164, 165, 166, 167, 168, 169, 212, 213, 214, 215
Triune Brain, 77, 214
*Truth and Reconciliation Commission*, 44
TUTU, 20, 63
Type-A, 39
understanding, 14, 15, 19, 21, 24, 25, 39, 40, 42, 46, 54, 57, 60, 69, 72, 80, 86, 95, 96, 97, 98, 100, 108, 124, 132, 134, 135, 136, 138, 150, 154, 162, 169, 171-173, 183, 185, 186, 187, 190, 200, 201, 203
unforgiveness, 29
unworthiness, 69, 152
values, 35, 38, 95, 97, 98, 118, 134, 135, 148, 150, 152, 176, 184, 187, 188
Veterans, 167, 168, 211, 214,
victim, 16, 24,56, 64, 66, 73, 84, 96, 112, 127, 131, 142, 146, 152-155, 156, 159, 165 ,166, 184, 214
violence, 8, 16, 20, 25, 28, 61, 67, 83, 103, 136, 139, 150, 153, 163, 166, 202
**vision**, 12, 23, 27, 41, 46, 103, 108, 109, 115, 122, 144, 173, 177, 184, 187, 196, 201, 203
**WARNING**, 67
Warren, 60
Wild Bill, 103, 104, 115, 174
willingness, 12, 16, 17, 34, 41, 42, 55, 56, 67, 72, 73, 86, 98, 100, 101, 106, 108, 109, 110, 115, 122, 129, 130, 134, 140, 169, 174, 175, 177, 180, 181, 184, 191, 193
Worthington, 62, 197, 216

Made in the USA
Las Vegas, NV
16 December 2022

62841960R00122